The Modern Language Association of America

Approaches to Teaching Masterpieces of World Literature

Joseph Gibaldi, Series Editor

1. *Joseph Gibaldi, ed.* Approaches to Teaching Chaucer's *Canterbury Tales*. 1980.
2. *Carole Slade, ed.* Approaches to Teaching Dante's *Divine Comedy*. 1982.
3. *Richard Bjornson, ed.* Approaches to Teaching Cervantes' *Don Quixote*. 1984.
4. *Jess B. Bessinger, Jr., and Robert F. Yeager, eds.* Approaches to Teaching *Beowulf*. 1984.

Approaches to Teaching

Beowulf

Edited by
Jess B. Bessinger, Jr.
and
Robert F. Yeager

THE MODERN LANGUAGE ASSOCIATION
OF AMERICA   1984

Library of Congress Cataloging in Publication Data

Main entry under title:

Approaches to teaching Beowulf.

(Approaches to teaching masterpieces of world literature ; 4)
   Bibliography: p.
   Includes index.
   1. Beowulf—Study and teaching. 2. Anglo-Saxon literature—Study and teaching.
I. Bessinger, Jess B. II. Yeager, Robert F. III. Series.
PR1585.A66   1984   829′.3   83-22124
ISBN 0-87352-481-0
ISBN 0-87352-482-9 (pbk.)

Cover illustration in paperback edition: portion of *Beowulf* manuscript transcribed
by Ellen F. Higgins
Published by The Modern Language Association of America
62 Fifth Avenue, New York, New York 10011

CONTENTS

PREFACE TO THE SERIES

In his thoughtful and sensitive book *The Art of Teaching* (1950), Gilbert Highet wrote, "Bad teaching wastes a great deal of effort, and spoils many lives which might have been full of energy and happiness." All too many teachers have failed in their work, Highet argued, simply "because they have not thought about it." We hope that the Approaches to Teaching Masterpieces of World Literature series, sponsored by the Modern Language Association's Committee on Teaching and Related Professional Activities, will not only improve the craft—as well as the art—of teaching but also encourage serious and continuing discussion of the aims and methods of our teaching.

The principal objective of the series is to collect within each volume a number of points of view on teaching a particular work of world literature that is widely taught at the undergraduate level. The preparation of each volume begins with a survey of instructors who have considerable experience in teaching the work, thus enabling us to include in the volume the philosophies and approaches, thoughts and methods of scores of experienced teachers. The result is a source book of material, information, and ideas on teaching the work to undergraduates.

This series is intended to serve nonspecialists as well as specialists, inexperienced as well as experienced teachers, graduate students who wish to learn effective ways of teaching as well as senior professors who wish to compare their own approaches with the approaches of colleagues in other schools. Of course, no volume in the series can ever substitute for erudition, intelligence, creativity, and sensitivity in teaching. We hope merely that each book will point readers in useful directions; at most each will offer only a first step in the long journey to successful teaching.

In a time that increasingly demands a rededication to undergraduate teaching of the humanities and to the idea of a liberal education, it may well be that our sometimes divided and fragmented profession will rediscover a sense of purpose, unity, and community in its concern for and commitment to teaching. We hope that the Approaches to Teaching Masterpieces of World Literature series will serve in some small way to refocus attention on the importance of teaching and to improve undergraduate instruction. We may perhaps adopt as keynote for the series Alfred North Whitehead's observation in *The Aims of Education* (1929) that a liberal education "proceeds by imparting a knowledge of the masterpieces of thought, of imaginative literature, and of art."

Joseph Gibaldi
Series Editor

PREFACE TO THE VOLUME

We here boldly paraphrase the first paragraph of Joseph Gibaldi's preface in the first volume of the Modern Language Association's Approaches to Teaching Masterpieces of World Literature series, which was devoted to Chaucer's *Canterbury Tales*, the work of "the first great English poet." We present here a companion volume on a somewhat earlier great English poem.

Because of a notable decline in the study of language and history in North America, and indeed in England and in English-speaking enclaves abroad, perhaps no other major poem in the English language is so jeopardized in the universities. Heroically, it seems to be surviving. While the study of *Beowulf* declines in the universities, it flourishes in other places—in small liberal arts colleges, in community colleges, in secondary schools. Beowulf is too sophisticated a primitive hero to indulge in folkish or mythic shape shifting, but the teaching of the poem about him has done something of the sort. Former great scholar-teachers might feel at home, we may hope, in some graduate seminars or advanced Old English classrooms today; but they would scarcely be able to credit what is happening to their poem, or to pedagogical approaches to it, in formerly less privileged places.

Like the other volumes in the series, this book is concerned chiefly with teaching at the undergraduate level. We offer it, however, to all teachers of *Beowulf*, among whom we trust will be found many instructors of a traditional *Beowulf* course in a traditional Old English course sequence. Indeed, some such survivors of a venerable tradition have contributed essays to this volume. We hope then that both specialists and neophyte teachers, and perhaps some advanced students, will find matter to interest and assist them.

Our book begins with an introduction by the editors on the current phenomena associated with the study of *Beowulf*, and not just in the classroom or on the North American continent. The main body of the work is divided into sections entitled "Materials" and "Approaches." The editorial "Instructor's Library" includes a special survey of translations of *Beowulf* by Douglas D. Short, a section clearly aimed at undergraduate teachers and their students.

In our introduction we have drawn also on the spectrum of instructors' opinions about translations and other matters. The "Materials" section, dealing with such questions as choice of editions and recommended research and teaching tools, was formally the editors' responsibility, but it is based on information provided to us by the Beowulfians who took part in the survey that initiated the preparation of this volume. There were about one hundred of them, from North America, England, continental Europe, Hawaii, and Japan. We salute them here.

From these generous respondents the editors chose about twenty-five teachers of *Beowulf* for a series of clustered essays discussing approaches to the poem at various levels—whether adapted to graduate, undergraduate, or mixed classes, whether teaching primarily in Old English or in translation. These essays, and our own, suggest different approaches to teaching the poem, and we hope the variety makes clear our belief that today there can be no possible "best" approach to *Beowulf*.

An appendix of participants in our survey, a list of works cited throughout the volume, a discography, and an index complete the work.

We have thanked the respondents to our survey, the people who made the book possible. But we owe special thanks also to the general editor of the series, Joseph Gibaldi, and to his staff at the Modern Language Association for their auspices and for their timely, thoughtful, practical assistance. We also thank the members of the association's Committee on Teaching and Related Professional Activities for their endorsement of our contribution to the Approaches to Teaching Masterpieces of World Literature series. We are especially grateful to Thomas J. Garbáty and Stanley B. Greenfield, whose careful readings of the entire manuscript were both friendly and rigorous; their independent and overlapping corrections and suggestions were very welcome. Our gratitude also goes to Ellen F. Higgins for allowing us to use her transcription of a portion of the *Beowulf* manuscript as a cover illustration for the paperback edition.

Our volume is a joint effort throughout, so we jointly thank Leda Neale and Patricia Kaplan and her family for warmly appreciated practical assistance and for the hospitality that made available to us a summertime Anglo-Saxon factory on the Connecticut shore of Long Island Sound.

JBB
RFY

INTRODUCTION:
AN INTERNATIONAL SURVEY
ON THE TEACHING OF
BEOWULF

This volume grew out of a long-standing interest among members of the Old English Group of the MLA. About sixteen years ago, the *Old English News-letter* was founded in order to publish "A Survey of Old English Teaching in America in 1966," by Jess B. Bessinger, Jr., and Fred C. Robinson, in its first number. More than a decade later, Robert F. Yeager published a new assessment in the same journal: "Some Turning Points in the History of Teaching Old English in America." The general editor of the MLA's Approaches to Teaching Masterpieces of World Literature series then kindly invited us to prepare a volume on *Beowulf*, and with his help we drew up and distributed as widely as possible a questionnaire for teachers of the poem at all levels and in many kinds of educational institutions. We planned to use the responses to develop a collection of essays by invited contributors, to which we would add introductory matter in the format of the series.

In the spring and summer of 1982, when the digesting of our questionnaire materials and the editing of our contributors' essays were drawing to a close, it sometimes seemed to us that, however much the study of *Beowulf* might be flourishing in the classrooms of the world, there was a cult of *Beowulf* that had somehow escaped from the classroom or private study and emerged into the public consciousness. An animated musical film from Australia called *Grendel Grendel Grendel*, with the title role spoken by Peter Ustinov, was seen briefly in New York City and some other centers. The acknowledged basis for the film was John Gardner's novel *Grendel* (1971), but there was something of the comic-book cartoon in the film also, a reminder of the thematically and artistically ambitious (and incongruous) *Beowulf* comics of a decade earlier. Early risers in Manhattan were invited by the *Village Voice* (3 Aug. 1982) to 6 a.m. and 6 p.m. free performances of *Beowulf* in Central Park's East Meadow, "a ritual-ceremonial experience in six movements based on the medieval epic . . . a vision-quest or journey to attain consciousness." In London the *Observer* (1 Aug. 1982) reviewed a one-man performance of "an expurgated *Beowulf*" at the Lyric Theatre, Hammersmith, by Julian Glover, who later took his show to the Edinburgh Festival. During the summer recess, at any rate, it seemed that *Beowulf* was to be found almost everywhere in the world but in the usual English department classroom.

In the classroom, however, if our questionnaires are true indicators, the poem is flourishing as perhaps never before—see Joseph F. Tuso's chapter for some surprising figures. It flourishes, moreover, increasingly in translated form, before younger audiences than was customary a few decades ago, and often in novel company with other works of imagination and science.

After World War II, *Beowulf* was widely taught in translation from survey-course anthologies and studied in Old English graduate courses or seminars. The work was either read mainly for philology or else related diachronically, if in few other ways, to the history of English literature. It was the staple of the philological requirement in many graduate schools of English that were shortly to reconstitute the requirement in a linguistics category, then restrict it more narrowly to a history of the English language option, then eliminate the requirement altogether, sometimes (but not always) banishing *Beowulf* from the curriculum altogether. Nowadays *Beowulf* is still studied in Old English, but by no means so frequently as before and certainly not as an unquestioned and universal graduate English requirement. It is studied today by proportionately more undergraduates than ever before, often in classes of mixed graduates and undergraduates. It is read in various good verse or prose translations (see the chapter by Douglas D. Short) in high schools and preparatory schools, at community colleges, in undergraduate courses in a wide distribution of liberal arts institutions, and, to be sure, in those graduate schools that can still afford to cater to a taste or a need for the Dark Ages in an educational market increasingly and restrictively competitive, egalitarian, technocratic, professional, popular, and geared to preparation in law, medicine, and business.

If a musical performance of *Beowulf* as a consciousness-raising medium at dawn in Central Park is no longer an anomaly, neither is the teaching of the poem as an ancestor or analogue to a futuristic motion picture like *Star Wars*. "After all," an enthusiastic and outstandingly successful young teacher writes on his questionnaire, "Darth Vader's helmet looks like the Sutton Hoo helmet." (Darth Vader is the intergalactic villain in *Star Wars*.) "So I show them the Sutton Hoo helmet and we talk about *Star Wars* and *Beowulf*."

The merely terrestrial *Beowulf* of old is now taught in bracing and eclectic company. We asked our correspondents, "If you compare *Beowulf* with other works of literature, religion, and history, indicate which and for what purpose." The replies include *The Tain*, Tolkien's *The Lord of the Rings*, *The Heliand*, *The Song of Roland*, *The Nibelungenlied*, *Sir Gawain and the Green Knight*, the *Saga of Grettir* and *Njal's Saga*, John Gardner's *Grendel*, Old Testament heroic sagas and poems, space movies, Homer and Vergil, *Billy Budd*, *Lord Jim*, and *Huckleberry Finn*. The "purpose" inquired about is always pedagogical and markedly subjective. Most respondents discuss undergraduate students and do not think much about philology, but those who answered another question about teaching *Beowulf* in translation regularly said they take care to introduce when they can some elements of the original Old English: "I show them and read them short illustrative passages"; "I write the first three lines of the poem on the board and read them"; "I mention Old English words and discuss them, like *wyrd* and *scop*, which just mean "fate" and "poet" but in very special senses." This is minimalist philology but good teaching if a class has one hour per term for *Beowulf*.

When we asked which background and supplementary materials were used, we received in answer a conspectus of the most famous names and titles in our field, works by Chambers, Sisam, Whitelock, Klaeber, and many others, who are cataloged in other pages of the present volume. Along with these are mentioned the *Germania* of Tacitus, Claude Lévi-Strauss' *The Savage Mind*, Ker's *Catalogue of Manuscripts containing Anglo-Saxon* or Ogilvy's *Books Known to Anglo-Latin Writers from Aldhelm to Alcuin (670–804)*, Lord's *The Singer of Tales*, Havelock's *A Preface to Plato*, Beryl Rowland's *Medieval Women's Guide to Health: The First English Gynecological Handbook*, and many others—a list too various to categorize but indicative of a new pluralism in the *Beowulf* profession.

More prosaically, we asked our friends and colleagues, "If you teach other Old English works in conjunction with *Beowulf*, state which and how much each enhances understanding of *Beowulf*." We are directed, emphatically and repeatedly, to the so-called elegies, especially *Deor*, *The Wanderer*, *The Seafarer*, and *The Wife's Lament*; *The Battle of Maldon*; *The Dream of the Rood*; the story of Caedmon and his *Hymn*; and the *Maxims*. Interestingly, our stipulation about the enhancement of understanding was seldom replied to, perhaps because the answer is obvious. It is clear, rather, that *Beowulf* instructors see Old English literature as an organon, an interrelated inventory, and they habitually teach it that way to the full stretch of their abilities and opportunities.

Readers may be interested in a short review of some of the remaining items on our preliminary questionnaire. We received about one hundred responses from teachers of *Beowulf*, whether in Old English or in translation, at all levels. We learned that *Beowulf* is taught to:

(a) graduate students   approximately   15%
(b) undergraduate English majors   approximately   30%
(c) undergraduate nonmajors   approximately   45%
(d) mixed graduates and undergraduates   approximately   10%

It seems to us that category (c) is the most remarkable and prophetic.

Major Questions

1. "If you teach *Beowulf* in Old English, which edition(s) do you use and why?" The majority recommend Klaeber for quality of edition and apparatus, especially the magnificent glossary, and for availability. It is described as "the most for the money" and "the most complete even though not up-to-date." A considerable minority prefer Wrenn-Bolton for quality of edition, for less formidable and more accessible apparatus than Klaeber's, and for the welcome updating of the critical introduction. Another considerable minority favor Chickering for economy and for the facing-page translation, as well as for the overall excellence of a well-rounded presentation of the poem.

2. "If you teach *Beowulf* in a Modern English translation, indicate which you use and why." (The reader should also consult Douglas D. Short's chapter, for it was prepared independently of our collation of questionnaires.) The order of preference—probably not too significant in so small a sample but not without interest—is Donaldson by a large measure, followed by Raffel, Chickering, Kennedy, Alfred, Clark Hall, and Hieatt. (Greenfield's translation was not yet available at the time of our survey.) The responses to this question are notably emotional or else typically resigned: "Donaldson's is always reliably close to the original; its prose is conservative, so that one must or can *imagine* the poetry; it is surpassingly available, in three different formats." "Raffel's is simply splendid but too free." "Alfred's is fine, noble, stirring."

3. "What are your views on the teaching of *Beowulf* in a modern translation?" The views expressed here are moderate, grateful, or indignant, in about equal measure. One instructor declares that "The modern translations I have seen would never be read by someone not compelled to read them. They are difficult to teach because not worth teaching on their own merits. It's a delight to teach the poem in Old English. But when the poem must be taught in just one hour or not at all, one is forced to translations." Another writes: "This seems to me to be not a real issue, as the choice between teaching Chaucer in Middle English or in a modernized version is. Teaching *Beowulf* in Modern English is the only way most of us are ever going to be able to teach it. There are excellent translations, and it is an easy compromise. I almost *prefer* teaching a translation, so that the students can avoid the distraction of translating."

4. "If you use an anthology, which do you use?" The order of preference here is Norton, Tuso, Oxford.

The main text of this volume covers the remaining questions, except for one that asked for "approximately five to ten essential background, critical, or reference works with which you believe instructors of *Beowulf* should be familiar." We need not tally the responses here, because they make up the critical mass of well-known and permanently valuable work on *Beowulf*, as outlined in the "Instructor's Library" chapter. What deserves notice here is that, on the basis of our samplings, it would appear that people teaching *Beowulf* nowadays, and in particular those teaching the poem in translation primarily to undergraduates, are remarkably well-informed about *Beowulf* scholarship and evidently well-equipped with teaching materials.

Part One

MATERIALS

EDITIONS

Selecting a text to use in the classroom poses several choices for the teacher of *Beowulf*. Most basic of these is whether the poem will be taught in Old English or in translation. Because, for one reason or another, most instructors elect translations, Douglas D. Short provides extensive discussion of those available in "Translations of *Beowulf*." In that chapter, too, he covers dual-language editions, with Old and Modern English versions on facing pages, and translations in anthologies. Thus, our present concern is exclusively with Old English texts. While we supply no recommendations here as to the relative merits of particular editions over others, we include synopses of comments taken from the questionnaires returned by colleagues who have used or are currently using these texts. Such comments, we hope, will be valuable to instructors seeking a *Beowulf* edition suited to their individual needs. Full bibliographical data are provided in the Works Cited at the end of this volume.

Inarguably, the most complete edition of *Beowulf* in Old English is that of Frederick Klaeber, Beowulf *and the Fight at Finnsburg*. It is the text generally cited in scholarly studies of *Beowulf* and it is frequently used in graduate and undergraduate classes around the world. Klaeber's *Beowulf* is acclaimed because, in addition to a sound text, it contains extensive support material vital for a thorough study of the poem. Indeed, such material makes up the bulk of the book: of 471 numbered pages, only 120 are *Beowulf* text. The remainder are explanatory notes; the important Finnsburg fragment (with a valuable introduction, notes, and bibliography for it); four appendixes covering (1) analogues and parallel passages drawn from Anglo-Saxon genealogies, Scandinavian documents, and Roman, Frankish, and Gothic historians; (2) aspects of Old Germanic life touched on in *Beowulf*, indexed according to line number and with a full listing of synonymous terms; (3) textual criticism, citing anomalous forms and metrical incongruities; (4) the text of *Waldere*, *Deor*, and selections from *Widsith* and the Old High German *Hildebrandslied*; glossaries of words and proper names; and two supplements, each updating the notes, glossaries, and bibliographies of previous editions. There are also 187 pages of introduction, containing a bibliography, a table of abbreviations, general remarks, and eight black-and-white plates illustrating two pages from the Cotton Vitellius A. XV manuscript, objects and scenes from pre-Conquest life, and the geography of *Beowulf*, as well as specific discussions of eight important aspects of the poem: (1) "Argument of the Poem"; (2) "The Fabulous or Supernatural Elements"; (3) "The Historical Elements"; (4) "The Christian Coloring"; (5) "Structure of the Poem";

3

(6) "Tone, Style, Meter"; (7) "Language, Manuscript"; (8) "Genesis of the Poem."

It is characteristic of human nature that some make a vice of what others find virtue; and certainly the case stands thus with Klaeber's edition, which has not been found suitable for every classroom. The extensive support material is universally praised by teachers of *Beowulf* as indispensable for their own work, yet some report that its very thoroughness renders the edition "too sophisticated," even "daunting," for their students to use. These instructors cite the small print and great length of the appendixes and supplements, only parts of which are intelligible to or needed by beginning students, whether graduate or undergraduate. "Sorting through it all to pick out what can be understood is difficult and time-consuming—and it's discouraging when half the analogues are printed in Latin with no translation" is a comment typical of many. Similar criticism has been leveled at the explanatory notes, which one colleague deems "excessively grammatical." It is also pointed out that many notes need to be revised in light of recent scholarship, as of course does the bibliography, which contains no reference later than 1950. The placement of the notes—in the back of the book, and then in two different locations among the supplements—is "inconvenient" for some, who would prefer a text with notes on the same page with the item they explain. The glossary is also sometimes criticized for providing more information than one needs in a teaching text. "A list of every instance of a word and its variants," runs the argument, "goes beyond the requirements of students. It burns them out with too much information."

While all, or certainly most, of the many teachers who use Klaeber's edition in their classes recognize these criticisms, they tend to weigh more heavily the advantages they feel come with the Klaeber text. Courses that emphasize the historical context of *Beowulf* or study it alongside other literatures seem to benefit from the extensive appendixes and supplementary material. One teacher considers the Latin excerpts "enormously helpful, even if I do have to translate Saxo for the students myself." A number of colleagues justify placing the glossary in the rear of the book on pedagogical grounds, arguing that this deprives students of a crutch available in texts with marginal glosses. "If it's not already done for them, they have to think it out and then memorize the forms. Isn't that what it's all about, really?" A large number of teachers consider Klaeber's glossary "in every way superior to other editions," since its multitude of forms and citations clarifies for students the complex set of choices involved in acts of translation. Delicate but vital nuance and subtle shading of the language become apparent after careful study of Klaeber's glossary. "It's not for all students, perhaps, but for the good ones, who really want to know Old English, it's the only choice," sums up opinion of this kind. Indeed, it may be true to say that most instructors who use Klaeber do so because it was the edition they used in graduate school, and they believe—correctly—that this will remain the standard scholarly edition for some time to come. As one teacher of *Beowulf* in Old English to undergraduates put it, "I require Klaeber for all my students, so that if any go on to do advanced work, he or she won't have to buy another book."

As an alternative to Klaeber, quite a few teachers of *Beowulf* have turned to the edition of C. L. Wrenn, Beowulf, *with the Finnesburg Fragment*, available since 1973 in a revised form by W. F. Bolton. Wrenn developed his edition in 1953 in response to what he perceived as the failure of previous versions "to present *Beowulf* in its proper setting as a great *poem* to university students," rather than as linguistic artifact or historical monument. Thus, Wrenn answers many of the reservations expressed about Klaeber by respondents to the survey questionnaire. The format of the volume is much different from Klaeber, appearing rather streamlined in comparison. Supporting material remains substantial but fills fewer pages: there are 318 total in Wrenn's first edition, of which 86 are *Beowulf* and the Finnsburg fragment. Wrenn's introduction is broken into seven sections: (1) "The Manuscript"; (2) "The Title"; (3) "The Text"; (4) "Date and Place of Origin"; (5) "The Subject-Matter"; (6) "Structure of the Poem"; (7) "Verse Technique." Additional apparatus consists of a select bibliography, a list of abbreviations, commentary on the poem, a glossary, a select glossary to Finnsburg, and a glossary of proper names. There are no maps or illustrative plates. In his original edition, Wrenn followed the example of Klaeber and printed only textual notes (much updated) at the foot of each page, also citing, like his predecessor, the authors of variant readings and emendations. He modified Klaeber, however, by shifting the linguistic elements of Klaeber's notes to the glossary, so that the "commentary" is precisely that: it frequently offers translations of difficult passages, explains cultural patterns, identifies historically verifiable events, describes scenes, and fills in obscure sections of plot. Despite the shifting of linguistic material from the textual notes, Wrenn's remains a "students' glossary" in that it follows models established by Sweet's *Primer* and *Reader*. As Wrenn pointed out in a prefatory note to his glossary, he intended there "no *complete* record of every occurrence of all the forms." Each word in the poem is glossed, with spelling variants included, but regular inflectional forms do not appear separately, and headwords are spelled according to the "forms most frequently found in the text." No reference to textual location is made except when a passage supplies a meaning other than the blanket one listed first by Wrenn. Finally, Wrenn's text itself is generally more conservative than Klaeber's, since it incorporates fewer emendations of an editorial sort and represents the manuscript more strictly, supplemented (often silently) by Thorkelin's transcriptions.

It should be noted, however, that in his first and second editions Wrenn did lengthen forms that seemed to him contracted in the Late West Saxon of the manuscript, in order to "restore" the metrical pattern of lines in accordance with Sievers' system.

For his third revised edition, Bolton responded to a number of criticisms of Wrenn that had been offered over the years. Gone are the "decontracted" words of Wrenn's two editions; gone, too, is much of Wrenn's introduction, which has been shortened throughout and rewritten, most notably in the final three subsections. These now bear the titles (5) "Narrative Content," (6) "Verse Techniques," and (7) "Structure and Theme." A helpful two pages of genealogical charts preface them, illustrating the royal houses of Denmark, Geatland, and Sweden. These new sections represent Bolton's views and incorporate scholarship more recent (through 1970) than was available to Wrenn.

Other modifications made by Bolton include removal of the "Commentary" from a separate section toward the rear of the volume to the bottom of each page of text—a change requiring significant compression of the explanatory material available for students. This decision also enforces an entirely new attitude toward translation, since many of these now-marginal notes consist of difficult passages rendered in Modern English. The glossary itself has also been modified by the addition of a number of significant variant spellings of common words in the list of headwords. Finally, the bibliography has been thoroughly redone, with special emphasis placed on recent scholarship. Bolton has added brief annotations to most entries, indicating authorial point of view, character of translation, general drift of critical argument, and so forth. The edition also contains a discography.

Wrenn-Bolton, then, is designed primarily for use in the classroom, and a number of instructors have hailed it enthusiastically on this ground. They cite its greater accessibility, the advantages of marginal glosses, the annotated, relatively current bibliography, the sound—and wieldy—introductory matter as especially helpful. Certain colleagues have adopted this edition because, in their view, "students no longer have the linguistic sophistication to handle Klaeber, and Wrenn-Bolton provides a comfortable alternative." On the other hand, it has been charged that the page-bottom commentary in Wrenn-Bolton relieves students of the need to puzzle out demanding translations on their own. This results, in the words of one critic, in "homogenized translation: all my students sound just like Bolton in class, and on tests, too, because they memorize the commentary." Bolton's reduction of Wrenn's original commentary is regretted by some who have taught using all three editions, and some appear to feel that the excisions from the introduction constitute a loss as well. In general, Wrenn-Bolton receives high marks for layout and typography, being considered "readable and clear" by those who choose to remark on this, but one teacher observes that the lines are printed "too closely together to encourage students to produce their own interlinear glosses"—a fact that "merely goes along with the over-all tendency of these editors to do the students' work for them."

Two editions of *Beowulf* seldom used in classrooms are Beowulf *and* Judith, edited by Elliott Van Kirk Dobbie in the Anglo-Saxon Poetic Records series, and a volume of the same title produced by Francis P. Magoun, Jr., with revisions by Jess B. Bessinger, Jr. Magoun-Bessinger is, as its Foreword specifies, designed merely to facilitate "pleasure reading." Two other important editions, frequently cited in scholarly discussions, were mentioned also by our respondents, not as teaching texts but as supplementary references for instructors and advanced students. The highly respected Else von Schaubert's three-volume revision of the much earlier edition of Moritz Heyne, *Beowulf, mit ausfürlichem Glossar* (1863), as revised by Levin L. Schücking (1908), is one of these; von Schaubert's revision of Heyne-Schücking is now in its eighteenth edition. The second often-mentioned but seldom-taught edition has long been studied in England and America: Alfred J. Wyatt's Beowulf *with the Finnesburg Fragment*, revised by R. W. Chambers.

TRANSLATIONS OF *BEOWULF*

Douglas D. Short

Prose Translations

Although the original edition of John R. Clark Hall's prose translation dates from 1901, it has escaped obsolescence because of the periodic revisions and new apparatus by C. L. Wrenn and the addition of a chapter on diction and meter by J. R. R. Tolkien. The translation is quite literal, and it attempts to suggest the stately language of the original by using formal diction and the archaic pronominal forms "thou" and "thee" and the appropriate "-est" verbal inflection. But aside from the second-person constructions, Clark Hall's version makes sparing use of the artificially archaic style typically found in translations of that vintage. The one questionable feature of this volume is its running plot summary that alternates with the translation after nearly every paragraph.

Over the years R. K. Gordon's prose *Beowulf* in his *Anglo-Saxon Poetry* has remained popular with graduate students because it is included in an inexpensive volume that conveniently assembles translations of most of the surviving Old English verse. Advances in textual scholarship, however, have reduced the utility of the Gordon renderings as translational aids, and the virtual absence of any critical apparatus limits its suitability as a classroom text. Moreover, the volume has recently been replaced in the familiar Everyman's Library series by a new set of translations by S. A. J. Bradley. Commenting specifically on his rendering of *Beowulf*, Bradley explains that he has accommodated the "densely textured" language of the poem with "a slightly more expansive manner of translation" (411). What Bradley means is probably best reflected in his diction, which shows a decided preference for the ornate. Thus, Scyld Scefing "dispossessed" his enemies of their mead benches, and Grendel, first introduced as an "obdurate being," suffers in Beowulf's grip, and "in his shoulder a great lesion became conspicuous." The general view of ancient Germanic culture that emerges from a reading of Bradley's *Beowulf* has, like his diction, a distinctly Latin coloration; it is a culture that abounds in "chalices" rather than "cups." Still, Bradley's translations are reasonably accurate. The advanced student who seeks a broad familiarity with Old English poetry will definitely find the Bradley collection useful.

Although it captures little of the stylistic flavor of the original, David Wright's *Beowulf* is one of the most readable translations on the market. Wright achieves this distinction by working consistently in "the middle style," as he puts it. His diction is moderately formal with little hint of the archaic or poetic. But the factor that contributes most to its readability is the natural quality of the syntax, for Wright has eliminated most of the asyndetic coordination and appositional constructions that enrich the original Old English. Thus, while the general reader may find Wright's prose a comfortable if rather colorless vehicle for the narrative, the specialist will certainly miss the echoes of the compound diction, distinctive syntax, and other stylistic features of the original that most prose translations to some extent preserve.

William Alfred's prose version of *Beowulf* may interest teachers of medieval surveys since it appears in a volume that also includes *The Song of Roland*, *The Nibelungenlied*, and *The Poem of the Cid*. Aside from a tendency toward rhetorical embellishment, Alfred's rendering is moderately accurate, although not sufficiently so to serve the advanced student as a reliable pony. This translation may appeal to the mature reader with a taste for elevated style and a willingness to forgive an occasional lapse in diction.

With its short lines and unjustified right margins, Lucien Dean Pearson's *Beowulf* appears to be a verse translation, and in fact selected passages in the poem—such as the voyages to and from Heorot, the description of Grendel's mere, the lament of the lone survivor—are given in blank verse. Rowland L. Collins, the author of the introduction, characterizes the form as rhythmic prose interrupted by occasional passages of iambic pentameter with a four-beat pattern in counterpoint. Ultimately this alternation between prose and poetry seems rather idiosyncratic, since the only rule involved seems to be Pearson's impression that some passages in *Beowulf* are more lyrical than others and thus earn special treatment. Yet anyone who has studied the poem carefully can find many passages overlooked by Pearson that have equal claim to lyrical distinction. Moreover, his translational scheme may obscure other, more significant structural segmentation—namely, the episodes, digressions, and rhetorical set pieces that *Beowulf* scholars customarily identify in the poem. Another problem with the mixing of prose and poetry is that it may create a false impression of the original prosody. *Beowulf* may well vary in the quality of its lyricism, but it remains prosodically homogeneous.

The prose translation by E. Talbot Donaldson is probably the most widely circulated version on the market, a status owing partly to its availability in three formats: as an inexpensive paperback with a modest introduction, as the *Beowulf* translation included in the ubiquitous *Norton Anthology*, and subsequently as the focus of a Norton Critical Edition. Donaldson's is one of the most literal renderings of the poem ever produced that does not sound like an interlinear gloss, and it is thus an excellent choice for the student seeking a translational aid. The less sophisticated student, however, will likely find this version more difficult to read than most others because it preserves so much of the original syntax and compound vocabulary. Nevertheless, Donaldson shows good judgment in sensing the limits to which a literal rendering can be pushed; the style may seem formal and unidiomatic to the general reader, but it is never unnatural. In all respects Donaldson's translation well supports the extensive apparatus of a critical edition of the poem, although *Beowulf* scholars must regret the skimpy resources that W. W. Norton and Company committed to that undertaking, especially in light of the relative heft of virtually every other Norton Critical Edition. Joseph F. Tuso, the editor of the Norton *Beowulf*, made sensible choices for the secondary materials included in the volume, but the necessity of resorting to excerpts rather than complete essays reduces the usefulness of an otherwise attractive project.

For a successful compromise between strict accuracy and easy readability, Constance B. Hieatt's Beowulf *and Other Old English Poems* is a serviceable translation worthy of consideration. The introduction by A. Kent Hieatt is well suited to the needs of the nonspecialist reader, and the addition of seven other Old English poems, including *Judith* and Ezra Pound's version of *The Seafarer*, enhances the utility of the book as an undergraduate text.

George N. Garmonsway and Jacqueline Simpson's Beowulf *and Its Analogues* is probably most often consulted for its handy translations of several Latin and Germanic analogues to the poem, many of which are not readily available elsewhere. Not surprisingly in a work of this sort, the *Beowulf* translation is quite literal; furthermore, it has one rather distinctive feature. As much as possible Garmonsway and Simpson render individual Old English words and phrases with exact Modern English equivalents, formula for formula. They also try to reproduce each element in compounds, although in doing so they often generate lengthy circumlocutions and thus sacrifice some fidelity to syntax. Most of their various efforts to convey verbal subtleties will go unnoticed by the nonspecialist, who may sense only the formality of the diction, but the advanced student reading the poem in the original might find this translation particularly instructive.

Verse Translations

Most verse translations of *Beowulf* imitate Old English prosody by using accentual meter with four stresses per line and some degree of alliteration. Charles W. Kennedy's *Beowulf: The Oldest English Epic* is one of the best known of the type since it has been in print for some time and appears in the first edition of the *Oxford Anthology of English Literature*. While Kennedy's version remains unsurpassed in imitating the sound of the original Old English, many readers will find his emphasis on alliteration in heavily stressed syllables to be cloying, since, as *Beowulf* translators themselves often remark, the modern reader is unaccustomed to extended passages of hammering alliteration. Nor will all readers warm to the abundance of stilted diction, trite poeticisms, and inverted syntax in the rendering—" 'tis," " 'twas," "ween," "Whence come you . . . ," "Deed of daring and dream of honor / Bring you, friend Beowulf . . . ," and the like. These archaisms seem all the more jarring against the informality of pronominal contractions in the dialogue passages. Also, Kennedy's lengthy introduction, while still of interest, is beginning to show its age. For example, it gives credence to the theory that the poem incorporates a number of separate lays, a notion that few recent scholars are inclined to accept without considerable qualification. In fact, Kennedy uses italics and longer lines to translate the passages that he believes originated in this fashion. Similarly, the apparatus that accompanies the *Oxford Anthology* version of the translation has its problems, not the least of which is its curiously uneven editorial policy. For instance, the generously sprinkled footnotes added to the Kennedy text usually do little more than interrupt the reader to gloss terms that are perfectly clear in context—words like "battle-board," "bale," and "winsome." Yet elsewhere the same reader who presumably lacks the sophistication to infer that a battle board is a shield is invited to compare Beowulf's funeral with Jordanes' sixth-century Latin account of the funeral of Attila the Hun. The quality of the commentary in the anthology introduction is as disappointing as the textual notes. Typical is the remark on Beowulf's reaction to the gift of the heirloom necklace: "On that first occasion, a pang of mortality strikes Beowulf as he looks at the splendid neck-ring he has been given by Hrothgar as part of his reward for victory over Grendel" (25). Actually the poet never mentions that Beowulf looks at the necklace (given to him by Wealhtheow, not Hrothgar), much less that Beowulf experiences pangs of mortality. In sum, Kennedy's *Beowulf* gives a vigorous if somewhat taxing imitation of the original Old English prosody, but problems in diction and style and weaknesses in editorial apparatus keep it from being a wise choice for classroom use.

Edwin Morgan's *Beowulf* avoids most of the archaic diction so prevalent in Kennedy's version, but ultimately this is a dull and frequently awkward translation. Hrothgar's report of the attack by Grendel's mother illustrates the problem:

> "The fight she has avenged
> Where yesterday evening you destroyed Grendel
> In violent act with unlax fists
> Since he had deprived me of my folk and ruined them
> Longer than was right."   (1333–37)

It would be unfair to dismiss a translation on the weaknesses of a single passage, but unfortunately this excerpt from Morgan is painfully typical of the whole.

Burton Raffel produces one of the liveliest translations of *Beowulf*, but he takes considerable license with the original in doing so. He is concerned with reproducing the spirit rather than the letter of the original, and he goes about this task with a fair degree of success. His diction is consistently vivid, and he manages alliteration more skillfully than most verse translators, for although he uses alliteration extensively, it is rarely obtrusive. While this version will not serve those who want to gain a feel for the syntax and rhetorical strategies of the original, the general reader may find Raffel's *Beowulf* more aesthetically satisfying than translations of a more academic flavor.

Perhaps the most beautiful poetic rendering of *Beowulf* is that of Kevin Crossley-Holland, a work that achieves an irresistible blend of artistry and scholarship. Crossley-Holland finds just the right style to convey the dignity of the original poem without recourse to archaisms, stilted language, inverted syntax, and other such questionable devices. The diction is formal yet natural, the alliteration subtle yet effective, and the deviations from the strictly literal are always reasonable. The introduction by Bruce Mitchell reprints portions of his excellent article " 'Until the Dragon Comes . . .': Some Thoughts on *Beowulf*," an essay that ranks among the best general overviews of the poem. Mitchell also contributes a useful set of appendixes, including an uncommonly efficient discussion of the poem's complex array of episodes and digressions.

Like the translation by Burton Raffel, Michael Alexander's *Beowulf* is more concerned with capturing the spirit of the original than with giving a literal translation of it. But unlike Raffel, Alexander has occasional problems with diction that somewhat diminish his efforts. For instance, in one breath Beowulf refers colloquially to the "heap of treasure" given him by Hrothgar and then explains pompously that "The ways of that king accorded to usage: / I was not to forgo the guerdon he had offered" (2144–45). Elsewhere Alexander's flights of poetic fancy are so flashy they fairly well overpower the original:

> those scaly flesh-eaters sat not down
> to dine on Beowulf, they browsed not on me
> in that picnic they'd designed in the dingles of the sea.   (562–64)

For the reader interested in a lively translation that makes no pretense to accuracy, Alexander's version may be a viable choice, but Raffel's *Beowulf* may ultimately prove a more satisfying one.

Of all the verse translations of the poem, Stanley B. Greenfield's *A Readable* Beowulf probably comes closest to serving the needs of the general reader while still holding the interest of the specialist. As his title suggests, Greenfield's primary goal is readability, but unlike others with the same goal, he rarely strays very far from a literal rendering. He uses a nine-syllable line throughout to emphasize the accentual rather than metrical nature of Old English rhythm and also to give greater prominence to caesuras than is typical in lines with an even number of syllables. A further effect of the nine-syllable line is the compactness it gives to the translation. This version of *Beowulf* reads very quickly; in fact, the fixed line length probably makes this the shortest complete translation of the poem available. But the most outstanding feature of this translation is the number of subtleties in the original poem that it manages to reproduce or in some way suggest. For example, at times Greenfield varies the number of heavy stresses from the usual four per line to imitate the relative density of secondary stress in the original Old English. Also, he manipulates his syntax and diction so as to preserve many stylistic and rhetorical details of the original—not merely the obvious kennings that all translators recognize but also such smaller details as chiasmus, envelope patterns, antithesis, and other artistic jewels that adorn the original. Of course, most of these subtleties will be noticed only by those who have some expertise in Old English, but by including such matters while producing an eminently readable translation, Greenfield serves both the specialist and nonspecialist alike. He provides excellent notes on the text, and Alain Renoir contributes an introduction largely adapted from one of his previous essays, *"Beowulf: A Contextual Introduction to Its Contents and Techniques."*

Combined Texts and Translations

Howell D. Chickering's *Beowulf: A Dual-Language Edition* is one of two first-rate modern translations with the Old English on facing pages. This rendering employs a predominantly four-stress line with heavy emphasis on the caesura but with only a suggestion of the original alliteration. The translation is more accurate than most other poetic versions and would read smoothly were it not for the policy of highlighting the caesuras with gaps in the printed lines, a practice adopted from editions of Old English poetry. But while these may aid in the prosodic and formulaic analysis of Old English, they prove an annoying obstruction to the flow of a modern translation. As for the apparatus, Chickering's is by far the most extensive of any translation currently available. The introduction includes a plot summary together with sections on style, narrative technique, structure, and critical interpretations. Following the text and translation is a lengthy chapter of background materials incorporating such topics as the history of the manuscript, the provenance of the poem, sources and analogues, and Germanic social traditions. But most striking of all is Chickering's commentary, a monograph-length chapter of interpretation with extensive references to previous criticism.

Michael Swanton's *Beowulf* is another modern translation with the Old English on the facing pages, but it differs from Chickering's in three respects: it is written in prose rather than in verse, it is less extensive in its apparatus, and it generally avoids references to *Beowulf* criticism. This volume is suitable for advanced students, especially those studying the poem in the original language, for the translation is extremely literal and is accompanied by a scholarly edition of the text. Eighteen pages of textual and interpretive notes elucidate the most problematic passages in the text. In his introduction Swanton places emphasis on Germanic backgrounds and gives special attention to sources and analogues.

There are a few other translations that merit notice but that, for various reasons, may not be suitable for the college classroom. James L. Brown's prose *Beowulf* remains faithful to the original and includes a detailed introduction, but its availability is probably limited since it appears to be the product of a hand-operated letterpress. Albert W. Haley's verse *Beowulf* is an attractive and literal version, but it has no critical apparatus. Ian Serraillier, Robert Nye, Frederick Rebsamen, and Rosemary Sutcliff have each authored an adaptation or abridged translation appropriate for younger readers but unacceptable for college students. For quite different reasons college students should also avoid Benjamin Thorpe's antiquated facing-column version, originally published in 1855. While this book may be of interest to the veteran scholar studying the editorial history of the poem, the translation has been obsolete for over a century and is thus clearly unsuitable for nonspecialists. Unfortunately, the publication of the reprint in the familiar Barron's Educational Series has promoted the book to the wrong readership and misled many an unwary student looking for a convenient aid in translating the original. Another dual-language edition, John Porter's *Beowulf*, takes the concept of a literal translation to a bizarre extreme, as a random sampling readily illustrates: "You the speech words wise Lord in mind sent; not heard I more intelligent at so young age man make speech" (lines 1841–43). Obviously this is not a translation in the conventional sense but, rather, a verbatim gloss on the poem.

There are so many subjective factors involved in selecting a *Beowulf* translation that any recommendations must be viewed cautiously. What appeals to one reader as a dignified style may strike another as stilted bombast; what one reader takes as vigorous prosody may seem alliterative doggerel to another; even translational accuracy, the sine qua non to many, may be dismissed as slavish pedantry by others. Fortunately, we have such a variety of translations that nearly everyone—from the inexperienced freshman to the seasoned scholar—can be assured of finding a version that will make reading *Beowulf* not only a pleasant experience but a rich and memorable one as well.

AIDS TO TEACHING

Audio

For most teachers of *Beowulf*, whether in Old or Modern English, the sound of the original language is important. Instructors working with the poem in translation frequently read passages aloud to their students in Old English or play them tapes or records made by others. Many teaching *Beowulf* in the original also use such aids to sharpen students' ears and to provide experience in listening to Old English in voices other than their own. Assigned hours in language laboratories are not uncommon for students in a number of institutions, as an integral part of their courses on *Beowulf*. For instructors who do not make their own tapes, as some do, such aural aids are available in various forms.

To put the language of the poem in historical perspective, the two-record set prepared by Helge Kökeritz, *A Thousand Years of English Pronunciation*, is clear and effective. Kökeritz reads nearly one hundred lines of *Beowulf*, along with examples of English from later periods. A comparable historical survey is provided by a three-record (or three-cassette) set by Jess B. Bessinger, Jr., *A History of the English Language*. Other selected readings from *Beowulf* on record include Jess B. Bessinger, Jr., Beowulf *and Other Poetry in Old English*, accompanying himself on a replica of the Sutton Hoo harp or lyre (now available only on cassette tape); Arthur G. Brodeur, *Beowulf* (a limited-edition recording produced for subscription among his friends and students); Nevill Coghill and Norman Davis, *Beowulf*; Charles W. Dunn, *Early English Poetry*; Francis P. Magoun, Jr., *Beowulf*; and John C. Pope, *Beowulf, Chaucer*. A complete reading of the poem is that of Kemp Malone, short-titled Beowulf *in Old English*.

A recording of a different sort is *Lament for Beowulf*, a musical composition for mixed chorus and orchestra by Howard Hanson. It was completed in 1925 and first performed at the Ann Arbor Festival in 1926. The funeral dirge is greatly modified from the translation of William Morris and Alfred J. Wyatt, *The Tale of Beowulf, Sometime King of the Folk of the Weder Geats*. The attempt of the composer was, apparently, to capture the "tone" of *Beowulf* in music and song.

A tape of a two-hour public radio broadcast, featuring Robert Creed reading selections from *Beowulf* to the accompaniment of a lyre, as well as discussion of the poem and readings by John Foley, Donald K. Fry, Bruce Rosenberg, and Creed, may be purchased from Charles Potter. All proceeds from the sale of this tape go as contributions to Radio Arts of New York, which sponsored the original panel. Another tape, of twenty-nine minutes' length, is available on cassette and has Fred C. Robinson lecturing on *Beowulf* as an introduction for the nonspecialist. Finally, Caedmon Records also has *Kemp Malone on Old English Poetry: A Lecture with Readings in Old English, with the Kemp Malone Translations*. This is a general discussion with references to *Beowulf*.

Beowulf: A Musical Epic, by Betty Jane Wylie and Victor Davies, is a contemporary setting of the poem for soloists, chorus, and symphony orchestra, on three records or cassettes.

Visuals

Just as many teachers employ aural aids in their classes, both to further enjoyment of the poem and to promote understanding, so also do many turn to various visual materials in helping students to perceive the meaning of passages, to locate themselves in the world of *Beowulf*, and to discover the social and psychological dimensions of the poem. Because of the growing use and availability of visual aids, we have included specific discussion of them in the chapter "Visual Materials for Teaching *Beowulf*," by Donald K. Fry.

Derivative Works

As Constance B. Hieatt points out in her chapter "Parallels, Useful Analogues, and Elusive Sources," many literary works share elements with *Beowulf* and a number of historical documents contribute to our knowledge of the events of the poem. *Beowulf* also bears relation to various modern pieces, both of poetry and of prose. Perhaps the best known of these is J. R. R. Tolkien's trilogy *The Lord of the Rings*, which has found its way into genre courses. Some instructors find such derivative works as Tolkien's helpful when teaching *Beowulf* itself. A poem by a contemporary writer may sometimes illuminate a point as well as or better than a picture or a recording; a historical novel may be assigned to achieve the same effect or to help students get the "feel" of life in Anglo-Saxon England.

Teachers of *Beowulf* describe a variety of works as particularly useful. Kingsley Amis' poem "Beowulf" and Richard Wilbur's poem by the same title are short, intense lyrics that suggest contrasts between our contemporary attitudes and values and those motivating Anglo-Saxon society. Jorge Luis Borges makes a similar point, albeit less directly, in another brief lyric, "Compositión escrita en un ejemplar de la gesta de *Beowulf*." A lengthy poem "in the spirit" of *Beowulf* was published in 1901 by Samuel Hardin Church, entitled *Beowulf: A Poem*. Church imitates Old English poetic style, using material drawn from *Beowulf* and elsewhere. Roughly at the same time as Church, Percy Mackaye composed and published a play, *Beowulf: An Epical Drama of Anglo-Saxon Times*. Apparently it was never performed.

Novels based on or derived from *Beowulf* include, most recently, John Gardner's *Grendel*, which approaches the poem from the monster's point of view, helped along by a hefty infusion of existentialist argot and not a little amateur psychologizing. This novel has served as the outline for a film, *Grendel Grendel Grendel* (see the chapter "Visual Materials for Teaching *Beowulf*"). Informative discussions of the original poem and Gardner's version are those of Jay Ruud, "Gardner's *Grendel* and *Beowulf*," and Norma L. Hutman, "Even Monsters Have Mothers." *Beowulf* and particularly Finnsburg also form the subject of an earlier fictional work, John O. Beaty's *Swords in the Dawn: A Story of the First Englishmen*.

Finally, for those who want both their historical fiction and their visual aids, *Beowulf*-inspired comic books exist in at least two languages. *O Monstro de Caim*, in Portuguese, an attempt to render *Beowulf* in words and pictures, appeared in a single printing in 1955. More available is a series published in the United States, beginning in 1975, entitled *Beowulf, Dragon-Slayer*. Featured—in addition to "the usual cast" of Hrothgar, Unferth, Beowulf, Wiglaf, and the "rest of the gang"—are Satan, "Swamp-men," an independent-minded consort for Beowulf called Nan-zee (after Nancy, the wife of the illustrator), and "a host of others."

THE INSTRUCTOR'S LIBRARY

Introduction

Such a vast store of scholarly work on *Beowulf* has accumulated over the years and in several languages that few libraries, let alone individuals, can hope to possess it all. For what we are not required to study and know, many of us can breathe a sigh of relief; yet perhaps the great quantity of research contains a lesson for us, simply by virtue of its bulk. "Good" teaching of *Beowulf* demands, in addition to creative approaches and a vigilant sensitivity to the needs of one's students, a continued effort to read, to learn, to stay current. No list of books and articles, no matter how carefully prepared or how up-to-date, can possibly take the place of thoughtful diligence.

The works noted in the next few pages, then, will not automatically complete an instructor's critical commitment to *Beowulf* studies, nor is the list intended to exhaust all worthy, or even most current, research. Rather, what follows represents a collection of publications identified as particularly important by active teachers of *Beowulf* who returned survey questionnaires, supplemented by certain other works that, in the opinion of the editors, an ideal instructor's library might contain.

Of course, even as these pages go to press, they are in some ways out of date; they miss that helpful essay by a teacher of *Beowulf* invariably published too late for citation. Readers of this volume, and of others in this series, are urged to add to the necessarily minimal entries included here by informing themselves further about recent criticism and scholarship. Several journals publicize new Beowulfiana in print and in progress and thus become valuable tools for the specialist and nonspecialist alike. Perhaps the most useful of these is the *Old English Newsletter*, published by the Center for Medieval and Early Renaissance Studies at the State University of New York, Binghamton (Paul Szarmach, editor; Carl T. Berkhout, bibliographer). Since 1967, the first issue of each volume of *OEN* has contained a survey of the previous year's work in Old English studies. The second issue of each volume (beginning in 1968, with vol. 2) has included a copiously annotated bibliography. Two other sources of Old English bibliography are *Anglo-Saxon England*, which has published an annual bibliography under the supervision of Martin Biddle since 1971, and *The Year's Work in English Studies*, which lists and reviews most important new research. Also worthy of mention is "Old English Research in Progress," a standard feature each year since 1964 in *Neuphilologische Mitteilungen*. Such a list—of works not published but under way—indicates the immediate direction of Old English studies and informs teachers of *Beowulf* about colleagues who share a particular interest or might answer a question on a troublesome point. Finally, on pedagogical issues specifically, readers may find two publications helpful: *College Eng-*

lish, which from time to time carries essays and evaluative articles touching on *Beowulf* and Old English literature in the classroom, and *SMART: Studies in Medieval and Renaissance Teaching*, edited by Robert V. Graybill, Robert L. Kendrick, and Robert E. Lovell (Dept. of English, Central Missouri State Univ.), which offers a forum where instructors of medieval literature can discuss problems and methods of teaching.

The following pages are not designed to substitute for perusal of the books and articles listed. The purpose of this volume and of this series is to guide, not carry, teachers through the maze of available *Beowulf* materials in order to initiate more enlightened classroom instruction.

Reference Works

Dictionaries and Concordances

Because *Beowulf* is written in Old English, even the instructor who teaches it in translation may need lexicographical help from time to time (see Stephen A. Barney's chapter "The Words"). Fortunately, our language resources are good and getting better as a result of technology and modern scholarship. The major complete dictionary of Old English in print is *An Anglo-Saxon Dictionary*, compiled by Joseph Bosworth and T. Northcote Toller. To this have been added a supplement by Toller and the *Enlarged Addenda and Corrigenda to the Supplement* by Alistair Campbell. The governing principles of Bosworth-Toller are essentially historical; that is, like the *Oxford English Dictionary*, Bosworth-Toller attempts to present a chronological profile of contexts illustrating each definition offered. The resulting volumes are compendious and unsuited to classroom use. A handier dictionary is that of J. R. Clark Hall, *A Concise Anglo-Saxon Dictionary for the Use of Students*, with a supplement by Herbert D. Meritt. This is a single-volume work, without the examples of words in context. The range is wide, however, and the scholarship thorough and inclusive. Another dictionary designed with students in mind is Henry Sweet's *The Student's Dictionary of Anglo-Saxon*, now available in reprint from Oxford University Press. More specialized but often useful is Ferdinand Holthausen's *Altenglisches etymologisches Wörterbuch*. Particularly helpful for instructors teaching *Beowulf* in a normalized text (see the "Editions" chapter) is *A Short Dictionary of Anglo-Saxon Poetry in a Normalized Early West-Saxon Orthography*, produced by Jess B. Bessinger, Jr. Also available is Arthur R. Borden, Jr.'s *A Comprehensive Old-English Dictionary*. Finally, a word should be said about the Dictionary of Old English project currently in progress at the University of Toronto. Under the general editorship of Angus Cameron, the Toronto dictionary will provide a complete record of every instance of every word from all known Old English manuscripts, thereby validating definitions with the maximum available information. Such inclusive work is made possible through advanced and exacting computer techniques. Descriptions of the plans and progress of the dictionary have been published; see John Leyerle and Ashley C. Amos.

Another tool frequently needed by instructors of *Beowulf* alongside a good dictionary is a concordance. The earliest of these was published by Albert S. Cook under the title *A Concordance to* Beowulf in 1911. Owned by many libraries, Cook's concordance is elegant but not comprehensive. Cook omits some five hundred "of the commoner words," such as articles, prepositions, and a number of the most important (that is to say, most frequently occurring) words in the language. The textual base for Cook is the first edition of A. J. Wyatt, and thus the concordance does not reflect the many revisions R. W. Chambers made for the second edition in 1920. Vowel quantities are marked as in Wyatt, so that words like *god* 'God, god' and *gōd* 'good' are separately grouped. A complete treatment of all words, including the most common, is the computer-aided *A Concordance to* Beowulf, by Jess B. Bessinger, Jr., and Philip H. Smith, Jr. (programmer). Bessinger-Smith is based on Dobbie's edition in the Anglo-Saxon Poetic Records series; hence, unlike Cook, it makes no distinction for vowel quantity but groups all words according to spelling alone. A more broadly conceived concordance, again the work of Bessinger and Smith, is *A Concordance to the Anglo-Saxon Poetic Records*. This too is computer-aided and helps to place the sometimes-specialized vocabulary of *Beowulf* in the larger context of the total Old English poetic corpus, as edited by Krapp and Dobbie. Most recently, as part of the ongoing Old English dictionary project at Toronto, *A Microfiche Concordance to Old English* has appeared, edited by Richard L. Venezky and Antonette di Paolo Healey. This makes available at much reduced cost the entire word collection to be incorporated into the dictionary, less the 197 "stopwords" issued in separate fiches and prepared by Venezky and Sharon Butler. Finally, for instructors wishing a useful survey of the subject of computers and Old English studies, there is *Computers and Old English Concordances*, edited by Angus Cameron, Roberta Frank, and John Leyerle.

Two word lists of particular interest to instructors of *Beowulf* need to be added here. *Word-Hoard: An Introduction to Old English Vocabulary*, compiled by Stephen A. Barney with the assistance of David Stevens and Ellen Wertheimer, is designed especially as a classroom text. Its purpose is to bring together Old English words joined etymologically and phonemically, to demonstrate relations of one to another within groups, and also to illustrate connections between Old English and various European languages. Because the book is intended to facilitate learning of vocabulary for beginning students of Old English, it might seem to be most applicable in classes where *Beowulf* is taught in the original. Teachers in translation will perhaps still find Barney helpful, however, in demonstrating links between Old English and languages their students know or are studying. An earlier and simpler tool is *A Grouped Frequency Word-List of Anglo-Saxon Poetry*, compiled by John F. Madden and Francis P. Magoun, Jr. This prints together words and word families used in all poetic texts surviving, according to how often they appear. Thus, the *Grouped Frequency Word-List* is useful both for those learning Old English for the first time and for advanced students involved with word-field studies.

Bibliographies

Several excellent bibliographies exist, some general to Old English, some specific to *Beowulf*, that provide comprehensive guides to scholarship dealing with the poem. Much can be learned from the *New Cambridge Bibliography of English Literature*, volume 1 (A.D. 600–1600), edited by George Watson. The *New Cambridge* lists studies of *Beowulf* under a separate heading and takes note of works concerned with other Old English literature; it is not annotated, however. Bibliographies citing only direct discussions of *Beowulf* have been published by George K. Anderson, W. F. Bolton, Donald K. Fry, and Douglas D. Short. Anderson's "*Beowulf*, Chaucer and Their Backgrounds," though highly selective and limited in subject, is carefully annotated. Bolton's "Select Bibliography" is included in his revision of C. L. Wrenn's edition of *Beowulf*. Though only a few pages in length, the bibliography is intelligently chosen so as to include major work on *Beowulf* since about 1925. Most items are annotated briefly. Fry's Beowulf *and the Fight at Finnsburh* is nearly comprehensive through 1969 but offers no annotations. The best and most recent bibliography treating only studies of *Beowulf*, then, is Beowulf *Scholarship* by Short. Selective for the years 1705–1949, comprehensive from 1950 to 1978, Short's volume is compactly but skillfully annotated, providing precise synopses of each work mentioned.

Instructors of *Beowulf* should also be aware of three other bibliographies of studies of Old English literature in general, two of which contain special sections on the poem. Earliest and briefest is Fred C. Robinson's *Old English Literature: A Select Bibliography*, a thoughtfully assembled and presented catalog. As part of the Toronto Medieval Bibliographies series, it appears in paperback, and it might reasonably be assigned as a classroom text for advanced students. By far the finest general bibliography covering the subject is that of Stanley B. Greenfield and Fred C. Robinson, *A Bibliography of Publications on Old English Literature to the End of 1972*. The most comprehensive collection ever to treat Old English poetry and prose, it includes notice of more than 1,500 items related to *Beowulf*. It also is available in paperback. Readers should be aware too of *Anglo-Saxon Scholarship: The*

First Three Hundred Years, edited by Carl Berkhout and Milton McC. Gatch. Part bibliography, part survey of the recovery and evaluation of the Old English corpus, the volume offers essays on the earliest work performed in the field.

Linguistic Aids

Just as teachers of *Beowulf* may sometimes require dictionaries of Old English, so may they also need to refer to various language reference works if they are to respond thoroughly to situations arising in the classroom. Quite a number of such aids have appeared over the years and address quite different purposes. The most complete presentation of Old English phonology is Karl Luick's *Historische Grammatik der englischen Sprache*, revised and supplemented by Friedrich Wild and Herbert Koziol. Eduard Sievers' *Angelsächsische Grammatik*, newly revised by Karl Brunner and retitled *Altenglische Grammatik*, remains for many the first source of grammatical information, although others find they turn more frequently to Alistair Campbell's *Old English Grammar*, which, unlike Luick and Sievers, is in English. Classroom grammars, as well as reference grammars, are available, and they may be more helpful to instructors who wish their students to see paradigms of declensions, conjugations, and so forth. Texts frequently cited by our respondents are *Sweet's Anglo-Saxon Primer*, edited by Norman Davis; *The Elements of Old English*, by Samuel Moore and Thomas A. Knott; *Bright's Old English Grammar and Reader*, edited by Frederic G. Cassidy and Richard M. Ringler; and Bruce Mitchell's *A Guide to Old English*, now in a new edition with readings and glossary by Fred C. Robinson.

Background Studies

Because *Beowulf* often seems to students the product of a culture much removed from our own, teaching it well requires some degree of background preparation. Three colleagues who make extensive use of background materials in their classes—Fred C. Robinson, Constance B. Hieatt, and John Miles Foley—have written descriptions of various essential sources in the section "Teaching the Backgrounds." Readers are encouraged to examine these, as well as the seven essays in the section "Specific Approaches." What follows here is intended as a supplementary guide to be used alongside these essays. It is by no means comprehensive; rather, it is designed to point out a limited group of studies of potential value to most instructors of *Beowulf*.

Among works dealing with Britain during the Old English period, Frank M. Stenton's *Anglo-Saxon England* is widely held to be a fine base upon which to add further reading. Such reading might well include *A History of the Anglo-Saxons* by R. H. Hodgkin, *The Beginnings of English*

Society by Dorothy Whitelock, *Everyday Life in Roman and Anglo-Saxon Times, including Viking and Norman Times* by Marjorie Quennell, *From Alfred to Henry III, 871–1272* by Christopher Brooke, and *Roman Britain and Early England, 55 B.C.–A.D. 871* by Peter Hunter Blair. Also worth examining is Blair's earlier *Introduction to Anglo-Saxon England*, as well as *English Historical Documents, ca. 500–1042*, edited by Dorothy Whitelock; John Halverson's essay "The World of *Beowulf*"; *Life in Anglo-Saxon England* by R. I. Page; *Loyalties and Traditions* by Milton McC. Gatch; Richie Girvan's Beowulf *and the Seventh Century*; *England before the Conquest: Studies in Primary Sources Presented to Dorothy Whitelock*, edited by Peter Clemoes and Kathleen Hughes; *The Anglo-Saxons: How They Lived and Worked* by G. A. Lester; and *Alcuin and* Beowulf: *An Eighth-Century View* by W. F. Bolton.

The single most important find of Anglo-Saxon remains was unearthed at Sutton Hoo, Suffolk, in 1939. Artifacts discovered there have helped confirm the accuracy of many descriptions of objects and life in *Beowulf*. A good beginning for a study of relevant archaeology is David M. Wilson, *The Archaeology of Anglo-Saxon England*, or Bernice Grohskopf's *The Treasure of Sutton Hoo*. The British Museum's *The Sutton Hoo Ship-Burial: A Provisional Guide*, by Rupert L. S. Bruce-Mitford, makes an interesting early-stage comparison with the same author's massively magisterial summary volumes, the first in a series: *The Sutton Hoo Ship-Burial, volume 1, Excavations, Background, the Ship, Dating and Inventory*, and volume 2, *Arms, Armour and Regalia*. Bruce-Mitford's *The Sutton Hoo Ship-Burial: Reflections after Thirty Years* is among other things a careful record of some of the more important revisionary reconstructions of objects in the find, helpfully illustrated for the expert and nonexpert reader. See also Charles Green's *Sutton Hoo: The Excavation of a Royal Ship-Burial* and "*Beowulf* and the Harp at Sutton Hoo" by Jess B. Bessinger, Jr. More general studies are Hilda R. E. Davidson's "The Hill of the Dragon: Anglo-Saxon Burial Mounds in Literature and Archaeology" and her "Archaeology and *Beowulf*." Studies relating to specific artifacts in the poem include Arthur T. Hatto's "Snake-Swords and Boar-Helms in *Beowulf*," Davidson's book-length study *The Sword in Anglo-Saxon England: Its Archaeology and Literature*, and A. Margaret Arent's "The Heroic Pattern: Old Germanic Helmets, *Beowulf*, and *Grettis Saga*."

Several different approaches can be taken in delineating the characteristics of the people who composed and listened to *Beowulf*. One method is essentially demographic: see Josiah Cox Russell's *British Medieval Population* or Kenneth Sisam's "Anglo-Saxon Royal Genealogies." These could be followed by J. E. A. Joliffe's *Pre-Feudal England: The Jutes*; two considerations of the Geats as imaginary or not—Jane A. Leake's *The Geats of* Beowulf: *A*

Study in the Geographical Mythology of the Middle Ages and a reply by G. V. Smithers, "The Geats in *Beowulf*"; and Robert T. Farrell's recent monograph, "*Beowulf*, Swedes and Geats." Also of great usefulness is *An Atlas of Anglo-Saxon England* by David Hill.

Another approach to presenting the folk of *Beowulf* is trying to reconstruct them from the poem itself, using clues left among the lines and between the lines. This is the tack taken by Robert M. Lumiansky in "The Dramatic Audience in *Beowulf*" and by Dorothy Whitelock in *The Audience of Beowulf*. Such clues might also reveal the nature of *Beowulf*'s author, who must have been culturally bound to the people described in the poem. Suggestive recent studies discussing the question of authorship and the poet's role are Norman Eliason, "The þyle and Scop in *Beowulf*"; Frederic G. Cassidy, "How Free Was the Anglo-Saxon Scop?"; Godfrid Storms, "The Author of *Beowulf*"; Jeff Opland, "*Beowulf* on the Poet" and, more lately, his *Anglo-Saxon Oral Poetry*.

The belief systems of *Beowulf*'s audience have been the subject of much modern scholarship. Two valuable general studies of the subject are *Gods and Myths of Northern Europe* by Hilda R. E. Davidson and Gale R. Owen's recent *Rites and Religions of the Anglo-Saxons*. Eric G. Stanley, in his *The Search for Anglo-Saxon Paganism*, addresses the question of the nature and extent of their non-Christian heritage most thoroughly; but also worthy of note are "The Religion of the Anglo-Saxons" by Charles D. Cannon; "The Pagan Coloring in *Beowulf*" by Larry D. Benson; "The Essential Paganism of *Beowulf*" by Charles Moorman; and "Bede, *Beowulf*, and the Conversion of the Anglo-Saxon Aristocracy" by Patrick Wormald. Beliefs of a more social sort have been examined too. Readers should consider George Clark, "Beowulf's Armor"; William A. Chaney, *The Cult of Kingship in Anglo-Saxon England: The Transition from Paganism to Christianity*; Stanley J. Kahrl, "Feuds in *Beowulf*"; Kathryn Hume, "The Concept of the Hall in Old English Poetry"; Anne F. Payne, "Three Aspects of Wyrd in *Beowulf*"; and Kenneth Florey, "Stability and Chaos as a Theme in Anglo-Saxon Poetry."

Mythological and folktale elements in *Beowulf* have shared some of the attention currently paid to systems of belief in the poem. Specific application of folklore criteria to a reading of *Beowulf* is made by Francis P. Magoun, Jr., in two articles: "*Béowulf* A': A Folk-Variant" and "*Béowulf* B: A Folk-Poem on Beowulf's Death." A counterview on the same subject is taken by Arthur G. Brodeur in "*Beowulf*: One Poem or Three?" Two recent attempts to understand how *Beowulf* might be related to earlier English mythologies are "Interlocking Mythic Patterns in *Beowulf*" by Albert B. Lord and "*Beowulf* in the Context of Myth" by Michael N. Nagler. Significant efforts have also been made by early and contemporary scholars to place *Beowulf* in the context of international myth, including "Beowulf and Watanabe-no-Tsuna" by Frederick Y. Powell, "*Beowulf* and the *Ramayana*: A Study in Epic Poetry" by I. S. Peter, *The Cultivation of Saga in Anglo-Saxon England* by C. E. Wright, and "Beowulf and Bear's Son in the *Vishnu Purana*" by George Clark.

As several of these titles suggest, the search for *Beowulf*'s mythic roots has connected the poem with others in various non-Western literatures. For a number of reasons, including the traces of oral heritage apparent in it, *Beowulf* has been connected or compared with classical epic many times. General studies that might help reveal *Beowulf*'s proper relation to Western European literatures are *Folktale, Fiction, and Saga in the Homeric Epics* by Rhys Carpenter and *The Singer of Tales* by Albert B. Lord. Both stress the oral qualities of the poem. Other helpful discussions include Tom Burns Haber's *A Comparative Study of* Beowulf *and* The Aeneid, Alistair Campbell, "The Old English Epic Style," Stanley B. Greenfield's "*Beowulf* and Epic Tragedy," Lord's subsequent "Beowulf and Odysseus," and William Whallon's *Formula, Character, and Context: Studies in Homeric, Old English, and Old Testament Poetry*. Taking a completely opposite view—that *Beowulf* has little connection with the other great European epics—is E. M. W. Tillyard in *The English Epic and Its Background*.

Finally, a number of scholars have taken up the question of the true nature of Beowulf's heroism. Since the topic is a common one for classroom discussion, instructors may find the following approaches supply valuable background: Maurice B. McNamee, "Beowulf, a Christian Hero"; G. N. Garmonsway, "Anglo-Saxon Heroic Attitudes"; John Leyerle, "Beowulf the Hero and King"; G. V. Smithers, "Destiny and the Heroic Warrior in *Beowulf*"; Gwyn Jones, *Kings, Beasts, and Heroes*; Harry Berger, Jr., and H. Marshall Leicester, Jr., "Social Structure as Doom: The Limits of Heroism in *Beowulf*"; Robert W. Hanning, "*Beowulf* as Heroic History"; Bernard F. Huppé, "The Concept of the Hero in the Early Middle Ages"; Michael Swanton, "Heroes, Heroism, and Heroic Literature"; and William Reynolds, "Heroism in *Beowulf*: A Christian Perspective." A suggestive and learned counterweight to the critical tendency to inflate Beowulf's heroic exploits to greater-than-human proportion is offered by Fred C. Robinson in "Elements of the Marvellous in the Characterization of Beowulf: A Reconsideration of the Textual Evidence."

Critical and Stylistic Studies

For many instructors, particularly those coming to teach *Beowulf* for the first time, a good place to begin is with the introduction to the edition selected for class. Readers are therefore referred to the chapter "Editions" and also to the chapter by Douglas D. Short, which evaluates translations and their introductions. Another beginning point is one of several available surveys of Old English writings. Stanley B. Greenfield's *A Critical History of Old English Literature* is a frequently used and highly respected introduction to the subject. Others include *The Literature of the Anglo-Saxons* by George K. Anderson, *A Study of Old English Literature* by C. L. Wrenn, *Form and Style in Early English Literature* by Pamela Gradon, and *Old English Literature* by M. W. Grose and Dierdre McKenna. Shorter (though still inclusive) considerations by Morton W. Bloomfield, "Understanding Old English Poetry" and by Derek Pearsall, "*Beowulf* and the Anglo-Saxon Poetic Tradition," are helpful. Also of value is Greenfield's *The Interpretation of Old English Poems*, a general study but one that makes frequent reference to *Beowulf*.

Comprehensive book-length readings of *Beowulf*, many of which relate the poem to its historical and literary context, may be examined as well. Particularly valuable in the opinion of a number of instructors are Arthur G. Brodeur, *The Art of* Beowulf (see also John C. McGalliard's related essay, "The Complex Art of *Beowulf*"); R. W. Chambers, Beowulf: *An Introduction to the Study of the Poem, with a Discussion of the Stories of Offa and Finn*; Kenneth Sisam, *The Structure of* Beowulf; Edward B. Irving, Jr., *A Reading of* Beowulf, and his more general *Introduction to* Beowulf; Margaret E. Goldsmith, *The Mode and Meaning of* Beowulf; Andreas Haarder, Beowulf: *The Appeal of a Poem*; and Thomas A. Shippey's slim, simply titled volume, *Beowulf*. Briefer general studies worthy of mention begin with what is perhaps the most influential modern article on the poem, J. R. R. Tolkien's "*Beowulf*: The Monsters and the Critics," and include Bruce Mitchell, "'Until the Dragon Comes . . .': Some Thoughts on *Beowulf*"; Eric G. Stanley, "*Beowulf*"; Robert E. Kaske, "*Beowulf*"; John Gardner, "*Beowulf*"; and Alain Renoir, "*Beowulf*: A Contextual Introduction to Its Contents and Techniques." Other discussions, with broad range but concerned with specific topics, are "The Originality of *Beowulf*" by Larry D. Benson, *Cruces of* Beowulf by Betty S. Cox, Martin Puhvel's Beowulf *and Celtic Tradition*, and R. Mark Scowcroft, "The Hand and the Child." Like Puhvel, Scowcroft treats the Irish analogues to *Beowulf*.

Anthologies of *Beowulf* criticism exist and are often used to introduce students to scholarly treatments of the poem. Two such collections published in paperback are edited by Lewis E. Nicholson and Donald K. Fry. Nicholson's volume contains eighteen essays, including early appreciation pieces by F. A. Blackburn, H. Munro Chadwick, and Levin L. Schücking (in translation), as well as Tolkien's "The Monsters and the Critics," Morton W. Bloomfield's two essays, "*Beowulf* and Christian Allegory: An Interpretation of Unferth" and "Patristics and Old English Literature: Notes on Some Poems," D. W. Robertson, Jr.'s "The Doctrine of Charity in Medieval Literary Gardens: A Topical Approach through Symbolism and Allegory," Francis P. Magoun, Jr.'s "Oral-Formulaic Character of Anglo-Saxon Narrative Poetry," and Robert E. Kaske's "*Sapientia et Fortitudo* as the Controlling Theme of *Beowulf*." Less weighted in the direction of Christian interpretation is Fry's anthology. In addition to Bloomfield's "*Beowulf* and Christian Allegory," Magoun's "Oral-Formulaic Character," and Tolkien's "The Monsters and the Critics," Fry reprints six others, including Joan Blomfield, "The Style and Structure of *Beowulf*," Robert M. Lumiansky, "The Dramatic Audience in *Beowulf*," Rosemary Cramp's "*Beowulf* and Archaeology," Alain Renoir's "Point of View and Design for Terror in *Beowulf*," and Kenneth Rexroth's "Classics Revisited—IV, *Beowulf*." Collections of original and previously published essays have also been edited by Robert P. Creed (*Old English Poetry: Fifteen Essays*), Jess B. Bessinger, Jr., and Stanley J. Kahrl (*Essential Articles for the Study of Old English Poetry*), Martin Stevens and Jerome Mandel (*Old English Literature: Twenty-Two Analytical Essays*), and John D. Niles (*Old English Literature in Context*). Creed contains pieces on *Beowulf* by Adrien Bonjour, Stanley B. Greenfield, Neil D. Isaacs, Robert E. Kaske, John A. Nist, Paul B. Taylor, and others; Bessinger and Kahrl include relevant work by Henry C. Wyld, Frederick G. Bracher, Robert P. Creed, Robert E. Diamond, Morton W. Bloomfield ("Patristics and Old English Literature"), Robert D. Stevick, and others; Stevens and Mandel offer essays touching on or dealing with *Beowulf* by Creed, Stevick, Bessinger, Dorothy Whitelock, Godfrid Storms, and Bonjour; Niles presents ten new essays, of which half (those by Theodore Andersson, Philip Damon, John Miles Foley, Albert B. Lord, and Michael N. Nagler) treat *Beowulf* directly. Finally, special mention should be made of two volumes of essays collected and revised by their authors, each a prolific Anglo-Saxonist: Adrien Bonjour's *Twelve* Beowulf *Papers, 1940–1960, with Additional Comments* and Kenneth Sisam's *Studies in the History of Old English Literature*. Both books provide convenient access to papers previously published in an assortment of journals and, for the most part, revised.

Festschriften honoring the many great medievalists who have worked in the area of Old English are still another source of useful studies of *Beowulf*. Particularly important among these are *Studies in English Philology: A Miscellany in Honor of Frederick Klaeber*, edited by Kemp Malone and Martin B. Ruud; *English Medieval Studies Presented to J. R. R. Tolkien on the Occasion of His Seventieth Birthday*, edited by Norman Davis and C. L. Wrenn; *Studies in Old English Literature in Honor of Arthur G. Brodeur*, edited by Stanley B. Greenfield; *Early English and Norse Studies Presented to Hugh Smith in Honour of His Sixtieth Birthday*, edited by Arthur Brown and Peter Foote; *Franciplegius: Medieval and Linguistic Stud-*

ies in Honor of Francis Peabody Magoun, Jr., edited by Jess B. Bessinger, Jr., and Robert P. Creed; *Nordica et Anglica: Studies in Honor of Stefán Einarsson*, edited by Allan H. Orrick; *Philological Essays: Studies in Old and Middle English Language and Literature in Honour of Herbert Dean Meritt*, edited by James L. Rosier; *Medieval Literature and Folklore Studies: Essays in Honor of Francis Lee Utley*, edited by Jerome Mandel and Bruce A. Rosenberg; *Old English Studies in Honour of John C. Pope*, edited by Robert B. Burlin and Edward B. Irving, Jr.; and *Anglo-Saxon Poetry: Essays in Appreciation for John C. McGalliard*, edited by Lewis E. Nicholson and Dolores Warwick Frese.

Festschriften and other collections of essays are highly important as reflections of trends in *Beowulf* scholarship, since relatively few book-length examinations of the poem have been written. Recommending particular shorter studies from among these, or from journals at large, is a problematic business in many ways. Nonspecialist readers might look, however, at the following additional pieces, which address specialized topics.

On characters: Adrien Bonjour, "Monsters Crouching and Critics Rampant; or, The *Beowulf* Dragon Debated"; Kenneth Sisam, "Beowulf's Fight with the Dragon"; Joseph Baird, "Grendel the Exile"; Jane C. Nitzsche, "The Structural Unity of *Beowulf*: The Problem of Grendel's Mother"; John C. Pope, "Beowulf's Old Age"; Geoffrey Hughes, "Beowulf, Unferth, and Hrunting: An Interpretation"; Norman E. Eliason, "Beowulf, Wiglaf, and the Waegmundings"; James L. Rosier, "Design for Treachery: The Unferth Intrigue"; Carol J. Clover, "The Germanic Context of the Unferth Episode"; A. P. Campbell, "The Decline and Fall of Hrothgar and His Danes"; Robert E. Kaske, "Hrothgar's Sermon" and " 'Hygelac' and 'Hygd' "; and Fred C. Robinson, "Is Wealhtheow a Prince's Daughter?"

On structures: John Leyerle, "The Interlace Structure of *Beowulf*"; Donald K. Fry, "Variation and Economy in *Beowulf* (1967–68)"; Michael D. Cherniss, "*Beowulf*: Oral Presentation and the Criterion of Immediate Rhetorical Effect"; Constance B. Hieatt, "Envelope Patterns and the Structure of *Beowulf*"; Kathryn Hume, "The Theme and Structure of *Beowulf*"; H. Ward Tonsfeldt, "Ring Structure in *Beowulf*"; and Brian A. Shaw, "The Speeches in *Beowulf*: A Structural Study."

On themes: Francis P. Magoun, Jr., "The Theme of Beasts of Battle in Anglo-Saxon Poetry"; Adrien Bonjour, "On Sea Images in *Beowulf*" and "*Beowulf* and the Beasts of Battle"; and David K. Crowne, "The Hero on the Beach: An Example of Composition by Theme in Anglo-Saxon Poetry."

On the digressions: Adrien Bonjour, *The Digressions in* Beowulf; Michael D. Cherniss, *Ingeld and Christ: Heroic Concepts and Values in Old English Christian Poetry*; Donald K. Fry, *Finnsburh: Fragment and Episode*; William W. Lawrence, "*Beowulf* and the Tragedy of Finnsburg";

Kemp Malone, "The Finn Episode in *Beowulf*"; Thomas E. Hart, "Tectonic Design, Formulaic Craft, and Literary Execution: The Episodes of Finn and Ingeld in *Beowulf*"; Bruce Moore, "The Relevance of the Finnsburh Episode"; and John F. Vickery, "The Narrative Structure of Hengest's Revenge in *Beowulf*."

Manuscript Studies and Facsimiles

British Library manuscript Cotton Vitellius A. XV is an important artifact and would be so even if the poem it contained were not a great one. Instructors often try to bring home to their students the remarkableness of the manuscript and use it to explain various cruxes, and they frequently need sources of informed opinion about the *Beowulf* manuscript itself. There are, of course, a great many of these: arguments about the character of the manuscript began early.

A good place to start is Kenneth Sisam's articles "The *Beowulf* Manuscript" and "The Compilation of the *Beowulf* Manuscript." Other significant early studies include Max Förster's monograph *Die* Beowulf-*Handschrift* (with two reproductions, of pages from the "Life of St. Christopher" and the "Letter of Alexander" found in the Nowell codex); Stanley I. Rypins, "The *Beowulf* Codex," "A Contribution to the Study of the *Beowulf* Codex," and the introduction to his *Three Old English Prose Texts in MS. Cotton Vitellius A. XV*; Johannes Hoops's "Die Foliierung der *Beowulf*-Handschrift"; James R. Hulbert's "The Accuracy of the B-Scribe of *Beowulf*"; and Eduard Prokosch's "Two Types of Scribal Errors in the *Beowulf* MS." An article by A. H. Smith discussing "The Photography of Manuscripts" is a pioneering study in the use of ultraviolet and infrared light for paleography; it contains important plates and analyses that were used in the facsimiles by Zupitza-Davis and Malone. Kemp Malone has also written about the manuscript (see "The Text of *Beowulf*") and Thorkelin's transcriptions of it (*Thorkelin Transcripts of* Beowulf and "Readings from the Thorkelin Transcripts of *Beowulf*").

More recent studies are those of N. R. Ker, whose *Catalogue of Manuscripts containing Anglo-Saxon* is the best general source of its kind; Sisam, "The Authority of Old English Poetical Manuscripts"; Paul B. Taylor and Peter H. Salus, "The Compilation of Cotton Vitellius A. XV"; and Tilman Westphalen's book-length examination Beowulf *3150–55: Textkritik und Editionsgeschichte*. Robert D. Stevick has also contributed an interesting manuscript study in the form of an edition of the poem (*Beowulf: An Edition with Manuscript Spacing Notation and Graphotactic Analysis*) that reproduces "the incidence and measure of spacings between the symbols in linear order" with the aid of a computer.

Current interest in the manuscript of *Beowulf* centers on renewed attempts to determine the poem's date. Out of a conference on this topic convened in Toronto in 1980 came a volume of collected papers, *The Dating of Beowulf*, edited by Colin Chase. Of these, most touch on the manuscript in various ways, although those by Kevin S. Kiernan ("The Eleventh-Century Origin of *Beowulf* and the *Beowulf* Manuscript"), Leonard E. Boyle ("The Nowell Codex and the Poem of *Beowulf*"), and Angus Cameron et al. ("A Reconstruction of the Language of *Beowulf*") are particularly useful. By far the most thorough reexamination of the manuscript—and the most controversial new theory about the composition of poem and manuscript—is by Kiernan, who argues at length in Beowulf *and the* Beowulf *Manuscript* that both are products of an eleventh-century scribe.

For many instructors of *Beowulf*, giving their students a "feel" for the original language and period of the poem involves sharing with them photographs of the manuscript. Several facsimile editions of British Library MS. Cotton Vitellius A. XV (c. A.D. 1000), which contains the unique copy of *Beowulf*, have been published. There are also many scholarly studies that can be helpful background aids for teaching the poem using the manuscript. A selected list of such studies appears in the chapter "The Instructor's Library." Interested readers should consider as well Jess B. Bessinger, Jr.'s "Forgeries and Facsimiles: Paleography without Tears" among the essays in the section "Special Approaches."

The earliest published facsimile of the *Beowulf* manuscript was edited by Julius Zupitza for the Early English Text Society in 1882. The volume, a remarkable achievement given early photographic processes, contains collotype reproductions of each page of the manuscript faced by Zupitza's transliteration. Although Zupitza attempted to render the leaves exactly as they were in the original, technical failures caused the size of the photographs to vary so that, in general, they appear somewhat reduced in scale from the original. A few are also unclear. These difficulties were partly overcome in 1959, when the society issued a second version of the facsimile, edited by Norman Davis. This edition reprints Zupitza's transliteration photolithographically, a testament to its accuracy (it contained but one copying error) and, in Davis's words, to its "permanent value as a record of what he could see in the manuscript in 1880–82." The manuscript itself was completely rephotographed, sometimes under ultraviolet light when this produced a clearer image, and printed true to scale. There is a short introduction by Davis in which he discusses photography of manuscripts and the edition's indebtedness to A. H. Smith's essay "The Photography of Manuscripts." The question—raised by Zupitza in his examination of the manuscript—of later "freshening up" by an unknown hand is also discussed.

A larger edition is that produced by Kemp Malone in 1963, in the Early

English Manuscripts in Facsimile series, which now contains some twenty volumes. Using the same photographic plates as Davis for the poem's text, Malone includes as well the other texts bound together with *Beowulf* in a single codex (designated "Nowell" by Malone, after the British antiquary Laurence Nowell, who owned the manuscript in 1563). There are thus four separate texts reproduced in Malone's volume, in addition to *Beowulf*: (1) a fragmentary English life of Saint Christopher; (2) the "Wonders of the East," an illustrated collection of monsters and miracles, translated from the Latin; (3) Alexander's purported letter to Aristotle describing his Eastern travels, also translated from Latin to English; and (4) the fragmentary Old English poem called *Judith*. Malone's is a magnificent oversize volume with two leaves to the page, a format that makes possible the examination of four photographs simultaneously. The reproductions are clear, sharp, and exactly to scale. There is an excellent 120-page introduction by Malone, bringing together all the best textual studies of the manuscript then available and adding to them the editor's considerable scholarly insight. The heart of this introduction is an exhaustive description of the manuscript, with particular attention paid to the two scribal hands and to elucidating passages difficult to read. Unlike Zupitza-Davis, Malone contains no transliteration of the text.

A facsimile of a slightly different sort, but of probable interest to teachers of *Beowulf*, was published by Malone in 1951 as the first volume in the series that later included his edition of the Nowell Codex. This volume reproduces the two transcriptions of the poem left us by the Icelandic archivist G. J. Thorkelin, one of which he had copied for him (the A transcript, so-called) and one (the B transcript) that he made himself. Both of these copies bear the date 1787, some fifty-six years after fire swept Ashburnham House, leaving the library of Sir Robert Cotton, including the *Beowulf* manuscript, scarred and damaged. Since most of the codex containing *Beowulf* escaped direct contact with the flames, losses were primarily subsequent, when scorched portions of the leaves crumbled under handling. This deterioration was halted by 1870, about which time the British Museum (then the owner of the Cotton collection) had the manuscript protectively rebound. Between the time of the fire and this rebinding, however, our best source of lost readings is Thorkelin's transcriptions. All compilers of serious editions of *Beowulf* have used Thorkelin, as well as partial transcriptions by Wanley and others, in piecing together the defective text. Malone's facsimile contains an introduction, as well as the facsimiles in clear photographs.

Part Two

APPROACHES

BEOWULF COURSES TODAY

THE STATE OF THE ART: A SURVEY

Joseph F. Tuso

Drawing on many excellent tools that Old English scholars have provided in recent years, teachers of *Beowulf* in the early 1980s are using a variety of imaginative approaches to present the poem to many thousands of students ranging from the middle grades through the graduate level. The dustcover of Betty S. Cox's *Cruces of* Beowulf maintains that more has been written about *Beowulf* than about any other single English literary work. Alan K. Brown's 1971–75 bibliography, prepared for an MLA seminar, listed close to 300 entries or, as Brown put it, "more than one per week." The *Old English Newsletter* (*OEN*) Spring bibliographies for 1972–76 list 144 entries on *Beowulf*, for an average of 29 per year. In 1977–81, however, the number rose to 229, or an average of 46 per year—a 60% increase. The past ten years have been especially fruitful ones for *Beowulf* studies and, in turn, for *Beowulf* pedagogy.

We now have new translations by Rebsamen (1971), Swanton (1971), Alexander (1973), and Greenfield (1982), which have moved into our classrooms along with Kennedy (1940), Clark Hall (1950), Raffel (1963), Donaldson (1966), and Hieatt (1967). Other studies have also contributed to a greater pedagogical awareness of and accessibility to *Beowulf* since 1971. On our shelf of essential teaching works we must now place, next to Bessinger's *A Concordance to* Beowulf and Fry's bibliography, Greenfield and Robinson's bibliography of Old English literature to 1972, Short's annotated *Beowulf* bibliography through 1978, and the useful annual bibliographies of the *Old English Newsletter* (1967–   ) and of *Anglo-Saxon England* (1972–   ), the latter, because of its fresh essays, a valuable source book for teaching *Beowulf* at any level.

A number of other works have also appeared in the last decade that are useful in the classroom. Lee's *The Guest-Hall of Eden* includes an extensive section on thematic elements; Cable's *The Meter and the Melody of* Beowulf and Luecke's *Measuring Old English Rhythm* must now be considered along with Sievers' and Bliss's views on *Beowulf's* prosody; and Opland's *Anglo-Saxon Oral Poetry* adds much that is useful to our notion of the oral tradition. The advanced student can benefit from Bolton's *Alcuin and* Beowulf and Puhvel's Beowulf *and Celtic Tradition*, while Kiernan's Beowulf *and the* Beowulf *Manuscript* fulfills Jerome Mandel's hope, expressed at an MLA seminar, that future studies would concentrate more on the *Beowulf* text itself.

To help us teach that text, Bolton has revised Wrenn's edition, Stevick has given us a highly specialized new version, and Chickering has provided a popular dual-language edition that has already been reedited. Student access to the text has been facilitated by Cassidy and Ringler's new version of an established grammar, *Bright's Old English Grammar and Reader*; by Marckwardt and Rosier's *Old English: Language and Literature*, and by a new edition of Bruce Mitchell's *Guide to Old English*, with texts and glossary by Fred C. Robinson. Barney's *Word-Hoard* has proved especially useful in teaching Old English vocabulary, including as it does some two thousand key words drawn from J. C. Pope's *Seven Old English Poems* and Klaeber's edition of *Beowulf*.

As for general studies useful in class, Burlin and Irving's edition of *Old English Studies in Honour of John C. Pope* has proved a veritable gold mine of Beowulfiana. This must go on the teaching shelf, together with several useful journals in addition to *Anglo-Saxon England*, such as *In Geardagum* (1975–   ) and the *Journal of the Rocky Mountain Medieval and Renaissance Association* (1980–   ).

While the teacher of *Beowulf* has acquired many and in some ways more useful tools to present the work to students both in Old English and in translation, there has been a dramatic change in where and how *Beowulf* is being taught. In a survey of 88 representative English departments in the United States and Canada (1973), Frances Randall Lipp found a decline in Old English requirements at the graduate level but an increase in courses in Old English for undergraduates. Only 29% of the responding Ph.D.-granting departments required an Old English course for doctoral students, with most departments offering an average 2.5 Old English courses per year and few requiring courses in *Beowulf*. Lipp challenged the profession to improve this situation: "The health of our field depends . . . on our pedagogical skills both as teachers and as textbook writers" (9).

A similar, more recent study by Robert F. Yeager (1980) reveals a further decline in the Ph.D. Old English requirement, from Lipp's 29% to 23%, in seven years' time. Yeager also reports that 40% of the schools offer Old English literature exclusively to undergraduates in translation, 23% to undergraduates in Old English, and that virtually no schools have an Old English requirement for the M.A. Whereas Lipp's survey showed departments offering an average of 2.5 Old English courses per year in 1973, Yeager's figures show them offering 2 such courses per year in 1980. Again, since *Beowulf* courses are included under Old English offerings, the teaching of *Beowulf* has probably remained relatively stable in graduate schools from 1973 to 1979 or so, while at the same time *Beowulf* is increasingly being taught at the undergraduate level in the original and in translation. The appearance and sales of related textbooks over the past ten years seem to verify this conclusion.

In a recent survey, Art Young discovered that 3 responding schools out of 66, or 4.5%, offer relatively successful elective courses in medieval literature (1980). We can safely assume that at least one of these three courses includes *Beowulf*. If we apply the 4.5% to the approximately 1,700 four-year colleges and universities and the 950 junior and community colleges listed in the 1982 *PMLA* Directory, we can conclude that some 120 such elective courses, with perhaps 40 including *Beowulf*, are currently being offered. Moreover, if even half of the 1,700 schools listed in *PMLA* have required or elective English, humanities, or world literature survey courses that include *Beowulf* in translation, the poem is currently being taught in about 900 undergraduate courses. If we assume an average section enrollment of 20 students, we have about 18,000 American college students studying *Beowulf* in translation each year, and doubtless more in Canada, in the junior colleges, and elsewhere. One popular text (my own) used primarily for teaching *Beowulf* (in the translation by E. T. Donaldson) to undergraduates, has sold about 3,500 copies each year since its appearance in 1975. Because it features but one of a number of translations presently being used, a figure of some 18,000 undergraduates currently studying *Beowulf* may even be a bit low. As a discipline, we have indeed met Lipp's challenge to keep our field healthy through our pedagogical skills as teachers and as textbook writers. The teaching of *Beowulf* in Old English at the graduate level has somewhat stabilized, if at a lower level than in the 1960s, and increasing numbers of students are now studying the poem in the original and in translation at other college levels.

In the 1980s, then, we have the pedagogical aids and we have the students.

We also have the teachers. In the study already referred to, Yeager reports that 40 institutions produced 150 Old English Ph.D.'s during 1974–79. During that same period the *MLA Job Information List* featured but 51 Old and Middle English positions, according to Ann G. Kirschner. Not considering the positions that went to pre-1974 Old English Ph.D.'s, this means that roughly two thirds of the Old English Ph.D.'s were hired as composition teachers, as generalists, or for other functions, if they were hired at all. Since faculty who specialize in Old English and in *Beowulf* have a charming penchant for adapting their specialty to enrich other courses they might teach, there is little doubt that the burgeoning of *Beowulf* studies at the undergraduate level is one of the less unhappy results of the tight Ph.D. job market of recent years. Thus today we find a few faculty members teaching a course in Old English grammar and vocabulary followed by a course in *Beowulf* from Klaeber or Wrenn for graduate students. Those who have not gained positions in the specialty may teach elective courses that include *Beowulf* for graduates and undergraduates in Old English or in translation, or they may use *Beowulf* in translation in large survey courses of various kinds.

Though there is little documentation of the state of the art of *Beowulf* pedagogy at the graduate level, some published studies pay special attention to thematic and other broad concerns that would be useful at the graduate level. John J. Pollock, for example, uses Jungian concepts at San Jose State University to show how Hrothgar and Beowulf might represent two sides of the same psyche: the impotent and the restorer of manhood. At Illinois State University, Samuel M. Riley requires his students to distinguish throughout *Beowulf* between statements of the poet that reflect concepts of Germanic fate on the one hand and Augustinian providence on the other. These distinctions set the stage for fruitful discussion of the Germanic and Christian cultural elements pervading the poem. Similarly, Melvin Storm focuses on the genealogies of the poem's ruling families. His Emporia State University students soon move from the genealogy to the ideas of kingship and kinship and then to related central themes.

We have somewhat more information on the teaching of *Beowulf* in undergraduate or in mixed graduate-undergraduate courses, with most of these pedagogical approaches hallmarked by dedicated, imaginative efforts on the teacher's part. Norma J. Engberg of the University of Nevada, Las Vegas, devised with her students' help a teaching text featuring ten excerpts from *Beowulf* in Old English. The excerpts, from nineteen to forty-four lines long, include Modern English versions interlinearly. Each excerpt in turn illustrates one aspect of the Old English language, with excerpts linked by Modern English prose summaries of the poem's action so that the students get all of *Beowulf* in sequence, partly in Old English, partly in summary.

For example, section 1, "Grendel First Visits Heorot" (86–125), includes a discussion of Old English metrics; section 5, "Grendel's Mere" (1345–82), features Old English pronouns; and section 10, "The Destruction of the People is Foretold" (3007–27), illustrates Old English sentence structure.

Engberg's text can be used to supplement a modern *Beowulf* translation or to provide an introductory overview to the original, but in either case she requires no prior knowledge of Old English from the student. The notes on Old English language features complementing the *Beowulf* readings are painstakingly done. In section 2, for example, "The Geats Arrive at Heorot" (320–39), the discussion of Old English consonants includes tables comparing and contrasting Old English consonant phonemes to those of Modern English. Engberg places this discussion early in her text to enable her students to apply what they learn as they read aloud later excerpts in class. Logically, a discussion of Old English vowels follows in section 3, and all language discussions employ the appropriate linguistic terminology.

Also useful in the mixed graduate-undergraduate class are a number of aids developed over the past few years by Douglas Butturff of the University of Central Arkansas. One of his most recent is a programmed approach to *Beowulf*'s Old English vocabulary on inexpensive eight-by-ten dittos. A column of Old English words and phrases on the left builds on material added from top to bottom, with corresponding Modern English equivalents in the right column. Students work down the page, covering each line successively with a card, mastering new words and phrases at their own rate, and having an immediate check on the correctness of their responses; errors can then be circled and restudied in minimal time. In the future, aids like Butturff's might be computerized, and students may be able to learn Old English vocabulary and grammar in a language lab, working at a keyboard with an electronic display.

Constance B. Hieatt and Loren C. Gruber also teach *Beowulf* courses to undergraduates in Old English. In Hieatt's twenty-six-week honors course at the University of Western Ontario, the first half is devoted to grammar, vocabulary, and three selections from Pope's *Seven Old English Poems*. The remaining weeks are spent on the first 1,235 lines of Wrenn's *Beowulf*, the section before Grendel's mother assaults Heorot. Hieatt's students are then expected to study and to read the rest of the poem in translation. At Simpson College, Gruber offered *Beowulf* three times between 1973 and 1978. Study of the poem was always preceded by a course in Old English grammar and vocabulary, either in an intensive January term or in a regular semester. One of Gruber's in-class techniques was to require his students to be prepared to translate each day's selection from Klaeber at sight, without using notes or prepared translations.

In a course on the epic and romance for mixed graduate-undergraduate students, W. Ken Zellefrow at New Mexico State University balances *Beowulf* against *The Song of Roland, The Nibelungenlied,* and *The Poem of the Cid.* Through reading these epics together in translation, his students usually find *Beowulf* more skillfully wrought and interesting than they first suspected. At the United States Air Force Academy, James R. Aubrey teaches *Beowulf* in two or three lessons in an undergraduate Western world literature course. Aubrey focuses on the monsters as perversions of human values such as valor, hospitality, or ring giving. Grendel is thus opposed to Beowulf, Grendel's mother to Wealhtheow and the other female characters, and the dragon to Beowulf and the *comitatus* ethic.

Three other approaches are typical of many that work well in survey courses. Bruce V. Roach teaches *Beowulf* together with the film version of Ken Kesey's *One Flew over the Cuckoo's Nest* at Stephen F. Austin State University. He has found that the works complement each other well, since both dramatize institutions, the individual's relation to them, and the passing on of behavioral codes. Marie Michelle Walsh assigns a research paper on *Beowulf* as part of a sophomore English major course in literary research at the College of Notre Dame of Maryland, using the Old English riddle form to motivate her students toward *Beowulf*'s language. And many teachers, such as Ann Hernández, have included the poem even in freshman courses; at Berkeley, she got good results by using *Beowulf* in a course with the central theme of conflict between the individual and the state, juxtaposing the poem with *Hamlet, Gulliver's Travels,* and *Animal Farm.*

Beowulf in translation is also appearing in continuing education programs to illustrate or support a central theme running throughout an entire course. At Georgia College in 1976, for example, the departments of art, English, music, and philosophy collaborated on an evening course called "The Idea of Christ in Literature and the Arts," using the Norton Critical Edition of *Beowulf.* The class met weekly for ten weeks to discuss "The Savior Figure in Classical Mythology," "Christ in the Old and New Testaments," "*Beowulf*: A Germanic-Christian Christ Type," "*The Grapes of Wrath*: Steinbeck's Pantheistic Savior," "Christ in Art," "Christ in the Asylum: *One Flew over the Cuckoo's Nest,*" "The Christ Figure in Modern Drama," "Huxley's *Brave New World* without Christ," "Christ in Poetry," and "Christ in Music" and closed with "*The Power and the Glory*: Graham Greene's Flawed Savior Figure." A course like this, when offered at the undergraduate level, affords an excellent opportunity for interdisciplinary cooperation and mutual faculty-student enlightenment.

In the 1980s *Beowulf* is also being taught in secondary and middle schools in a highly professional fashion that motivates younger students to reach beyond their grasp. Lenore Abraham has provided an approach so useful that parts of it can readily be adapted for use at more advanced levels as well.

Alain Renoir of the University of California, Berkeley, has stated: "I believe that *Beowulf* has tremendous value for human beings and is a very important poem for anyone who has the right to vote in the English-speaking world." This may be the ultimate justification for teaching the poem. The approaches to *Beowulf* highlighted in this essay and elsewhere in this volume give ample evidence that dedicated and innovative teachers at all levels, employing new and stimulating texts and techniques, are passing on to numerous students the values that we and Renoir appreciate in *Beowulf*.

TEACHING *BEOWULF* IN OLD ENGLISH TO UNDERGRADUATES

I.

Howell Chickering

I teach *Beowulf* in Old English for the same reasons that I teach Chaucer, Donne, and T. S. Eliot in their original languages: to increase students' responsiveness to poetry, their awareness of language itself, their critical thinking, and their sense of historical differences. With *Beowulf* I use many of the same strategies that I use when teaching a Frost poem to freshmen. For instance, the students and I declaim passages, taking turns trying to get the pace and tone of voice "right" at each point. We analyze why the words are arranged as they are and what would be lost by rearranging them. In the *Beowulf* course the students give oral translations of selected passages, which lead directly to problems of literary interpretation, large and small. We go around the room with each person first declaiming and then translating. Discussion follows as I ask philological and critical questions about the passage at hand. These classroom activities are extended by frequent short critical papers responding to questions about specific poetic features. The students' writing is treated as their most reflective form of reading, and I hold them just as responsible for the order of their words as they in turn hold the poem.

This approach derives from my conviction that undergraduate readers always need to pay close attention to the most immediate features of whatever writing they encounter: its texture and tone, how it *moves*. It doesn't matter whether the students are majors or nonmajors, seniors or freshmen. Too often they are either baffled or put off by the literary uses of language, or else they read only for the story or, worse, the message. So I take first things first, and often we never get beyond them, which suits me fine. There are no invitations to write on Grendel as Symbol, but we linger long over the fight in Heorot to see if we can find words adequate to describe its complex tone of terror and irony, the musical structure of the action, the manipulation of visual viewpoint. This combination of critical reading and reading aloud comes only with practice, naturally. And first the students must learn Old English.

I offer an open elective course in Old English in the fall and *Beowulf* in the spring. We start with six weeks on pronunciation and grammar, using drill tapes I have made and Sweet's *Primer* or Mitchell and Robinson's *Guide*. We also read Bede in translation, Tacitus, and several modern background works. I punctuate the classes on grammar with discussions of these books, especially Bede. I also tell the students that by the term's end they will be able to go from grammar to translation to literary appreciation as a single process, although these first appear to them to be separate activities. After they have translated four or five short prose texts, including Bede's sparrow simile, the syntax of which we examine as a metaphysical metaphor, they spend the last eight weeks of the semester translating four to six poems in Pope's *Seven Old English Poems*.

They first encounter Old English poetic rhythms when they write a short paper on the second paragraph of Ælfric's *Life of St. Edmund*, printed as prose in Sweet. They are asked to discover on their own the rules of its rhythmical organization and to break it up into lines. Many are surprised to find a regular rhythm in what they have just translated. Then they learn about Old English meter proper while reading *Caedmon's Hymn*, which also shows them poetic variation. From vocabulary they already know, I put together an ersatz hymn on the same subject, the Creation, to show them how oral-formulaic composition works and what makes *Caedmon's Hymn* a good poem. After they understand the rudiments of Old English poetic form, they write their first full literary exercise (three to five pages), on *The Battle of Brunanburh*. We go through their translations in class first so that everybody has an accurate understanding of the grammar and sense. I try to be very clear about what I want:

> Please reread lines 37–52 of *The Battle of Brunanburh*. First pay close attention to some of the poet's techniques. In some lines, stressed

words paired up across the caesura will add to the meaning or change the tone. Some lines have words whose very sounds seem meaningful. Notice the obvious repetitions in the passage. Are they good examples of litotes? Notice the variations, their extent, and where they fall. Are there kennings in them? What sort of images do you see in the kennings? All this as preparation for writing.

What does the poet do in this passage? Do not tell me merely that he uses the techniques you have inspected. What is his tone of voice? Is it altered anywhere by the imagery? How is a double perspective upon events created and controlled?

Now reexamine lines 57–65a. Does the poet's use of "the beasts of battle" theme bring you closer to the carnage? Or does it create a mythic distance? In either case, why?

Finally, in lines 65a–73, what perspective is established? How exactly—by what strokes of seeing and saying—does the poet create it?

They write similar papers on the other poems. By the end of the course, they can translate *The Battle of Maldon* at the rate of fifty to seventy-five lines per class. They can pass a final examination that reads: "For four of the seven selections below, identify approximately where the passage occurs and in what poem. Then describe the particular *poetic* properties of the language of the passage and the functions that the passage can have in the poem as a whole." They have not read reams of Old English, but they know a few of the best poems well and have practiced writing critical appreciations of them. They are ready to read *Beowulf* as poetry.

In the spring course the students translate selected passages totaling three hundred to eight hundred lines. They use Clark Hall's dictionary and the Old English text in my *Beowulf: A Dual-Language Edition*. The facing translation helps them begin to parse passages, but they must look up vocabulary and work out their own translations, which we go over in class (fifty lines per class). They write their papers on some of these passages, and they study the rest of the poem by reading my translation for the sense and declaiming the original for the movement and texture of the verse. I could justify this procedure by claiming that translating all of *Beowulf* in one semester is just too much a steeplechase for undergraduates, leaving no time for literary study. But a better reason is that any long narrative poem has peaks and valleys in its poetry, and the "big moments" where the poet is most fully engaged are the passages students benefit most from reading in the original. The new printing of my edition contains an appendix of glosses to some of these passages (1–52, 86–114, 710–836, 1345–96, 2231b–77, 2631–68, 2792b–820, 3156–82) to assist students in making their own translations.

The short *Beowulf* papers are still heuristic exercises in close reading, but the students also read up on major textual and critical controversies. I encourage skepticism toward interpretations that rest on emendations, toward the possibility of recovering an exact historical context for the poem, and toward any easy resolution of the ambiguities in its structure and viewpoint. I want them to learn to respect their own authority as readers of poetry more than received opinion. They obviously cannot learn everything about *Beowulf* or its scholarship, but they can establish their own positions toward its most problematic features by careful reading and critical thinking.

It helps to see *Beowulf* in relation to other heroic and epic works. Having already spent a semester together in close reading, both the students and I are ready to broaden our perspective while we are reading *Beowulf*. In recent years the spring course has been offered as "*Beowulf* and the Heroic Mode." Its guiding questions are: Why is *Beowulf* a great poem? How does it test the Anglo-Saxon view of heroism? What are the values and limitations of the heroic mode of experience? In addition to comparing passages in *Beowulf* with other Old English poems we have read (e.g., 2247–66 with *The Wanderer*), we read some Old Norse sagas, *Roland*, selections from Malory, and some modern literary responses to *Beowulf*, such as Richard Wilbur's poem "Beowulf" and John Gardner's *Grendel*.

I use the context of the heroic mode mainly as an interruptive device in the course structure, so that it will have some similarity to the structure of *Beowulf* itself. We spend half the semester on the poem, all told, turning away from the work of translating and declaiming it—usually at lines 1300, 1800, and 2200—to read and discuss these other works. With both interruption and continuity in their experience of the course, the students are better able to discuss the poet's method of composing by juxtaposition, by shifting his contexts, particularly in the Finnsburg episode and its environs and in his treatment of the hoard and its varying meanings throughout part 2. For these discussions, I have them read, among other things, Donald K. Fry's *Finnsburg Fragment and Episode* and A. J. Bliss's arguments about lines 3074–75 in *J. R. R. Tolkien, Scholar and Storyteller: Essays in Memoriam*, edited by Mary Salu and Robert T. Farrell. If my students are going to write about the truly problematic aspects of the poetry of *Beowulf*, then they must be acquainted with current scholarly views. And if they come to feel that there are no authoritative external contexts, literary or historical, to resolve the ambiguities they can discover in the text, it may only serve to increase their enjoyment of the poem, which need not rest on an irritable searching after certainty. Poetry has its own authority. So I set them a final longer paper on *Beowulf*, which comes due two weeks before exams.

Preparation

First, reread the whole poem in translation. Reread the Old English of passages that especially interest you.

Second, describe for yourself, to your own satisfaction, the complete range of the poet's tones of voice in *Beowulf*. You may wish to make a list of the different tones. Also describe to yourself his significant silences, the moments of reticence in his style, his darker allusions, his ironies of expression, his recurrent themes and concerns.

Third, try to name for yourself the meanings of the poem's major action and the meanings of its "interlace" and "diptych" patterns. Structure is a form of meaning; what is the poem's structure?

Writing

Write a seven-page essay in which you bring together your most significant perceptions above in an attempt to define and describe, in all their complex manifestations, "The Viewpoint and Intentions of the *Beowulf* Poet." Let this be the title and the goal of your essay. Good luck, and have fun!

After these demonstrations of their sensibility as readers of poetry there is little need for a final examination. The course load lightens as the semester ends, and we terminate rather than conclude.

II.

Elizabeth Greene

Beowulf is many things at once—artifact, linguistic document, poem containing history, myth, elegy, and heroism—so I try to make my course complex enough to contain all these elements. I begin with the sound of the language, playing Jess Bessinger's harp-punctuated recording of *Caedmon's Hymn* and talking about the sounds of Anglo-Saxon and the shape of the poetic line. Through the year, I ask each student to read the Anglo-Saxon before translating, and I work in class, or privately, on pronunciation and rhythm. If a student does no more than develop an "ear for the sea-surge" (to use Ezra Pound's phrase), he or she has made a beginning. I find that if I do not stress the sound of the language, the words will remain unpronounceable, impenetrable mysteries to most of the class.

Early in the year, depending on the class aptitude for grammar, I show as many pictures as I can, usually reproduced from the Sutton Hoo treasure, the Bayeux Tapestry, the Book of Kells, the Lindisfarne Gospels, and the Book of Durrow. As I show the pictures, I talk about interlace, stylization, frames, and borders—and I ask my students to keep these images in their minds as they read the poetry. As the class is learning grammar, I also assign an epic in translation, usually the *Iliad* or *Njal's Saga*, for class discussion. The epic in translation should remind the students that there is life after grammar and introduce them to the heroic world, heroic conventions, and discrepancies between deserts and destiny (very different from the poetic justice most of us have come to expect from novels and postheroic poetry). Most difficult of all—and central to *Beowulf*—is the idea of living for an ideal that may lead to worldly disaster rather than to reward. I find it much easier to begin discussing these critical problems before language difficulties begin—we can then return to them as familiar issues at appropriate points in our journey through *Beowulf*. I do all this—besides grammar—in the first six weeks because I want it clear that Anglo-Saxon requires much more than rote memory and that I value "real thought," though as the year goes on "real thought" becomes increasingly difficult without mastery of the mechanics. I remember that as a student I had surpluses of time and energy at the beginning of the year that only my most expert teachers turned to account; I try to use this early time to create a context for *Beowulf*. I also try to point much of what we do in class toward *Beowulf*. As we do grammar and begin poetry, I point out words, themes, and constructions that we will encounter later, such as the dual form and high-frequency verbs in Quirk and Wrenn; the poetic variation and careful structure of *Caedmon's Hymn*; the themes of the *comitatus*, perception, and the last survivor in the *Dream of the Rood*. We follow these themes, among others, through *The Wanderer*, *The Seafarer*, and *Deor*, so that we have the beginning of a critical context by the time we reach *Beowulf*—and we can build from there.

Once we have reached the poetry, we necessarily settle down to the standard routine of a language class—reading, translation, and commentary. My classes have always been small enough (under twenty) that I can ask each student to give a short talk on widely varying topics. This procedure breaks up the routine (as long as the talks don't grow like pachysandra and take over the yard) and allows me to weave my students' interests and points of view into my commentary. Some students choose a research topic (Tacitus' Germans, Anglo-Saxon law, Anglo-Saxon swords); some choose an artifact (the Franks Casket or the Bury St. Edmund's Cross); some choose to analyze a character in *Beowulf*; some explicate passages from the poem—with good management, these passages are from that particular day's assignment. I ask these students to consider, in addition to the obvious, the poetic effects of the passage and its place within (or anomalous to!) the whole poem. A few students formulate their own topics, such as treasure in *Beowulf*, the *scop* in *Beowulf*, linguistic perspective on language in *Beowulf*. I sometimes have to scramble to keep up with my students' varied interests, but I prefer the struggle to dragging them after me, weary in the dust—though I'm prepared to do that too, if necessary.

As I teach *Beowulf*, I find that each passage presents its own particular problems and leads in its own direction. R. W. Chambers' Beowulf: *An Introduction*, G. N. Garmonsway and Jacqueline Simpson's Beowulf *and Its Analogues*, Rupert Bruce-Mitford's *Sutton Hoo Ship-Burial: A Handbook*, E. B. Irving's *A Reading of* Beowulf, Herbert G. Wright's "Good and Evil . . . in *Beowulf*," and George Clark's "Beowulf's Armor" consistently help me pursue these different directions. I resemble most other teachers of *Beowulf* in wanting my students to see for themselves the beauties of the original (word by word, line by line), which no translation has yet caught.

III.

George Clark

Near the beginning of the term I decide how much of the original a given class can handle, I select that much text (continuous or not), and I divide it into graduated weekly assignments of which the first is very brief (e.g., lines 1–52). In the first week the students read twice through a good prose translation, learn the story, unravel its basic chronology, and acquire a sense of the persons and places named in *Beowulf.* I frequently ask students to identify and relate groups of names: for example, Heorogar, Hrothgar, and Halga; Ongentheow, Athils, Eanmund, and Onela. From the names we reconstruct, order, and begin to interpret the stories. I try to place the persons, places, and actions of *Beowulf* in space and time by referring to genealogical tables and maps and by retelling and reordering the interlocking and related stories that make up the poem so that the whole becomes visible as we deal with a single passage.

Robert Frost compared writing free verse to playing tennis without a net. One teaches or studies *Beowulf* with the net in place. Students of *Beowulf* must begin with an eagerness to know what the text means taken line by line, to know the things the words refer to as well as the words in their cases and moods and genders, to discover how the words create a work of art and an idea of the hero, society, and the world. Inevitably a *Beowulf* course becomes an introduction to a classical body of scholarship and criticism, but on reflection my course seems to become an annual reinterpretation of the poem and its established scholarship touched off by a new, sometimes unclassical, or even unacceptable study or argument. For me, the classical tradition begins with the apparatus in the editions of Klaeber, Wyatt and Chambers, Dobbie, Wrenn, von Schaubert, and Wrenn-Bolton, but I urge the students to begin with the apparatus in Chickering's dual-language edition as their best introduction to the body of learning that has illuminated the poem. The required text and apparatus are Klaeber's. For the historical and legendary matter of the poem and analogues to its basic story, I trace the classical tradition to Chambers' Beowulf: An Introduction, Lawrence's Beowulf and Epic Tradition, and Panzer's study, which deserves a fuller summary than can be found in English. Garmonsway and Simpson's Beowulf and Its Analogues enables modern students to recreate a comparative context for the poem, and N. K. Chadwick's important but difficult "The Monsters and Beowulf" suggests a radical revision of Panzer's thesis and of the genre and literary traditions of the poem. Fontenrose's study of the "combat myth" makes possible, from another perspective, a complementary revision of the traditional view. I usually outline a possible unitarian reading of Beowulf that takes Chadwick's Norse analogues (and Beowulf itself) as reflexes of a mythic pattern also visible in the later folktales.

Most recently Kiernan's book (1981) became the instrument of renewal and variation. We started at line 2200; I brought Zupitza's facsimile to class regularly, began most reading assignments with some lines from the (reproduced) manuscript, discussed paleography, codicology, textual criticism, and specific textual problems. At line 2226b (MS mwatide) I illustrated Dobbie's argument with a bit of chalk shaped like a pen point: the effect was electric, Dobbie the man of the hour. I survey a number of unitarian readings of Beowulf with attention to the particular strengths of each: Tolkien's "Beowulf: The Monsters and the Critics," Kaske's "Sapientia et Fortitudo as the Controlling Theme of Beowulf," Leyerle's "Beowulf the Hero and King," Clark's "Beowulf's Armor," Irving's A Reading of Beowulf, and Shippey's Beowulf. But their common weakness usually provides matter for some discussion or debate: none of these studies makes an entirely convincing case of the thematic unity of Beowulf. Kiernan's I think unintentional disintegrationism gave the debate new edge since the thematic, structural, and codicological discontinuities of Beowulf seem to coincide; and the end of term found us grappling with the question, can we see Beowulf steadily and still see it whole?

IV.

Paul B. Taylor

The proposition that a critical grasp of the major works in English literature requires a firm grip on their sources ensures the place of Old English studies in the undergraduate curriculum of the Faculty of Letters at the University of Geneva. Since the degree in letters is earned chiefly in examination and not by course credits (although three advanced seminar credits are tickets to the final exam sessions) and since both written and oral exams are fixed individually with each student, instruction in Old English cannot afford to be formally rigid in coverage and emphases. In practice, it points to analysis and criticism rather than to linguistic description.

At Geneva, the upper-level medieval courses are taught in the last two years of a four-year degree program. The core of the instruction in Old English is a year-long two-hour seminar that alternates its subject matter in a two-year cycle, either year of which should be sufficient to prepare students for the minimum exam requirement and varied enough in texts and scope to incite them toward wider studies in the field. Any student of English may choose to prepare as many as two of the obligatory three seminar credits in medieval English. In the first year of the cycle, a winter semester seminar (sixteen or seventeen weeks) is entitled "Introduction to Old English Language and Literature." Current texts are Bruce Mitchell's *Guide* and J. C. Pope's *Seven Old English Poems*; these are supplemented by numerous prose and poetry handouts. O. D. Macrae-Gibson's *Learning Old English* course on tape is available for listening in the faculty *médiathéque* as an aid to rapid learning of the grammar, but unless it is referred to frequently in class it is seldom used. A mimeographed version of Madden and Magoun's *Grouped*

Frequency Word-List is used in class as a guide to the poetic vocabulary. The summer semester (eleven or twelve weeks) is devoted to a rapid critical reading of *Beowulf*, emphasizing analysis rather than translation. No more than a thousand lines are actually translated in class. To facilitate understanding of the poetic structure, students use the Donaldson translation in the *Norton Anthology*, which is readily available. The primary text is that of Wrenn-Bolton, used because of its price and availability, but students learn to use Klaeber's glossary and notes. To reinforce classroom discussion of the prosodic features of the poem, students are directed to the tapes made from the Bessinger reading available in the *médiathéque*. I do not object to the use of the Swanton bilingual edition of *Beowulf*.

The second year of the cycle consists of a year-long two-hour seminar on *Beowulf*, with only brief excursions elsewhere in the literary corpus. The first meeting of the year looks at the opening lines of the poem, and for some six weeks the first fifty-two lines of *Beowulf* are pressed for a study of Old English phonology, morphology, prosody, and poetic style. Students are asked to have Mitchell's *Guide* at hand, and there is a reserve shelf in the English Reading Room with copies of Alistair Campbell's *Old English Grammar* as well as basic critical studies. Besides photocopied offprints of articles, there are collections such as Nicholson's *Anthology*, Bessinger and Kahrl's *Essential Articles*, and popular studies such as Brodeur's *Art* and Irving's *A Reading*. These are the titles the students themselves reach for most readily. In the weeks that follow, *Beowulf* is translated in its entirety in class, although in the later weeks the seminar emphasis shifts from skill in translation to textual problems and then to analytic criticism. Some time is spent in the last sessions on comparative problems; these are of particular interest to students here, almost all of whom have had exposure to Old High German or Old French, if not to both. Since few of our students are native speakers of English, translations of *Beowulf* into Modern English have a special fascination as critical problems. Students here are also attracted to Modern English revisions of the Beowulf story (John Gardner's *Grendel* and Richard Wilbur's "Beowulf"), as well as to modern English poetic views of the older tradition (Geoffrey Hill's *Mercian Hymns*), and all of these are covered, from time to time, in classroom reports.

If a student chooses Old English as a subject for one of the obligatory seminar "certificates," or credits, I prefer a paper that works with the language and the prosody of the poem in terms of performance. I strive to interest the student in the problems of establishing the bounds of meaning as well as in the many ways performance of the verse line can inform sense. My own critical emphasis in class is on the inextricable bond between the language of Old English poetry and the critical issues it occasions. My approach is textual rather than structural.

Probably the most important aspect of the curriculum here, however, is the independent work the student does to prepare for tailor-made exams, since exams are not normally course-related. The one obligatory exam demands that the student be prepared to compare, for example, genealogies in *Beowulf* and *Four Quartets* or *Absalom! Absalom!*, heroism in *Beowulf* and *The Faerie Queen*, tales and tellers in *Beowulf* and *The Tempest*, wisdom in *Beowulf* and *Moby-Dick*, fidelity in *Beowulf* and *Hamlet*, praise in *Beowulf* and *The Winter's Tale*, magic in *Beowulf* and *The Canterbury Tales*, and so forth. Preparation for this and the other oral and written exam possibilities consists of an individual investigation into the prominent tendencies of current literary criticism.

V.

Robert F. Yeager

I first prepare my students to translate *Beowulf* by teaching them Old English, developing an interest in Old English poetry strong enough to carry them through an elective course in grammar and odd prose texts; then, and only then, am I able to work with them on *Beowulf*. I am teaching *Beowulf* all the time, in one stage or another: either I am actually working on the poem with students (about once every two years, as my schedule now stands), or I am grooming the next group of students to read the poem a year or two hence. The approach is geared to the conditions at my institution and has been tailored to fit the unique needs and potential of a specific place.

I teach *Beowulf* in Old English to undergraduates at Warren Wilson College in Swannanoa, North Carolina. Warren Wilson is a private liberal arts college and may be the smallest institution in the country in which *Beowulf* is so taught. It has approximately 520 students, of whom some twenty percent are from overseas, primarily from third world countries. The college is one of a half-dozen work-study institutions in the United States. This means that at Warren Wilson, all students, regardless of financial circumstances, must work three hours a day, or a total of fifteen hours a week. Their labor covers the cost of room and board, and they perform a wide variety of tasks. There is a sawmill for processing some of the college timber into boards, fenceposts, and so forth. Somewhat less than half the 1,100 acres are farmed. We raise cattle and hogs, their feed, and vegetables for human consumption. The students are responsible for the farming and lumbering operations, as well as for college-maintenance jobs such as carpentry, kitchen, and secretarial help. Faculty work regularly with them to get the big jobs, like haying or winter feeding, completed ahead of bad weather.

Such an environment affects teaching in a number of ways: most classes are small, ranging between five and twenty students; a large class is thirty. Because the college resembles a diminutive town or village, students and faculty know each other outside the classroom as well as in and frequently share many things, including first names. Thus the teaching is often intense and extremely personal. It is also quite diverse and, I would expect, surprising from the standpoint of other colleges and universities. A class at Warren Wilson is likely to have elbow-to-elbow students from seven or eight states, an African or two, a Thai, a Colombian, a Portuguese, some from rural backgrounds, some from New York or Atlanta or Nairobi, some whose families have little money, others quite well-to-do. It certainly is the only college I know where the students frequently arrive in class direct from the cow barn or the farrowing house, leave their soiled boots at the door, and parse sentences from the *Anglo-Saxon Chronicle*.

Because Warren Wilson is the sort of place it is, I work on getting the students interested in *Beowulf* and the Middle Ages almost from the time I meet them. The size of the college and its work orientation bring me in contact with students more frequently and in a greater variety of conditions than perhaps would be the case on other campuses. Outside class, I have made it a point to illustrate some of my remarks in general conversation with bits from *Beowulf* I like particularly. Usually, I give a paraphrase, identify the source, and mumble something about *Beowulf* being a great poem. This kind of "teasing" has provoked some good questions in rather odd places: a silo, the tailgate of a pickup truck, mending a barbed-wire fence. It has been responsible for bringing more than one student into classes in Old English and eventually to read *Beowulf* with me. Since few of my students have heard of the poem or much about Anglo-Saxon culture before they get to college, this "casual" activity is a necessary aspect of my approach to teaching *Beowulf*.

What I do outside the classroom, I repeat—albeit in a different form—in class. I teach *Beowulf* in translation in two courses, one a survey of English literature, in which *Beowulf* forms the first text on the syllabus, the other a conglomerate course entitled "An Introduction to Medieval Life and Literature." In both of these, I read extensively from *Beowulf* in Old English, pass around photographs of the manuscript and copies of the passages I read aloud, and let the students follow along in the original and in their translations. I comment on ambiguities in the original text that translations perforce are unable to reveal, in order to hint that reading the poem in Old English is preferable. Usually the discussion turns at some point to the language itself, and I try to show the classes how Old English is both like and unlike the English they speak. I even follow a somewhat similar procedure in my composition classes. I explain points of spelling, usage, and grammar as often as possible by showing the relation between Modern English and Old English. Sometimes in individual conferences with composition students I flip open my *Beowulf* to give examples of various forms. I'm sure students have left my office feeling bludgeoned by a fifteen-minute answer to what seemed to them a routine "yes/no" question, but I persist because from their subsequent responses I know that they have become more aware that Old English exists and that it has relevance to difficulties in the modern idiom. Introduced in these ways, Old English seems less removed a thing, and a course in it less abstruse and unthinkable, than the students might earlier have supposed.

If I'm successful at this sort of pump priming, I fill my beginners' Old English language class. I have taught it three times in six years, each time to around fifteen students. To some degree, I have been assisted in enrolling students in Old English because the college has a distribution requirement, one section of which may be fulfilled in this way. Since, however, there are many other choices that fit the requirement (some with a reputation for being "easier" than mine), I seem to get few students who take the course for that purpose alone. Most have discussed taking it with me before they sign up, and appear to know what they're getting into before class starts.

One of the reasons my beginning Old English class is thought of as a "hard" course is that I view it as a preparatory exercise for reading the "real stuff"—poetry, and *Beowulf* in particular. I'm clear about this from the first class. I point out that the goal is to be good enough at Old English to enjoy *Beowulf*. I get a little challenging about it, telling the class that most people in the world cannot do this, much to their loss. I promise the students that if they do very well in the beginning course, they will be allowed into the advanced Old English class that I teach by appointment only the following term and that there, by the end, they will be able to read *Beowulf*. I keep the notion alive in their minds throughout the term, sometimes breaking off a grammar lesson to look at passages of poetry containing a particular grammatical structure we're studying, sometimes asking them to try sight-reading poetry they've never seen, to show them how far they've come. As the term draws on, I use bits of *Beowulf* for this, and we discuss the bits (once we've broken them down and translated them) in relation to prose passages we've read or may be reading. I find this practice helps my teaching poetry, and *Beowulf* in particular, in several ways. First, it "demystifies" poetry somewhat if students get a little almost from the beginning of their work. Of course, I edit the snippets heavily, as the students come to find out (indeed, as I tell them at the time), but this doesn't appear to lessen their pleasure and sense of achievement. Another advantage to this method is that it gives a set of welcome "oases" or "islands" in poetic texts that can seem quite long the first time through. Suddenly, out of the lines they don't know and are laboring over come a few they have read, or know already, from the beginning Old English class. But most important, perhaps, is the inspirational quality of the poetry. Reading it early in gobbets offers a rationale, or purpose, for the slogging grammar study of the beginners' class. The poetry soars; can the students, once they've found their linguistic wings, follow to those heights? Some answer in the negative, naturally, and choose not to continue to the advanced class. Others, however, truly seem held by the prospect of achievement that reading *Beowulf* holds out.

Once in the advanced class, my students find I continue another technique for teaching I have used in the beginning course. I try to tie cultural and environmental issues raised by the text to situations familiar to the students in their own lives. This, of course, is hardly a technique I have invented; every instructor does it to some degree. I have come to rely on it heavily at Warren Wilson for teaching *Beowulf*, however, because there is so much in the college routine that illuminates certain passages in the poem. The river twisting through the pasture grows icicles in the winter; its banks hang hoary and dark with roots. By chance, there is a large Indian burial ground on campus under excavation by the college and a major university. Every summer, a number of Warren Wilson students work on the site and have helped unearth skeletons, jewelry, and spearpoints. A few black bears live yet in the mountains not far from Swannanoa, and deer and foxes are occasionally observed in the fields. The woods at night are very dark and at times can feel quite wild. Since we slaughter our own cattle and pigs, many of the farm-crew students are familiar with floors awash with blood. I call on my students to describe for the others what it was like to do certain things—say, stand in the abattoir on butchering day or wake up in the middle of the night with the fire out and a strong sensation of not being alone. If a student has worked at the archaeological dig, I draw on that knowledge when we talk about Sutton Hoo and the dragon's hoard in *Beowulf*. I strongly believe that the greatest power of *Beowulf* comes from its tones and "colors," and the emotions they evoke. Thus I employ vigorously any means I can find to transport my students emotively "into" the poem by calling on what they have themselves felt. I even try to use my international students to this end, since many of them are able to portray vividly tribal loyalties and concerns essential to understanding *Beowulf* but unfamiliar to suburban Americans. The same can be said for the Appalachian students in my classes. One of the best descriptions I have heard of the blood-feud mentality came from such a student, a girl who normally said very little but who was able to put the "Fight at Finnsburg" into chilling perspective by reciting a short history of family members who had died over the years in the mountain coves where she grew up.

What might be useful to others about the way I teach *Beowulf*, then, is not so much what I do every day in class (that's actually rather standard— about five hundred lines per week, mostly covered in class sessions of ninety minutes each five days per week) but, rather, the strategies I employ in the course and outside to bring students to the poem, put them inside it, and give them a "real" experience of demanding academic work and an Anglo-Saxon world view to take away with them. That they seem satisfied with these things satisfies me, as does the apparent fact that, with a bit of calculation and cajolery, *Beowulf* in Old English can draw students in reasonable numbers, even in a small, work-oriented liberal arts college in the mountains of North Carolina, "right down there with the hogs."

TEACHING *BEOWULF* IN TRANSLATION TO UNDERGRADUATES

I.

Elaine Tuttle Hansen

I currently teach *Beowulf* in translation to undergraduates in a course entitled "Topics in Medieval English Literature: From Epic to Romance." The course is designed chiefly for English majors with previous work in introductory and intermediate literature classes. We begin with *Beowulf*, read in Howell D. Chickering's dual-language edition, and end with Malory. We have at most four class meetings to devote to *Beowulf*, and since it is also the first work we study, I am obliged to use some of that class time to introduce the course as a whole.

Fortunately the Old English epic serves as a fine initiation not only into the texts and contexts of its specific historical period but also into the general strategies of reading, interpreting, and discussing medieval poems—or for that matter literary discourse of any period. Although I adjust my approach to the particular needs and skills of any given group of students, in theory my unit on *Beowulf* proceeds in the following way. The class meets for an hour and a half twice a week. On the first day, the students have no text but we also have no time to waste, so after completing course business I hand out copies—untitled—of the first fifty lines of *Beowulf* in Old English. I ask the class to imagine that they have just discovered this strange piece of writing, with no clues to its language, date, title, or author, and to tell me all they can about what it might be. They turn out to be eager and fairly successful detectives: They quickly decide that what they have is a poem, or part of one; they note the alliteration, the half-lines, and enough cognates (so they claim) to know that the language is somehow related to Modern English. (I later show them a facsimile of the manuscript so that we can talk briefly about the conventions of typography and punctuation on which modern readers implicitly depend and for which students of medieval texts are so indebted to editors.) The students might also speculate that it is a poem in which war or battle—a felicitous misreading of *blæd wide sprang* 'his fame sprang wide'—and God (whose modern name appears in 1.13b) play a part. After we have done all we can with our mystery guest, I hand out a titled translation of these same fifty lines and ask students to tell me all they now know about the poem and the kind of culture that might have produced it. Again, this seems to be an engaging and productive enterprise; everyone is roughly equal and can (and must) say something, and the students can astonish themselves on this first day with the power as well as the limitations of their reading and interpretive skills. They want to talk about the fact that the poem begins with a funeral and with the celebration of a hero who is apparently not the titular hero of the work; they note the importance of the king and his fame, the stance of the storyteller and his intrusive comments in the middle and at the end of the passage. We keep a record of their first impressions, none of which I "correct" at this juncture, and at the end of our time on *Beowulf* we can compare the students' initial responses with their later interpretations.

There are several purposes to this opening exercise. First, I am hoping to persuade students who have had a minimal and sometimes unpleasant exposure to medieval literature that something as uninviting, even forbidding, as an Old English poem is indeed different, but not so different that it cannot speak to them. This discovery introduces a central concern of the course as a whole with "alterity" and "modernity." As Larry Benson has recently put it, "It is this combination of strangeness and familiarity that allows us even on the briefest acquaintance to discover in the medieval period, as in no other, a true sense of 'otherness,' of alternate ways of thought and feeling." The accompanying recognition that "society is a construct rather than a given" is, in turn, a distinguishing characteristic of the modern world (Benson, "Why Study the Middle Ages?"). Furthermore, our initial encounter with the Old English at least makes students less uncomfortable with glancing to the left as they read Chickering's translation of the poem and, more significantly, serves as an early reminder of the problems of studying any work in translation. When we are later discussing central or difficult passages, students will often ask me what the Old English "really" says, and since I usually cannot answer the question simply or definitively, my comments on the richness and often the ambiguity of the Old English may reinforce a sensitivity to verbal detail that will carry over into their own short papers on this poem as well as to their later study of texts in original languages. Of course this first consideration of *Beowulf* also sets them to the task of reading closely and "milking" any text for all they can find in it. Finally, my approach is designed to fill up time on the first day with something other than a lecture, to underline my explicit intention that students should collaborate in class work and that to do so profitably they must pay attention to themselves as readers, to the assumptions on which they depend to make sense of a text, to the kinds of questions they have been trained to ask, and to the answers they feel satisfied with.

By the second class meeting, students have read approximately 1,250 lines of *Beowulf* (or more, including the introductory material in their text, if a weekend has passed). They have also been asked to write a paragraph about their experience as readers of this poem to serve as a basis for discussion. At first I read aloud in Old English and they try a little too; then I talk briefly about the language, its history, dialects, and development. I show them some easy Old English prose, which they can "translate" with very little help, and we look at examples of basic poetic techniques, such as alliteration, meter, kennings, and variation. In the remaining time we discuss the reading and the students' responses and problems. I have advised them to read this poem with one general rule in mind: if something seems odd or inappropriate or confusing or boring, it is probably important. This rule focuses our attention immediately on issues like boasting and digressions and the "Christian coloring" of the work, and it enables me to talk in a rudimentary way about historical and sociocultural contexts. We begin, in other words, by noting how *Beowulf* differs from modern poems (or plays or novels), and we always slide over into a consideration of how it is the same, which is the other half of the point I am trying to make.

By the third class meeting, students have finished *Beowulf* and we have a tremendous amount to discuss. We focus in this way: at the end of the previous class, I circulate some standard questions and concerns I am currently thinking about—everything from structure (two parts or three?) and narrative technique (repetition, foreshadowing, understatement, gnomic commentary, etc.) to monsters, the question of Beowulf's tragic flaw (does he have one?), and the role of women in the poem. I might ask the class to think about ambiguities and ironies in the story or the treatment of time and space or the function of imagination, memory, and storytelling in terms of narrator, characters, and audience. I then ask each student to choose at least two questions, one of mine and one of his or her own devising, and to bring to the third meeting a paragraph written in response to each question. We begin the discussion by hearing a number of their questions (which we can often relate to the issues I have raised) and answers; this generates a useful degree of consensus on important problems and a healthy amount of disagreement about solutions.

On our fourth and last meeting on *Beowulf,* students review and focus their interpretations of the poem by choosing one passage that they think is crucial, puzzling, an interpolation, or otherwise memorable and writing a short explanation of how the passage lights up the poem as a whole for them. If the class is small enough, I try to hear all these passages and explications and to underscore the readings that I find most accurate, fruitful, and interesting. This seems to be another useful way of encouraging individual responses, clearing up specific problems, and summarizing, without suggesting that such a brief look at the poem in translation can catch more than a glimpse of the goodly things in *Beowulf* and the ways in which they may be recovered by the modern reader.

II.

Bernice W. Kliman

After a year of composition, liberal arts students at Nassau Community College choose two electives to fulfill their English requirement from an array of thirty course offerings. As one of these electives, some choose English 205, "English Literature I: The Works of the Major English Writers from the Anglo-Saxon Period to the End of the Eighteenth Century." These vocationally oriented students hope this course will be fairly easy so they can concentrate on the courses they feel will be important to their careers. To reach them, the instructor must enable the great works of early literature to generate excitement. Fortunately, the poetry explored in English 205 seldom fails to exert its magic on the students.

Starting with *Beowulf*, we read whole works, such as *Sir Gawain and the Green Knight*, Chaucer's General Prologue and one tale (often the Wife of Bath's Tale), and a play by Shakespeare (often *Henry IV, Part 1*). In addition, we read short poems from the entire period, from Caedmon through Pope. Of twenty-nine class sessions, each seventy-five minutes long, the five spent on *Beowulf* set the tone and pattern for the whole course. To prepare for each class, students must read, take notes, and write answers to questions; in class, they must be prepared to notice, write, discuss, and read aloud. The students learn how to read for values in addition to character, plot, setting, and themes; this mastery enlivens their appreciation of all the works. Since *Beowulf* also provides the opportunity for a short course-within-the-course on the history of the language, I use the poem to introduce the idea of an evolving language.

On the book list I distribute on the first day, I include the Lord's Prayer

(Matt. 6.9–13) in an Old English dialect, in the King James version, and in a modern version. Because these students have had little language training, they do not at once see any similarities between the first two. It's something of a revelation to them to recognize the common elements. Then I ask the class to notice differences in word order, in spelling, and in diction. Their preference for the King James version—which, I point out, is from Shakespeare's time—over the modern version gives them a positive attitude toward Shakespeare's language even before they encounter it. Samuel Moore's chart on Old English inflections (in *Historical Outlines of English Sounds and Inflections* 22–23) can also be useful on the first day because he includes many familiar words.

In connection with the language materials, I tell the romance of the *Beowulf* manuscript. Students respond to the mystery and miracle of the *Beowulf* as a survivor from long ago. Because our text is a translation, with only a few Old English passages, I depend on xeroxed, dittoed, and projected pages to demonstrate the alliterative patterns and incidentally to point out the absence of punctuation and capital letters, the abbreviations, and the run-over verse lines in the manuscript. I want them to be aware of the poem as an artifact. From the Wyatt and Chambers *Beowulf*, I use the reproductions of the manuscript showing the two hands that copied it and the modern orthography on facing pages. We can compare parallel passages in Thorpe, which has Old English and word-for-word Modern English in facing columns, and the related sections in our text. I don't try to cover more than ten lines of verse this way. That is quite enough to give students a taste. A few will want to find out more on their own, but the comparative study opens vistas for all they hadn't imagined—about language, about scholarship, about translators' choices.

Rather than use an anthology, I choose separate volumes for each work because I want to acquaint my students with the pleasure of holding in the hand a small text with thicker-than-tissue pages and comfortable print size. I've selected the Burton Raffel translation because he is a poet whose verse moves. On reserve in the library are Bede's *Ecclesiastical History of the English Nation*, Tacitus' *Germania*, *The Penguin Atlas of Medieval History*, John Gardner's *Grendel*, and several additional translations of *Beowulf*, including Thorpe's. In class I employ these texts in various ways—simply showing them, having students come forward to see them, passing them around, or reading from them. *The Penguin Atlas*, for example, clarifies the early history of Britain in relation to the rest of the world. Having paper-clipped the important pages, I have students crowd around the front desk, where I point out the features of the ten or so maps that concern us. At appropriate times, I introduce them to Bede's wholesomeness and humane geniality by reading the story of Pope Gregory's first encounter with the

Angles (bk. 2, ch. 1), the conversion of the Northumbrians (bk. 2, ch. 13), and the story of Caedmon (bk. 4, ch. 24). A few passages from *Germania* depict attitudes toward women and the concept of *comitatus*.

In addition to these ancillary texts, I bring in a number of nontext materials. Not all of these will be useful each semester, but I draw on a store I have gathered. Sutton Hoo photographs never fail to arouse awe and admiration and to awaken students' imaginations at the outset. Postcards on the Book of Kells demonstrate the high skill of early Celtic art. These can be spread on my desk, where students can come up to examine them, and may be used with an abbreviated slide show from the Metropolitan Museum, *Early Irish Art* (with my own commentary rather than the cassette's). Though Celtic art has little to do with *Beowulf*, Celtic designs found among the Sutton Hoo artifacts establish a link between the Anglo-Saxon and Celtic communities; the illuminations show the admiration for gold that the *Beowulf* poet describes; and these beautiful works of art dispel notions about the "dark ages." I refer to these Celtic materials again when I sketch in the British background of the Arthurian legend for our study of *Gawain*. I also distribute a map of Britain with key dates, places, and personages penciled in, to be used the entire semester. Booth's cartoon in the *New Yorker* depicting an encounter between an innocuous, lame-brained dragon and a caveman gives a moment of pleasure. We can usefully compare this dragon to the *Beowulf* dragon to see why one like the latter is needed for the former to be funny. An article in the *New York Times* by Harold M. Schmeck, Jr., on "monsters" produced by optical illusions lends a scientific note that most students find interesting but unnecessary; they are more than eager to accept the "reality" of monsters. Upon application by the instructor, publishers readily grant permission to xerox items for class use; alternatively, an overhead projector can flash them on the wall. By varying these resources, I not only surprise and delight the students but also quicken the pace of the course.

The reading of *Beowulf* takes four sessions: prologue to fitt 9, fitts 10–20, 21–30, and 31–43. For each reading assignment I ask focusing questions; students must hand in brief answers along with a one- or two-sentence summary of each fitt and a listing of the values they have inferred. I might ask the class, for example, "What does Beowulf reveal about his character in his first speeches?" and "How do the reactions of other characters and the narrator's comments contribute to his portrayal?" Drawing on their answers, I can list on the board the manifold attributes connected with the topic *sapientia et fortitudo* (here Robert Kaske's article "*Sapientia et Fortitudo* as the Controlling Theme of *Beowulf*" has been important for my preparation). These questions will also be the basis for the weekly quiz that is my chief tool to persuade the students not to fall behind in the reading, to keep me aware of what they are not clear about, and, along with classroom participation and homework, to provide grades for the course. I give no midterm or final, require no term paper: the students' gratitude energizes their study for homework and the weekly quiz. During the semester, I assign no more than two outside papers. If I assign one on *Beowulf*, it might be to compare a key passage in three different translations and to draw conclusions about the effect of each translator's choices or to read *Grendel* by John Gardner and then rewrite a passage of *Beowulf* from yet another point of view—say Unferth's or Freawaru's—or to see the movie *Grendel Grendel Grendel* and compare it with Gardner's book and *Beowulf*. A visit to the Cloisters Museum later in the semester always provides the topic for one of the two papers. For many students, this museum visit is the most memorable part of the course.

That of course is the point of the whole semester—somehow to make this material a part of the students' lives. Discussing *Beowulf*'s values, connecting these to other poems from the Old English period as well as to later works, tracing these values as they change or remain the same—this aspect interests students and seems relevant to them. The depiction of women, for example, has been a useful starting point for class discussion. Students begin to feel competent to discuss such ideas as Christian and pagan elements, joys of the court, youth and age, realism and idealization, women's and men's roles, morality, custom, and ceremony. Though they are initially less interested in the poet's artistry than in his or her values and though it is indeed difficult to convey some of the nuances because we are reading a translation, ultimately students must be able to notice a poet's style if literature is to offer them its unique pleasure. Within discussions of character and values, which the students grasp readily, I interweave questions and comments about alliteration, stress, caesura, kennings, synonyms, Homeric similes, oral formulas, and other oral signals; about dramatic irony, understatement, tone, and narrative point of view; and about narrative movement, repetition, and parallelism. Students do begin to notice these stylistic details in *Beowulf* and are thus prepared to enjoy the artistry of the *Gawain* poet and of Chaucer later in the semester.

Appreciation for these works convinces even the most vocationally-oriented student that perhaps there is something to literature after all. I have the sense that students are going out to their work in industry and business with fond recollections of days spent with *Beowulf* and the other works of English 205.

Edward J. Rielly

Teaching *Beowulf* to undergraduates is a demanding challenge, though certainly a worthwhile one. The challenge is heightened at those many colleges and universities where the one-volume *Norton Anthology* is used, for then *Beowulf*, the first selection in the text, inevitably becomes part of the instructor's introduction to the course. It is precisely this situation that I face in a two-semester sophomore-level course that all English majors and minors are required to take at the college where I teach and that other students may take to satisfy their sophomore literature requirement. Consequently *Beowulf* is the first early classic that many of my students study during their college years. An obvious concern is whether the poem can survive the multitude of preconceptions students bring to types of literature with which they are unfamiliar. Will students reject *Beowulf* out of hand because they see it as too old, too difficult, or generally irrelevant to their lives?

The idealistic approach might be to say that *Beowulf*, as a great work of literature, can stand on its own without an apologist and that students inevitably will respond to both its spirit and its substance. We know, however, that reality intrudes. People tend not to like what they see as foreign.

I believe, though, that only on the surface, so to speak, is *Beowulf* "foreign." Its essence—its spirit and ideals—is a part of me, is a part of my students. That message, above all, is what I want my students to carry with them as they leave the classroom, not only so that they will neither reject *Beowulf* nor avoid a major or minor in English but, more importantly, so that they will not write off centuries of magnificent literature.

What makes a classic classic, after all, is that it speaks to us across the span of many years, and it does so because it transcends mechanics and techniques. It transcends questions of structural unity, historical veracity, time and place of authorship (so many of the questions that have inspired generations of *Beowulf* scholars but have failed to inspire generations of undergraduates) in order to speak to that complex emotional and intellectual matrix that is human nature. Can we not feel and lament, for example, the passing of a way of life, as the *Beowulf* poet does at the end of the poem, as we do in our own lives as we move from one period to another, when present becomes past without altogether leaving us? Do we not admire the individual who stands alone against great odds, who sacrifices everything for a losing cause (which, for that precise reason, is not a losing cause), whether that person turns out to be Beowulf facing his final adversary, Christ sacrificing himself on the cross, or a modern student taking a stand on a controversial issue?

I concentrate on this topic of heroism because I find much of the relevance of the poem in this theme. Beowulf's heroic nature is complex, of course, for he is several types of hero. I focus particularly on Beowulf as a pagan hero, as a Christian hero, and, finally, as an elegiac hero.

I hope that my students will perceive that the categories of pagan hero and Christian hero are not mutually exclusive. An event that comes to mind is the death of Beowulf. Though weakened with age, he resolves to face the dragon alone. It seems clear as Beowulf begins his battle that he is no longer confident of victory; perhaps he is even a bit reluctant to carry out his intention. Being older and wiser, he may see more clearly now what the future holds for his people after his own departure. But he goes forward, alone, not only because fate "goes as it must" but also because it is right that he do so and not right that any other man, as he says, "should spend his strength against the monster," do the king's work.

Though Beowulf's death and burial are overtly pagan, it is easy for a Christian to see in them, as Frederick Klaeber does (pp. li, n. 2; 212; 217), many reminders of Christ's last hours. For example, Christ is also deprived of his friends, who fall asleep while he prays in the Garden of Gethsemane. Christ prays that God might remove the cup from him, yet, as Wiglaf says of Beowulf, holds "to his high destiny." Finally, having rejected the armed assistance of Peter, Jesus meets death alone (Matt. 26, Mark 14, Luke 22, John 18). The point here is not that the *Beowulf* poet may have been writing an Imitation of Christ but that laying down one's life for others (or perhaps making a lesser though still important sacrifice, such as sacrificing one's popularity for a just cause) is an essentially heroic act regardless of the cultural or religious context in which the sacrifice is made.

My students are apt to agree that there are universals (or at least common traits) in heroism, but they are likely to argue that there are few true heroes

today, certainly few of Beowulf's type. Each year, in fact, I ask my students
to list their personal heroes. They put few names on paper, yet they tell me
that heroes are not just for children, that they would be willing to have
heroes, that it would even be good to have some. At this moment, ironically,
my students are very close to the mood of the poem. The poet, while
obviously valuing many changes that had occurred over the years, including
the new vision of a life eternal, must have felt the trade not altogether
satisfying, for the elegiac tone of the poem is so pronounced that Beowulf
functions as a true elegiac hero, as a concrete manifestation of a way of life
both passing and mourned. The poet says what my students, after these
many centuries, are still saying, that we live in a world increasingly short
of heroes.

Still, the poem implies a corrective to this lament. After all, we have seen
many heroes during the intervening centuries, so perhaps heroism never
really dies out. Perhaps we are too prone to look outward for our heroes
rather than at ourselves. How many students who sit in front of me in a
classroom are capable of sacrificing for others, for a just cause, for whatever?
Many of them are, I think. We sacrifice within the context of our lives, as
others did within the context of theirs.

IV.

Diana M. DeLuca

I teach a survey course, "British Literature to 1800," to undergraduate nonmajors in a Hawaiian community college. My students are familiar with many cultures—Chinese, Japanese, South Pacific, Hawaiian, mainland American—but they are not noticeably interested in British literature until some effort on my part shows them why a literature so foreign is still important to them. We read *Beowulf* in the verse translation that appears in our anthology. We have about two weeks, or five hours of class time, to study the poem. I try to show them a universality in *Beowulf* that corresponds, in its two major adventures, to real and legendary figures in Hawaiian mythology and history.

The young Beowulf comes to life for them when compared with people in early Hawaiian history. In some ways, early Hawaiian society can be compared with the British, though I don't insist on this—the comparison breaks down after a while. The older Beowulf, heavy with the responsibilities of kingship, recalls the great king Kamehameha, who was responsible for uniting the Hawaiian islands into one kingdom. Having launched into the work by this kind of analogy, I talk about *Beowulf* as a study in heroism and about the burdens a people place on those they call heroes. We talk about differing kinds of heroism and move naturally into comparing Beowulf with Sir Gawain, for *Sir Gawain and the Green Knight* is the next work on our list. Finally we talk about the particular kind of society that created a work such as *Beowulf*.

I hope by this kind of approach to achieve two things: first, to give students a sense of the particular nature of *Beowulf* by acquainting them with the techniques, expectations, and challenges of a specific poem created for a definite audience. They approach this particularity, during and between our class discussions, with readings in Dorothy Whitelock's *The Audience of Beowulf*, Burns and Reagan's *Concepts of the Hero in the Middle Ages and Renaissance*, the anthologies of *Beowulf* criticism edited by Nicholson and by Fry, and Fisher's "The Trials of the Epic Hero in *Beowulf*."

Second, I try to give students a broader appreciation of how literature can "mean" both within its time and beyond. For this expanding realization of the poem, they can read in Bowra's *Heroic Poetry*; and I often assign a past issue of the *Saturday Review* with pointed articles by Reynolds Price, "The Heroes of Our Times," and Paul Zweig, "The Hero in Literature." In teaching *Beowulf*, I want students to recognize the difference between the young hero attempting to establish his reputation and the old king who must act as he is expected to precisely because of his youthful heroics.

As for the mechanics of the course, I avoid lecturing as much as possible. Each day I am fully prepared to lead discussion and to answer all manner of questions; however, my goal is to make the students independent and curious on their own. I want them to have a direct response to the story and to find the answers to their own questions, if possible, from the list of reserve texts.

I duplicate the first fifty-odd lines of the Klaeber text and make photostats of the Zupitza-Davis facsimile edition. I read aloud the first twenty-five lines to demonstrate sound associations and special characters like the thorn. The class then tries to piece together the possible content of the following lines, which we then compare with the translation. My students must read the poem in a translation, but I make sure that they know what the original looks and sounds like. We play the Bessinger recording of the poem. Some students indicate that they would like to tackle the original later in their careers.

I try to vary my classes with different approaches. I am fond of the British Library's Sutton Hoo Ship Burial slides. Students have worksheets distributed ahead of time; they must complete and turn these in before our discussions of such topics as the Sutton Hoo treasures, the oral-formulaic question, and the Christianity in *Beowulf* and *Gawain* compared. I have students give five-minute presentations to the class all through the semester. Some of them choose to do their report on something germane to *Beowulf*—medieval monsters, Germanic arms, wedding customs. The most amusing report was a comparison of John Gardner's *Grendel* with *Beowulf*. The most enjoyable activity was a panel discussion during which students assumed the identities of characters in the poem and answered questions directed at their personae from the general class. I have the students try to create some alliterative lines in the formulaic style and include a kenning or two. They are delighted to find that "gas guzzler" is a kenning. I challenge them with a "hands-on" experience: to try to find anything in the poem that suggests an oral delivery. This is not too hard for them, since Hawaiian chants use many common oral-traditional techniques.

The overall pattern of our *Beowulf* unit begins with the students' reading the first few hundred lines of the poem and answering worksheet questions about them, to stimulate discussion and understanding. If all goes well, we look at the poem's internal evidence for the Anglo-Saxon background, and I ask them to look at Dorothy Whitelock's book on their own. Meanwhile, one of their worksheets has required them to rank a series of personal values (money, power, education, reputation, service, freedom, stability, hedonism, etc.) for themselves and then in small groups. Finally they do it once more, but this time to discuss the ranking *as if they were Beowulf*. Discussion is likely both within and between groups at this point. The students become aware of the poem as an artifact that is based on premises differing from their own, but they have also begun the practice of using personal criteria in literary analysis.

So we move along through the great poem, a shadow of its real self in an abbreviated translation. We arrive at the dragon. Someone will elect to give a report on medieval bestiaries; we get a lurid description of general dragonish morbidity. It's rather fun. By the time it is over, the students have a general appreciation of Beowulf's struggle. I introduce the figure of King Kamehameha now as an analogue for Beowulf. Like the young Beowulf, Kamehameha was a warlike hero. In his old age he too was a great lawgiver and more the servant of his people than of his own fame. Beowulf thus comes to serve as a link between European and Polynesian cultures.

TEACHING *BEOWULF* IN OLD ENGLISH TO MIXED UNDERGRADUATE AND GRADUATE CLASSES

I.

Michael D. Cherniss

My approach to the teaching of *Beowulf* is an eclectic one, neither wholly philological nor historical nor literary-critical, but rather a mixture of these approaches as well as others. My primary goal in the one-semester *Beowulf* course is simply to familiarize my students as thoroughly as possible with the text of the poem in Old English. Secondary goals include expanding the students' knowledge of the historical and cultural contexts of Old English literature, introducing them to a variety of significant critical approaches to and views of the poem, stimulating in them some degree of thought about the poem in a comparative literary context, and enriching their knowledge of the language in which the poem is written. While it is obvious that any one of my proposed goals might easily serve as the focus for an entire course, I have nonetheless found it possible to offer the students a fairly substantial variety of material that can at least set them off on paths approaching these goals.

The course in *Beowulf*, which I teach with some regularity, is open to both graduate and advanced undergraduate students. This mixture creates no very difficult pedagogical problems, although the occasional undergraduate, rather heavily outnumbered by more advanced students, may at first feel slightly intimidated. In actuality, the graduate students are normally more familiar with the methodology of literary study, but their backgrounds give them virtually no advantage over the undergraduates in studying Old English language and literature. All the enrolled students must have taken the prerequisite course, "Introduction to Old English"; few have done any other formal work in Old English.

Although they may have read a bit of Old English literature in translation, perhaps in an undergraduate survey course, and may know some Middle English literature in its original form, the students entering the beginning Old English course that is prerequisite to *Beowulf* generally have almost no knowledge of the earliest form of the English language. This makes my task as their instructor wonderfully uncomplicated; I can treat them all equally, as reasonably bright illiterates. Their text is Cassidy and Ringler's edition of *Bright's Old English Grammar and Reader*. Guided by me, they are required in the first four or five weeks of the semester to learn the basics of Old English grammar and phonology and thereafter to read certain prose and verse selections in *Bright*. Also, on a schedule of two pages per week, they memorize a substantial portion of the vocabulary in the Madden-Magoun *Grouped Frequency Word-List of Anglo-Saxon Poetry*. I supplement *Bright* with some cultural and historical background and some attempts at literary insight through informal lectures and discussions, as the students read aloud and translate their assigned selections. By the end of this first course, they are presumed to be ready to confront *Beowulf* in Old English, and some of them usually choose to do so.

At the beginning of the *Beowulf* course, I outline for the students its general configuration and give them their preliminary instructions and materials, together with assurances that they are, indeed, adequately prepared for the tasks at hand. The students are advised that, especially if they have not done so before, they should at the outset read a modern translation of the poem so that they will be generally familiar with its plot, characters, and overall structure. This preparation should enable them to make some sense of the secondary materials—and of their instructor's rambling, allusive monologues—as the semester progresses. The prose renderings of R. K. Gordon or E. T. Donaldson are recommended, since these make better, more literal "ponies" for struggling student-translators than do verse renderings. I also recommend strongly that they acquire and read in, if not through, either Greenfield's *Critical History of Old English Literature* or Wrenn's *Study of Old English Literature* for a description of the literary context in which *Beowulf* appears. Finally, they are given a two-page bibliography for *Beowulf* and its backgrounds. This bibliography is necessarily introductory and highly selective but not intolerably idiosyncratic; a similar one might be assembled by selecting what one considers key items from the (already selective) bibliographies of William Matthews, Fred C. Robinson, or Joseph Tuso, together with whatever more recent items one might wish to include. I distribute my own list to provide the students with a manageable number of books and articles that I consider essential reference works, reliable informative background studies, or provocative discussions dealing with interpretation and related matters such as audience, archaeology, heroic aspects, and meter. Among the items included are Chambers' *Introduction*, Bessinger's *Concordance*, Blair's *Introduction*, Hector Chadwick's *The Heroic Age*, Brodeur's *Art*, Irving's *Reading*, Whitelock's *Audience*, Cable's *Meter and Melody*, and well-known articles by Benson, Donahue, Farrell, Hulbert, Leyerle, Smithers, and Whallon.

The primary classroom business of the *Beowulf* course is that of the traditional second course in Old English: the students prepare at home an average of about 230 lines per week in Klaeber's edition of the poem for translation and discussion in three one-hour classes. Klaeber's introductions and footnotes, whatever their deficiencies, prove useful in class as stimulants to discussion of the many major and minor linguistic, textual, historical, mythical, and interpretive aspects of the poem. It is, of course, not possible to deal with all of the problems and questions that might be raised concerning the poem's successive passages, particularly if the class is to maintain its pace, but one can try to introduce the students to the wide variety of issues and approaches that have occupied serious readers, past and present. To this end, as relevant lines and passages are read in class, I attempt to supplement Klaeber with brief lectures and observations that are intended to supply pertinent information and to initiate discussion. I thus hope to demonstrate to the students the imperfect state of our present knowledge and understanding of the poem.

Outside the classroom, the students are also required to read representative scholarly studies of *Beowulf*. My aim, again, is to expose them to a broad spectrum of approaches that bear upon the poem. Additionally, this assigned reading may perhaps serve as an antidote to the various biases and areas of relative indifference that I must inevitably reveal. Over the course of the semester the students are therefore expected to read Lewis Nicholson's *An Anthology of* Beowulf *Criticism* in its entirety. Depending on class size, each student is assigned one or two oral reports of a descriptive and critical nature on selected books and articles for in-class presentation. The topics for these reports are selected from a short list provided by me that includes important single books (e.g., Brodeur's *Art* or Irving's *Reading*) as well as a few paired items (e.g., Lawrence's book Beowulf *and Epic Tradition* and Peter Fisher's article on the epic hero in *Beowulf*, or Goldsmith's *Mode and Meaning* and Halverson's article "Pitfalls of Piety"). Normally I exclude from this list items such as the articles in Nicholson, which I expect the entire class to read. I intend this outside reading and in-class reporting to stimulate discussion of key issues in the study of *Beowulf* and to enable the students to share their knowledge of important or otherwise controversial scholarship.

Finally, the students must exercise their critical and scholarly abilities by writing two assigned formal papers. The earlier of these must be comparative. From a list of early epic, romance, and historical narratives, which includes such works as the Homeric poems, the *Aeneid*, and the *Song of Roland*, they select one work (or offer a suitable alternative choice not included among my suggestions), read it (either in its original language or in translation), and write an essay comparing or contrasting some element that the selected work has in common with *Beowulf*. A student might, for example, deal with a particular kind of scene (e.g., battles, feasts) or a theme or topic (e.g., heroism, the role of women) or a literary technique (e.g., the handling of dialogue or of description). Since this assignment comes along relatively early in the semester, the students must lean on their knowledge of *Beowulf* in translation, and they are not expected to delve very deeply into secondary materials. Near the end of the semester, after the classroom lectures, discussions, oral reports, and outside reading have supplied matter for thought and investigation, a longer paper is assigned. Topics and overall length are left more or less open and are arrived at through consultation with me. At this point, the students may work at their individual levels of knowledge and training (e.g., in research skills and languages) on topics suited to their particular interests.

Mary Elizabeth Meek

Teaching *Beowulf* in Old English to a class comprising both graduate and undergraduate students does not, I feel, present such difficulties as might be encountered in mixed classes in later literature. It hardly needs saying that a student's ability to read any literature productively depends on his or her background in literature and history, and my experience has been that the cultural contexts of Old English poetry are just as new to graduate students as to undergraduates. Furthermore, again stating the obvious, the appreciation of Old English poetry is dependent on a thorough understanding of the language, and the graduates and undergraduates I have had in my classes have been on an equal basis to begin with, their mastery of the language depending partly on discipline and partly on a feeling for language, which not everyone is endowed with. Nevertheless, I think it important for graduate students to do some reading in *Beowulf* criticism and to report informally on their reading to the class as a whole. The problem is then to prevent a division between clergy and laity, but, with any luck at all, undergraduates as well as graduates will assess various views of the poem on the basis of their own reading of it and contribute to the discussions.

My *Beowulf* classes are made up of survivors from my introductory Old English course, generally five or six of them, including one or two graduate students. The introductory course establishes the procedure that will be used in the *Beowulf*: class members read aloud in Old English, translate, and comment. Inevitably some students will have trouble with the pronunciation and others with translating, but eventually most of them will be sufficiently at home with the language to be able to have some sense of the literary qualities of what they are reading. In fact, I choose the readings in the introductory course with the specific purpose of introducing themes that occur in *Beowulf*, so that the students may have some slight inkling of how to respond to different works coming from a common tradition. Included are Bede's account of the conversion of Northumbria and *The Wanderer*, to illustrate, among other things, the concept of the hall as the center of civilized life and the sense of the precariousness of that life, while the *Chronicle* story of Cynewulf and Cyneheard and *The Battle of Maldon* present the concepts of loyalty, revenge, and the *comitatus* spirit.

When the class is familiar with the methodology of the course, little remains but to start with the first line of *Beowulf* and forge ahead to line 3182 at the rate of about eighty lines per fifty-minute class session, but I always use the first day for an audiovisual review. In the introductory course, the class has already looked at pictures of the British Library reconstructions of the Sutton Hoo harp or lyre (in connection with Bede's story of Caedmon) and listened to the Bessinger recording of Caedmon's hymn and other short poems. The students have also seen pictures of early Germanic jewelry and weapons—I am now using the catalog of the Metropolitan Museum Viking exhibit (by Graham-Campbell and Kidd). In the *Beowulf* course I show pictures of the Sutton Hoo find in more detail, concentrating on the reconstructions of the helmet and pointing out the connection of the design on the purse lid with Leyerle's analysis "The Interlace Structure of *Beowulf*," an article that the graduate students will read toward the end of the term. We also listen to the Bessinger recording of the opening lines of *Beowulf* and as much else as time allows.

Once started on the actual reading of the poem, the students always have plenty to talk about: the mythic mysterious quality of the opening; the careful structuring of the three scenes in which Beowulf is challenged by the coast-guard, the herald, and Unferth; and, above all, the sense of a world as real as the world of Bede's Northumbria. At this point we are working just on the story level, though I do tell the class about the many conflicting views of the role of Unferth. But when we come to what Irving calls "The Great Banquet," I ask the graduate students to read his discussion of the scene (*A Reading of* Beowulf) and Sisam's *The Structure of* Beowulf and we start considering possible ironies, sinister suggestions of evil existing in the Danish court as well as outside, and the function of the story of the fight at Finnsburg.

If the class discussion of the first section of *Beowulf* focuses on the social or historical, that of the second is more literary. The emotional language of Hrothgar's lament for Aeschere and his sermon speech to Beowulf and the lyricism of the description of Grendel's mere are obvious points of departure, as is the whole topic of the marvelous. In addition, I encourage the class to look for ways in which the second part develops logically from the first by contrast and parallel in such motifs as the undersea battle with monsters, the race of Cain, and family feud and revenge. In line with these topics, the graduate students read Robertson's allegorical interpretation of Grendel's mere and Irving on the undersea hall and the Ingeld story. Leyerle's article on the interlace structure and Shaw's on the patterning of the speeches touch off consideration of other narrative patterns in the poem.

In similar fashion we discuss the way the third section of the poem develops from the second and concludes the overall structural design in the echoing of Scyld Scefing's funeral with Beowulf's. Again we look for recurrent themes and motifs, particularly the transitoriness of human happiness and the broadening of the motif of family feuds to that of wars with neighboring peoples. In addition, we focus on the character of Beowulf, his depiction as hero and king, starting with the parallels between his situation and Hrothgar's. In this connection, I like to have the graduate students reading and reporting on as many different views of Beowulf as possible, including those of Kaske ("*Sapentia et Fortitudo*"), Goldsmith ("The Christian Perspective"), and Irving.

As this sketch suggests, I like the class as a whole to deal with basic themes and structural patterns and the graduate students to become familiar with the relevant criticism. I emphasize structure because I feel that is the new direction in *Beowulf* criticism today, as the oral-formulaic theory was for my generation and the exegetical approach for the generation intervening. For the sake of the graduate students, I continue to use Klaeber as the text; not only is it the version most often cited in the criticism, but it is also a cenotaph for pre-Tolkienian criticism. I suggest that the students get the Norton Critical Edition of *Beowulf* (edited by Joseph Tuso) as well because it contains the Donaldson translation, useful when the difficulties of translation seem insuperable, and because the brief selections from representative criticism may attract some of the more adventurous undergraduates.

I do not require the graduate students to read the earliest criticism, but I do expect them to read Tolkien's "The Monsters and the Critics" and Magoun's "Oral-Formulaic Character of Anglo-Saxon Narrative Poetry." In addition, I ask them to pursue their own critical interests by reading selectively in collections like Nicholson's *An Anthology of* Beowulf *Criticism* or Burlin and Irving's *Old English Studies in Honour of John C. Pope*. I also point them toward whatever articles in the current journals seem to be of interest.

Because it takes longer to list the suggested readings in the critical literature than to list the various topoi in the text that prompt those readings, this sketch indicates a greater emphasis on the reading of criticism than in fact exists in my course. As I stated at the outset, the basic procedure is for the students to read out loud, translate, and comment, the comments engendering discussion. Any difficulties with the language are thrashed out in class since the three or four exams given during the term each test the student's ability to translate some six or seven passages, totaling about fifty lines, chosen from the preceding weeks' reading. The later exams may also require brief commentary on one of the passages. The final, a two-hour exam, is divided between a similar testing of the last weeks' translation and a choice of short essay topics asking the students to discuss the poem as a whole.

III.

Alain Renoir

At the risk of earning the censure of those readers who object to self-overvaluation in others, I believe that I have impeccable credentials for discussing what not to do in a *Beowulf* course intended for graduates and undergraduates alike: I have been teaching such a course for over a decade and have done a consistently terrible job of it. Nor do I think that I did a better job when the course was strictly a graduate preserve or even when it was a doctoral requirement; and I find no comfort in my conviction that many other Anglo-Saxonists are equally unsuccessful.

The extent of our collective failure may be inferred from the fact that Old English through *Beowulf* was commonly required of undergraduates in English at reputable institutions on both sides of the Atlantic until World War I, that it was required for the English M.A. at many American universities for over four decades thereafter, and that it was only in the 1950s that Harvard—soon followed by Johns Hopkins—abolished that requirement for the Ph.D. in English and thus took the lead in bringing about the debacle that has now turned Old English literature into a severely endangered species. Since the professors who voted the requirement out of existence had been exposed to it during their student days, they must have been less than enchanted with either the materials or the teaching thereof. Because I rank *Beowulf* among the great masterpieces of literature, I must necessarily opt for the latter alternative.

The foregoing remarks are not a call for public self-flagellation on the part of the Old English establishment but merely a recognition of the likelihood that any university subject that requires hard work and drudgery will be badly taught. If the subject be required, the professor will probably demand an unconscionable amount of work, base much of the final grade on the pettiest aspects of the drudgery, and impose his or her pet concerns on hapless students, who must pretend interest while waiting for the day when they will in turn become professors and abolish the requirement. If the subject be not required, the professor must recruit customers by claiming that rumor has grossly exaggerated the amount of work and that the materials are immediately relevant to every single student's most intimate concerns. Because these and other implicit promises must be made good in order to retain the clientele, much of the necessary drudgery is eliminated, and any relationship between completion of the course and competence in the subject matter becomes coincidental. In addition, perfectly foolish notions must be entertained during class discussion and occasionally on papers, and these often prove more relevant to the student's aberrations than to the materials under scrutiny. So far as I can see, a demanding course that loses its status as a requirement tends to retain only one aspect of its former self: the same professor who will compromise everything else in order to recruit students will make a stand to the death in order to indoctrinate them with his or her pet concerns.

Let us face it: a first course on *Beowulf* means lots of work and necessarily includes a staggering amount of drudgery. The students normally come with very little Old English behind them, so that they must spend interminable hours looking up words and paradigms in order to translate their assignments. In other words, the course is a prolonged exercise in translation by people ill-acquainted with the language from which they are translating. The task would be wearisome under the best circumstances, but it needs must seem even more so to physically grown-up students with scant practice in this kind of ego-shrinking discipline. They can hardly avoid comparing the ego-boosting experiences increasingly available in courses devoted to the kind of critical theory that denies the integrity of the text, the validity of the historical context, and the relevance of authorial intention to the critic's business.

If my own institution (the University of California at Berkeley) be at all representative, the situation is further complicated by the diversity of students: mostly undergraduates in English and in linguistics as well as doctoral students in comparative literature and in the program in the English language, with a substantial contingent from the English M.A. program, whose students are almost free from requirements and can accordingly undertake work considered irrelevant to the professional study of English and American literature. The three of us who teach Old English do a fair amount of recruiting among undergraduates. I make it a point to offer our freshman course every year and to include a Modern English version of *Beowulf* on the reading list, and I find perfectly spurious excuses for sneaking a great deal of Old English into my undergraduate courses on the English language and for bringing Old English materials into my lectures on Chaucer. Because duplicity pays off, I almost always find in beginning Old English and in the *Beowulf* course several students who took freshman English and either Chaucer or a language course from me and allowed themselves to be conned into something more demanding than they bargained for.

Implicit promises must be made good, and I attempt to do so by dividing the work into two categories. The first category consists of assignments and exercises that are the same for all the students: (1) reading nearly the whole of *Beowulf*, translating most of it in class, and reading aloud and discussing key sections of the day's assignment, (2) submitting to a midterm as well as to a final examination requiring translations, identifications, and an essay, and (3) producing by the end of the second week a brief paper consisting of the literary translation and analysis of an assigned passage not yet discussed in class, with special attention to contents, organization, vocabulary, imagery, and tone. The second category consists of individual discussions leading to a term paper on a topic selected by the student and preferably suited to his or her interests and academic preparation. This practice often results in papers that would have been unacceptable when *Beowulf* was a graduate requirement, but it also produces many genuinely challenging pieces as well as the occasional embryo of a doctoral dissertation. It also provides me with information on which I draw in class to make the students think that the poem is as immediately relevant to their understanding of the world as it is to mine. So as not to be accused of having irremediably prostituted a great poem in order to attract students, I hasten to add that I offer on my own time various follow-up courses in which prospective medievalists may experience all the drudgery formerly associated with Old English and learn about my pet scholarly concerns.

The only insoluble problem is one of logistics. At my institution as elsewhere, undergraduates must enroll for more units than the graduate students, so that a gross inequity is built into the course, even though one may encourage the undergraduates to choose easier term-paper topics than the graduates. Because this inequity is obvious, many undergraduates who would want to study *Beowulf* hesitate to do so, and I am accordingly convinced that courses designed primarily for undergraduates are desirable if we are to regain for early English literature the eminence that it once enjoyed and fully deserves in a civilized English-speaking society.

Subject to correction, I assume that what I have outlined corresponds to what most Anglo-Saxonists do in one way or another. All of us need students to justify the existence of our subject, and we must accordingly fill our classes as best we can. I submit that what we ought to do is not so much to search for new teaching gimmicks, however immediately successful they may seem, but rather to realize that what is happening to Old English is merely part of what is happening to our entire tradition of letters and that we should accordingly make common cause—and militantly so—with those colleagues who teach other segments of that tradition and may not even realize that the demise of Old English must necessarily foreshadow that of their own disciplines.

In other words, we must not attempt to justify *Beowulf* as a grand and unique phenomenon. If we form a united front with the appropriate colleagues, however, there will be enough of us to make a formidable case for a tradition that is our cultural lifeline, which includes Homer, Cicero, Vergil, Chaucer, Shakespeare, and Milton, and of which *Beowulf* is an absolutely indispensable part for culturally responsible citizens of the English-speaking world. If we do so and refrain from being either too pedantic or too silly in our teaching practices, then I suspect that it will matter little whether we address ourselves to graduates or to undergraduates or to both, for the poem will speak to all of them.

IV.

Victor L. Strite

A college course is taught only in a context, just as a word means something only in a context. The context of my teaching *Beowulf* in Old English to a mixed undergraduate–graduate student class has molded the course considerably. A declining enrollment of English majors, plus a requirement of offering the traditional year's sequence of Old English language and literature to a few Ph.D. candidates in alternate years, prompted me eight years ago to save the course by opening it up to undergraduates and M.A. candidates. My chairman added a new twist: offer both courses in one semester (every other year) for six hours credit, meeting five hours per week.

Thus, the course to teach *Beowulf* is not organized as a *Beowulf* course. It is a course in Old English literature. Its goals are (1) to translate about half of *Beowulf*; (2) to translate two or three other Old English poems for exposure to other styles, genres, and talents; (3) to read and discuss most of Old English poetry in Gordon in translation; (4) to research an interesting aspect of *Beowulf*—a paper or a "project." The course follows a semester of Old English language, in which a good bit of prose is studied. Undergraduate and graduate students are treated equally in class, but the latter are required to give an oral report and to do a more ambitious paper or project.

A brief explanation of these four goals and how they are developed follows.

(1) *Beowulf* is only partially translated because we need time for the other goals and because the students do read (during the first two weeks of class) and discuss (throughout the course) the entire poem in translation. I allow students to choose their own passages for translation in Klaeber. In addition, I select a few excerpts to provide a representative balance.

(2) Students usually translate an elegy (often *The Wanderer*), some of *The Dream of the Rood* or "The Phoenix," and something continental or secular (usually *Widsith* or a couple of riddles). For most of this literature, our text is John C. Pope's *Seven Old English Poems*. These works are compared with *Beowulf*. We consider the use of formulas, style, vocabulary, and so forth.

(3) I require students to read and discuss most of the extant Old English poetry because I think it is important literature in its own right and because I am annoyed by the ignorance of many English teachers who have taken a *Beowulf* course but are not acquainted with the sea passage of *Andreas* or the structure of "The Phoenix" or the contents of *Genesis B*, as I am acquainted with comparable aspects of major and many minor works in other periods of English and American literature. Thus, about a third of class time is spent discussing Old English poetry exclusive of *Beowulf*. I usually require graduate students to work up a half-hour oral report on a particular work, although these reports are quite informal, with many interruptions from me and the other students. I do not allow the dull graduate-student-report syndrome to prevail. The course, further, is designed not as a graduate seminar but as an introductory survey of Old English poetry.

(4) I am rather flexible about research topics and allow students to do most anything that they feel will further their understanding of *Beowulf* or Old English literature. I accept a paper or a project. The findings are shared orally toward the end of the course. I do require more of graduate students here, but only in the form of more ambitious and higher quality work, which I control by approving and guiding research. Projects are accepted in lieu of papers when I feel the student would benefit more from working with several topics than from researching and writing on one narrow topic. Projects might include reading and summarizing several diverse critical articles, additional translating, collecting data on some project larger than what might be covered in fifteen to twenty pages but not writing it up, or examining a semantic field in *Beowulf*. Projects are submitted in a variety of forms, usually notebooks, cards, or data sheets. When grading, I look for evidence that substantial effort and thought have been expended. Some students prefer the discipline (and familiarity) of writing a paper; others prefer the more flexible project. I think students usually learn more doing projects.

The materials and specific techniques I have developed include handouts, intensive and broad-ranging vocabulary study, and variety. Since my students are not being trained to become professional medievalists or Anglo-Saxonists, I de-emphasize (but don't ignore) literary criticism and emphasize instead teaching students to teach themselves how to read and appreciate *Beowulf*. My key technique is a series of handouts I have prepared that present in topical form major ways of approaching the poem. One handout, for instance, contains eight Modern English translations—in verse and prose—

of the Grendel's mere passage. Students compare their own translations with those of the professionals. With much discussion and detailed analysis, the class is thus initiated into the mysteries and pitfalls of translation. Another handout lists about two dozen interlace topics; we discuss how these patterns are used in *Beowulf* and other poems. Another handout lists alliterative patterns, verse types (from Sievers and Pope), and formulas so that the class can begin to wade through some of the criticism. Another handout, from which I more or less lecture, traces the history of *Beowulf* in manuscript. Another briefly introduces backgrounds—Christian, Celtic, and Germanic. (I discuss Anglo-Saxon history and the history of the English language in the previous Old English language class.)

I emphasize the importance of knowing what Old English words mean as a key to interpreting the poetry. Since my own research is primarily in Old English word fields (semantic fields), I often break up the work of translating in class with a digression (sometimes a handout) on a word field. I demonstrate with words for deities, weapons, the sea, emotions, and the like.

Classes are organized to emphasize variety. Because the course usually meets twice a week for a total of five hours, I do many different things to keep the students' attention focused. One two-and-a-half-hour class might include four or five activities: going over the translations of the assigned portion of *Beowulf*; discussing the assigned Old English poem; treating a topic that grows out of a handout; discussing some particular aspect of *Beowulf* (such as theme, style, structure, vocabulary). With an average of five students in a class, spending most of the class time translating *Beowulf* (the major teaching emphasis I remember from graduate school) just isn't satisfactory; it develops translating skill but not familiarity with *Beowulf* as literature. My overall approach, instead of the linguistic problems of translating or the forests of literary criticism, builds toward reading and appreciating *Beowulf* in the context of Old English poems as a work of literature, a work of art.

TEACHING *BEOWULF* IN OLD ENGLISH TO GRADUATE STUDENTS

I.

Stanley J. Kahrl

The approach I outline here has evolved out of my experiences teaching both in the graduate program at the University of Rochester, where a semester-long course in *Beowulf* was open both to graduates and undergraduates, and at the Ohio State University, where the course in *Beowulf* is ten weeks long and populated almost exclusively by graduate students.

In the first place, as literary critics have certainly known since the classical period and as Augustine himself firmly states, before there can be any interpretation there must be a sound understanding of the literal level of any text the student wishes to expound. I have found that this principle demands that both the teacher and the student must be able to give a full grammatical description of every word in the poem, a goal I found daunting when I first taught *Beowulf*. But the tools are available, and the rewards are real. Given the existence of such texts as Howell Chickering's facing-page translation of the poem, one can pick up the original poem and believe that, with a little work, one can quickly master the essence of the original language. As I have found, however, one cannot. The language is too intricate, the poetry too complex. But even after only an introductory ten-week course in Old English, students equipped with Wrenn's edition of the poem and Bruce Mitchell's *Guide to Old English* can learn to ask themselves the gender, number, and case of all the words they are translating and to find the syntactic puzzles of the poem as absorbing as any *Times* crossword.

Hand in hand with constant emphasis on grammar goes a struggle to understand the semantic riches of the poem. Students are ever willing to take the glossary of their text as a reliable guide to the poem. I first realized fully how much a glossary is an extended reading of a poem when I assigned the "Gnomic Poem" in Bolton's *Old English Anthology* to an introductory Old English class. As I prepared for class the night before we met, I discovered to my consternation that if one put together the glosses for the words in the poem offered by Bolton, one ended up with gibberish. The meanings (never more than one or two) he had chosen, apparently at random from some larger dictionary of Anglo-Saxon, did not fit the poem. To gloss a poem one must first interpret it. Thus, when *Beowulf* students take the readings of a glossary as final, they have essentially bought Klaeber's or Wrenn's reading of the poem.

The solution is to develop a healthy skepticism in one's students as to the offered meanings of important terms. Ideally each member of the class ought to own Clark Hall's *A Concise Anglo-Saxon Dictionary* and a copy of Klaeber's glossary as well as the Wrenn text used in class. But in this day of high costs, such a hope may be quixotic. At least one can develop in one's students a sense of what compounds are and teach them to see a complex word as a set of grouped meanings, all of which they know in part, instead of encouraging them to grab the first polysyllabic Latinate equivalent they run across in the back of their text.

If one accomplishes these purposes, one has done much. Certainly if one's students leave confident in an ability to translate any line on their own, confident in their own ability to argue with the literal readings of the poem offered by others, one has equipped them well. But we are talking of graduate students, of future teacher-scholars. I believe we have a duty to teach them not only how to read the poem but also how to go about offering one's own particular interpretation of a portion of that poem to an audience of one's peers. After years of hearing papers poorly delivered at scholarly meetings, I realized that no one in graduate school had taught me how to present my ideas in public or how to present them in writing for consideration by a board of reviewers for a scholarly journal. The activity of writing up ideas and presenting them to a public audience is one that many of our graduate students must undertake if they are to achieve any hope of permanent employment, yet few of my colleagues either at Ohio State or elsewhere seem to feel that time need be spent learning how to do these difficult things.

Thus, in each graduate seminar I teach, my students are required to do two things. First, from a list of suggested topics presented to them on the first day of the seminar, they choose a subject on which they might like to do some research. The topics are ones in which I am interested and on which I know interesting work is being done. Students beginning the study of *Beowulf* have little idea of how many different topics are currently under lively discussion. Furthermore, in a course in which the major emphasis must be on accurate translation, one cannot expect students to read widely in *Beowulf* scholarship in order to discover a topic on their own. The *Year's Work in English Studies* is an invaluable source of ideas for graduate seminar topics.

Students choose, then, a topic and one of a series of days on which papers will be given. On the appointed days, I ask the students to read their papers as they would at a scholarly meeting, such as that held annually at Kalamazoo. They are to dress as they would plan to dress there, and they are to deliver their papers in an interesting manner, standing behind a podium before their peers, taking no more than twenty-five minutes. Each paper is evaluated as an oral performance; I do not see the written version in any form at that time. If I fall asleep, the paper wasn't interesting. If the other students have no questions, it wasn't interesting. I need not go on. One has only, as a teacher, to remember the boring papers of the past and to recall, too, the marvelous successes so often heard in the meetings of Group I at the annual meeting of the MLA to be able to advise students what to do and what not to do. If you have a paper of your own, read it too, but if you do so early in the course, particularly if you are one of our more skilled orators, you may induce a feeling of despair. If you save your paper until the end of the course, the students will have the opportunity to rise to their own challenge, to set high standards for themselves, and then to see how far they still must go.

Oral reports are read no later than the eighth week of a ten-week quarter or the last week but one on a semester-long course. What I ask to see, at the end of the course, is the original argument and evidence presented orally, now revised in the light of class discussion and extensive reading of other critical and scholarly work, presented as it would be presented to a learned journal. I point out the differences between an oral presentation and a scholarly article and draw attention to the *MLA Handbook*. Those who submit their written paper as it was read in class, with nothing more than a small string of footnotes listing texts quoted, generally find their grade lower than those who show an awareness of the conventions of scholarly debate. The result? Papers are written on time in a format similar to the format our students will be using for their scholarly work for the remainder of their working lives. Because of the original form in which the papers were presented, the students find themselves choosing focused, manageable, interesting topics they really wish to explore instead of indigestible problems better tackled in a monograph. The best papers are regularly accepted at regional scholarly meetings, where they please their audiences. My students often return from such experiences with an increased sense of confidence in themselves as scholars. They have learned not only how to read *Beowulf* with care but also how to share their more adventurous readings as equals.

II.

John C. McGalliard

In an ideal program *Beowulf* would perhaps constitute the third semester or quarter of an Old English sequence. In the first, students would learn basic grammar and read some prose; in the second, they would encounter a variety of the shorter poems. Thus they would bring suitable experience to the study of *Beowulf*, the longest, the most difficult, and the most rewarding work in Old English. But this program is rare in American universities; ordinarily only two semesters are available, and the second is devoted to *Beowulf*. This is the situation in which I have taught the poem for three decades.

For teacher and student alike, the task is to comprehend the whole of a complex design: to see how a pair of folktale plots are given epic stature and moral significance by the way in which the poet handles them. The teacher of *Beowulf* can show how the poet's sketch of the Danish dynasty—from Scyld to Beowulf (the Dane) to Halfdane and his sons, including finally Hrothgar—furnishes an "authentic" background and setting for Grendel and his depredations. Thus also the poet achieves a Coleridgean suspension of disbelief: the listener or reader has no difficulty in accepting the evident distress of Hrothgar and his court as "real." The dragon plot of part 2 is equally surrounded by legendary-historical context; but here we are given first the dragon's wrath and its cause and then the outline of the aged hero's career since his conquest of Grendel, along with highlights of Geatish-Frisian and Geatish-Swedish conflicts over three generations—and the foreshadowing of more in the future.

If Klaeber is the text chosen, the instructor should act initially as a Vergilian sibyl, pointing out the numerous and diverse regions of the under-ground and overground. This might well occupy five minutes at the beginning of the first half-dozen sessions. Then, since art is long and semester is short, the reading of the poem should begin at once. The assignment for the second session may well be fifteen or twenty lines. The instructor will want to read the passage aloud before asking the class to do so—preferably in chorus at first, then individually (for the particular lines under scrutiny). Since the aim of the course is full and accurate understanding of the text, the instructor has a duty to ask students for the identification of forms—case of nouns, pronouns, and adjectives, tense and mood of verbs, and so forth. The use of translations need not be taboo, but it does not exempt the student from the obligation to see the relation of each word form to the rest of the Old English sentence. Of course, the time taken by this procedure can be grad-ually diminished, just as the number of lines read is gradually increased. Indeed, steady acceleration is essential and highly successful: the first third of the poem may occupy the first half of the term and time may still be left to reach the end with reasonable ease.

As for versification, I think it best to have students learn Sievers' five types. They offer the basic patterns of the oldest alliterative verse in all the Germanic languages and they fit most of the lines in Old English. Here again, the approach can be gradual: begin by asking the student to spot the "A" lines in the day's reading, next week go on to the "B" lines, and so on. The class should read the treatment of the "B" and "C" lines in Pope's *The Rhythm of Beowulf*. These phonetically light verses may include a pause or "rest" and thus are especially suitable for "slow," deliberate passages such as (some of) Hrothgar's lines on the inevitability of death (1761–68).

What should be required of a *Beowulf* class besides reading the entire poem in its original language? There is not time for much more. The teacher must resist the temptation to burden the course (and the students) with heavy assignments of secondary matter. Fixed requirements, if any, should come near the beginning of the course, when a relatively small amount of text can be covered in a day. I have often recommended and sometimes assigned Tacitus' *Agricola* and *Germania*. More often, also in the early part of the term, I have asked the class to read Bede's *History of the English People*, either in the Penguin translation or in the Loeb edition (Latin and English). The class read the *History* at the rate of one book a week for five weeks; discussion was limited to ten minutes a book and mostly consisted of responses to the question "What did you find interesting this time?" So far as I can judge (from an obviously partisan stance) students were grateful for this perspective on early English kings and saints—and ruffians.

Requirements aside, the *Beowulf* teacher has an unsurpassed opportunity to practice the "show and tell" pedagogy—with the teacher doing the showing and telling. Throughout the course the instructor can bring in a book, talk about it for five minutes at the beginning of the hour, pass it around the class, and offer to lend it. In this way, surely, all students should have a look at Bruce-Mitford's British Library *Provisional Guide* to Sutton Hoo when the class is reading about Scyld's ship funeral. (Showing slides of the Sutton Hoo treasures is a fine thing, if the slides are clear, the machine works smoothly, and the lecturer has all the facts in order!) I let the class glance at the histories of Collingwood, Stenton, Hodgkin, and others. Talking for a few minutes about each of the six volumes of the *Anglo-Saxon Poetic Records*—on different days—will help the student place *Beowulf* in the perspective of Old English poetry in general. And books of interpretation and criticism such as those of Kennedy, Nicholson, Wrenn, Irving, Greenfield, Brodeur, and others will make a firmer impression if the students handle them physically instead of merely seeing the titles in a bibliography. As intimated above, students won't have much time for the books during the course but can earmark them for the future.

For the student, a well-conducted *Beowulf* course is a strenuous experience, but it need not and should not be a hardship. I regularly told the class that they owed the course no more time in preparation than is due any other course carrying the same amount of credit. If a student was unable to finish the day's quota of lines, he or she should say so without distress. Another student, or sometimes the instructor, could take over.

The important thing is that the text should be read in class. Only on this basis, it seems to me, can questions and discussion—whether ad hoc or more general, whether factual, ideological, or aesthetic—shed adequate light on the poem. In many classes some or all of the narrative of the Geatish-Swedish wars is omitted; time presses, in the last third of the poem, and the account is not entirely chronological and can be initially confusing. Yet I think omission is unfortunate. It impairs the reader's perception of thematic structure and aesthetic effect. For there is a notable symmetry in the presentation of three generations of the royal families of Geats and Swedes; they form a counterpart to the royal Danes in part 1. As for the order of events, it is natural enough for the several narrators, namely, the poet, Beowulf himself, and the "Messenger" who survives his lord.

It is the responsibility of the teacher to show students that *Beowulf* does not "digress" arbitrarily in all directions. Instead, the poet carefully places the foreground of the narrative—the Grendel and the dragon stories—against a rich, abundant background of legendary history. The foreground—the present—is a stage between the past, known through tradition, and the future, which may be anticipated vaguely, as in the Messenger's prophecy, or vividly, as in Beowulf's conjecture that the Danish-Heathobard feud will be renewed on the marriage of Freawaru, Hrothgar's daughter, to Ingeld, the Heathobard prince (2024–69).

The ideological stature of the poem is sustained by a pervasive view of the human situation as definite as that in the *Aeneid* and as explicit as that in *Paradise Lost*. Men and women are presented centrally as morally responsible agents in the society of the Heroic Age (of the first millennium A.D.). As a thane, a man must be courageous and loyal to his lord; as a ruler, he must be just and generous, eschewing avarice and oppression. The poem provides many examples of these virtues and the contrasting vices. Hrothgar's wife, Wealhtheow, and Hygd, wife of Hygelac, exemplify the queenly virtues of concern for the future of the kingdom and the royal family; and Hygd is contrasted with a (possibly) anonymous princess who savagely suppresses would-be suitors—though there is precedent for the taming of a royal shrew. Young or old, a man cannot know the outcome of a brave venture; but he is to be admired if he risks his life in a good cause. Ultimately, all things depend on destiny (*wyrd*), an agent of omnipotent God; but this does not annul man's opportunity or obligation to act on the (tacit) premise of free will. The three essential terms, God, *wyrd*, and *mod* 'courage' (or, more broadly, "quality of mind and character") occur together in a single brief clause (1056–57). (I undertake to deal with the poet's moral precepts and judgments in "The Poet's Comment in *Beowulf*" 246–51.) The teacher should not neglect to point out the coherent ethical core of the poem.

Neither teachers nor students should be so preoccupied with translation that they fail to recognize the variety of poetic effects. Early on in the poem, consider the conclusion of Scyld's ship funeral:

> Men ne cunnon
> secgan to soðe,   selerædende,
> hæleð under heofenum,   hwa þæm hlæste onfeng.

People cannot say truly—hall counselors, men under the sky—who received that cargo.   (50–52)

The two appositives, by delaying the end of the statement, increase the solemnity of the occasion, reinforce the sense of wonder and mystery that it arouses. In a very different vein is the incremental repetition in the account of Grendel's approach to Heorot on the night when Beowulf and his men await him (702–21). The momentary delays heighten the listener's (or reader's) suspense and lead to increasing identification with the waiting hero. Not until the Gothic novels of the eighteenth century, I should think, is there such effective depiction of macabre landscape as that of Grendel's mere, part in Hrothgar's description, part in the poet's direct account (1357–76 and 1408–41). Two of the finest "elegiac" passages in Old English poetry— one might say in Old Germanic poetry as a whole—are found in *Beowulf*. One is the speech of the "last survivor" as he bids farewell to the buried

treasure (2247–66). The other is the scene of material and emotional deso-
lation in which an old man is described as lamenting the violent death of
his son (2444–62). The opening of Beowulf's reply to Unferth's slander reveals
a mastery of polite insult:

> "Hwæt, þu worn fela,   wine min Unferð,
>   beore druncen,   ymb Brecan spræce. . . ."

"Well, my friend Unferth, you, drunk with beer, had a great deal
to say about Breca. . . ."   (530–31)

Scavenging beasts and birds are the invariable props of battle scenes in
Old English poetry. Only the *Beowulf* poet lends a touch of drama to the
situation: "The dark-coated raven, eager over the doomed, will say many
things, will tell the eagle how it fared for him at the meal when he ravaged
the corpses, competing with the wolf" (3024–27). The intimate vividness of
a camera close-up is rare in the poet's tradition, but it appears when Wiglaf
revives the dying hero:

>   he hine eft ongon
>   wæteres weorpan,   oð þæt wordes ord
>   breosthord þurhbræc.

He began to sprinkle him with water, until the beginning of a word
broke through his breast.   (2790–92)

With all this variety, the poem steadily maintains an elevated style and
diction, as do the *Aeneid* and *Paradise Lost*. Thus *Beowulf* does not offer
the complete range from high to low that we find in the *Divine Comedy* or
the *Canterbury Tales*. But it offers a dependable competence in handling
its material, whether narrative, descriptive, expository, or argumentative.
Beowulf's first speech to Hrothgar and the Danish court is a good example
of the poet's skill and efficiency (407–455). From his home among the Geats
the hero has come to Denmark in the hope of fighting Grendel. But if this
is to happen, Hrothgar must accept the offer. If he does not, the enterprise
is a failure before it begins! His speech itself shows how decisive Beowulf
considers it—one way or the other. After the formal salutation and identification, he offers his credentials: his friends at home encouraged him to
undertake the task—because they knew at first hand of his conquests of sea
monsters. He is now ready to face Grendel. The next sentence (426–32) is
the heart of his speech, his offer, and his petition.

> "Ic þe nu þa,
> brego Beorht-Dena,   biddan wille,
> eodor Scyldinga,   anre bene:
> þaet ðu me ne forwyrne,   wigendra hleo,
> freo-wine folca,   nu ic þus feorran com,
> þaet ic mote ana   [ond] minra eorla gedryht,
> þes hearda heap,   Heorot faelsian."

"I wish now, lord of the Bright-Danes, to ask of you, protector of the Scyldings, one request: that you do not refuse me, shelter of warriors, friendly ruler of peoples, now that I have come this far, that I be permitted alone—with the troop of my men, this hardy band—to cleanse Heorot."

Several features of this sentence are notable. The first half line is made up of four little words—two personal pronouns and two temporal adverbs—none of which would ordinarily receive alliterative stress or rhetorical emphasis. Here þe 'you' and nu 'now' are the stressed elements of a "slow" C-verse. Modern English word order makes it impossible to keep the original phrasing: "I you now then." But in the Old English the phrasing sharpens the focus on Beowulf, the speaker, and Hrothgar, the hearer. The sentences preceding this one contain a few appositional constructions, which is normal for Old English poetry. But here they are piled up; four half lines are appositives of þe, or ðu, that is, Hrothgar. Is this otiose, an indication of indolence in the poet? Not at all; these delaying repetitions express the earnestness of the prayer and the pray-er. Again, the "periodic" pattern of the sentence is surely not accidental; it maintains suspense, for the Danes and for us: we don't know exactly what the "one" request is until we reach the end—"cleanse Heorot." Lastly, the negative phrasing of the petition, "that you do not refuse me," is a form of the traditional understatement. The rest of Beowulf's speech is also well designed for its purpose. Since Grendel does not use weapons, Beowulf will forgo them, relying on the strength of his grip; let God decide the outcome. This calm self-confidence includes full acceptance of the possibility of death; Grendel will devour him if he can. Here Beowulf is careful to relieve Hrothgar of all responsibility—only let him send back his coat of mail (if available!) to Hygelac. The reference to this as an heirloom from King Hrethel and the handiwork of the marvelous smith, Weland, lends added prestige to its wearer. Finally, the speech closes with a philosophic proverb (or sententious remark): "Gaeð a wyrd swa hio scel!" 'Destiny moves ever as it must!'

For many years we celebrated the completion of the poem with a *Beowulf Gebeorscipe* at the end of the term. In my living room or at a private room at the University Union, we had a long evening of talk, beer, and sometimes modern mead. Without any fixed program, members of the class offered views or queries about many of the topics that had come up in the course of the semester—the most probable date of *Beowulf*, eighth century or any time later, including the period of the manuscript; the relation of the poem to the oral tradition, with its formulaic diction; its structure, whether "Aristotelian" or other; the question of Christianity in the poet and in the characters of the poem; and many more. We seldom broke up before midnight—long after Grendel would have appeared if he had had designs on us. It was hall-joys without hangovers.

III.

Marijane Osborn

My primary aim in the first week is to establish momentum. I have been most successful when I have set things up so that my principal function in class is as facilitator and occasional participant; failure to establish such a dynamic nearly always results in reducing *Beowulf* to a schoolroom exercise. The Finnsburg episode and fragment have proved a rich but not too taxing unit for opening the discussion, but before introducing these materials I give a quick overview of the poem, incorporating my own approach to it, and I explain what is expected in the course.

Here are the main points of my set piece reviewing the general shape of *Beowulf* in the context of the society it celebrates. Against a historical background moving from mythic to real event, a hero battles three monsters in a progression moving toward myth: cannibalistic Grendel, his terrible mother, an apocalyptic dragon. Each fight takes place at a farther distance from the human center, the lighted gift halls of fellowship: in a darkened hall, an underwater hall, a barrow. Each monster in turn hurls itself unexpectedly from the wilderness on the halls where human beings, confident together, are enjoying *seledream* 'hall-pleasure,' oblivious to the fact that strife is always renewed. The poet's asides to the audience link these marauding monsters to a cosmic conflict, whereas Hrothgar's wisdom speech at the center of the poem offers us and Beowulf a secular philosophy that is essentially stoic and altruistic; the poet's vision of the cause of disaster is metaphysical, Hrothgar's advice for dealing with it moral, and the two supplement each other. This is as far as I go with textual authority. I then suggest tentatively that Hrothgar's speech points to magnanimity as a noble human response to fate, an implication that may foreshadow the final moving scenes of the poem.

Having offered this range of impressions and ideas and leaving that final idea hanging (as the poet does), I go on to what the students most want to know on the first day. By commenting on the following description in the English department catalog of graduate courses, I map out the ground to be covered:

> The purpose of this course is to enable students to read in the original as much of *Beowulf* as is possible in a ten-week quarter: probably two-thirds, which means two hundred lines per week. In twice-weekly classes we will both translate and read aloud in Old English. Chiefly through class reports on specified subjects and discussion of these reports, we will cover as much background material as time permits. The grade for the course will be based on weekly translation exercises, the class presentation, and a brief final paper that may develop from that presentation.

Using the format of Klaeber's introduction, I offer for distribution the following report topics (modified according to the number of students in the class): mythic backgrounds, folklore and analogues, history, Christianity, structure, style, manuscript, and dating and provenance. I advise students to confer with me about their choices as soon as possible and to read Klaeber's introduction to get a sense of each topic. Once they have selected their topics, I supplement Klaeber with more recent scholarship, explaining that I expect each student to become something of an expert in the area of his or her interest. I am always surprised by the commitment with which the students strive to fulfill this expectation.

These preliminaries over, I then enter the poem by way of the Finnsburg materials, concentrating particularly on history and style. I have three hand-outs ready, useful whether or not the students have come to class with Klaeber in hand. The first is a copy of my own translation of the Finnsburg episode in *Beowulf*; after reading this aloud I read them the original, having them follow with the translation and pointing out phrases where they can make an immediate connection with Modern English. I try to stress the sound and movement of the Old English, and I do not comment much on the story. The second handout is a chronology of postulated dates (to which I shall return later); I suggest that the Finnsburg battle might be placed in the mid-fifth century in order to become a traditional heroic tale being sung in Heorot around A.D. 515. The third handout is a glossed and annotated text of the Finnsburg fragment; we work through this heroic poem imme-diately after reading the episode, and in the course of the exercise the students discover for themselves and comment on what seems to me the most striking feature of the style of *Beowulf*, its nonheroic reflectiveness. Their own discovery of this quality, I find, makes them sensitive to further stylistic features of the poem.

I reinforce their discovery by pointing out how the lines introducing the episode in *Beowulf* (1066–70) seem to describe the battle in the fragment rather than the aftermath of the battle that actually follows line 1070, so that the episode may be read as the poet's reflection on the heroic song in Heorot rather than a summary of it—hence the "reflectiveness" of the style. Moreover, Wealhtheow's concern for her sons when the song ends seems a response to the tragedy of the episode rather than to the heroism of the fragment; it is almost as though the story of Hildeburh's sorrow and Hengest's oathbreaking were Wealhtheow's own reflections as the Finnsburg fragment is sung. Thus I introduce the class to Bonjour's idea of the integration of the episodes into the text as a whole. I conclude with my own fantasy about why the poet places such a long and detailed digression at that point in his poem: Hengest is Bede's Hengist, so the digression is a link with England (and I refer to the chronology), and it offers a hint about what might have happened to the Geatish leaders after Beowulf's death—another link with England, possibly with Sutton Hoo, and possibly even one reason for composing such an ancestrally oriented poem. We all inevitably become engaged with this idea, so my last words on the subject are a warning about the fine line between scholarship and speculation, between the kinds of ideas fruitful to examine in class and the greater decorum expected in print or in a formal performance such as a paper read at a conference.

My presentation of the Finnsburg materials with handouts and discussion provides the format for the more condensed presentations that follow. I choose with some care the first student who will perform, as he or she will probably establish a pattern for the others. Though reports are moderately informal, students are urged to present their final papers in a format suitable for submission to a scholarly journal or a conference; a student organization has recently been formed by our graduates for the trial presentation of such papers. Last year there were two papers that, with some tidying up of argument and documentation, could in fact be sent out; one of the students has now submitted his, and I am confident that he will read it at a conference next year and get it published. From the same group I received a set of papers good enough to "publish" in a xeroxed "journal" for their benefit, including as an introduction a highly critical and detailed review of each essay, thereby impressing on them how public an endeavor scholarship is once we have left the classroom.

I append here the most useful handout I have devised, a chronology of the dates in *Beowulf* postulated from Klaeber's discussion (xxxvi–xl). Simple though it appears, this scheme offers students a framework in which they may associate *Beowulf* with other things they know; in my experience of teaching the poem, such orientation is vital. I have bracketed the dates of three events interesting in English history but not mentioned in the poem; I underline the dates of Beowulf's monster fights to demonstrate the richness of the detailed historical background against which they are set and the way the monster fights are a supernatural reflection of the recurrent theme of feuds in human history. Then of course I offer the question this correspondence raises, another question that we keep open throughout the course: How big a battle is Beowulf really fighting as "strife is renewed"? When Klaeber says of this phrase (at line 2287, when the dragon awakes), "Probably not 'strife was renewed,' but (lit.) 'strife arose which previously did not exist' " (210), how far can we agree?

From the beginning I try to get across the idea that *Beowulf* is a work continually opening out beyond itself, in terms of both ordinary history and "dreamtime" or symbolic history, and that we must be aware of that factor while being highly cautious about how we interpret it. These are the matters I introduce in the first meetings of the course. Where it goes from there, within the framework I have established, is up to the students. They have not so far let me down.

BEOWULF: A RECONSTRUCTED CHRONOLOGY

This chart is based on Klaeber's reconstruction, especially p. xlv. As he admits, the only date verifiable by outside evidence is Hygelac's death c. 521 (now thought by some to have taken place in 524); the other dates, calculated from Hygelac's death, are guesses based on legends, contemporary accounts, and archaeological finds. Beowulf and Wiglaf (but not Wiglaf's father Weohstan, Old Norse Vésteinn) represent the only family group mentioned below whose existence is not in some way confirmed by evidence outside the poem. Bracketed dates place *Beowulf* in a larger and more English historical context; these events are not referred to in the poem.

Key to tribes (alternative Old English tribal names in *Beowulf* are in parentheses):
D   *Danes* (Dene, Beorht-Dene, Gar-Dene, Hring-Dene, East-Dene, Norð-Dene, Suð-Dene, West-Dene, Healf-Dene, Scyldingas, Ar-Scyldingas, Here-Scyldingas, Sige-Scyldingas, þeod-Scyldingas, Ingwine)
F   *Frisians* (Fresan, Frysan)

G   *Geats* (Geatas, Guð-Geatas, Sæ-Geatas, Weder-Geatas, Wederas, Hreðlingas)

HB   *Heathobards* (Heaðobeardan)

S   *Swedes* (Sweon, Scylfingas, Guð-Scylfingas, Heaðo-Scylfingas)

[449]	[Bede's date; Hengist and Horsa come to Vortigern's aid in Britain.]
495 G, S(?)	Beowulf born, son of Edgetheow (a Swede?), grandson of the Geatish king Hrethel.
498 HB, D	Froda kills Halfdane of the Danes; Froda's son Ingeld born.
499 HB, D	Heorogar, Hrothgar, and Halga (Danes) kill Froda.
502 G	Hathcyn accidentally kills his brother Herebeald.
503 G	Their father King Hrethel dies of grief and Hathcyn becomes king of the Geats.
503 G, S	Swedes attack Geats at Sorrowhill: First Swedish-Geatish feud begins.
510 G, S	Hathcyn and Hygelac attack the Swedes and abduct their queen. In the ensuing Battle of Ravenswood both Hathcyn of the Geats and Ongentheow, the Swedish king, are killed. Hathcyn's brother Hygelac becomes king of the Geats and Ohthere king of the Swedes.
515 G, D	*Beowulf kills Grendel and Grendel's mother.*
[518]	[According to the tenth-century *Annales Cambriae*, Artorius (King Arthur?) wins an important battle at Mt. Badon.]
518 HB, D	Hrothgar, who with his brothers Heorogar and Halga had killed King Froda in vengeance for their father's death, gives his daughter Freawaru in marriage to Froda's son Ingeld to forestall a renewal of the feud (peace weaving).
520 HB, D	Ingeld attacks after all, burns down Heorot, but is then defeated by Hrothgar and Hrothulf.
524 G, F	Hygelac of the Geats is killed in his ill-fated Frisian raid; Beowulf escapes by swimming after killing Dayraven.
524 G	Heardred, Hygelac's son, becomes king of the Geats with Beowulf acting as regent.
525 D	Hrothgar dies; his nephew Hrothulf comes to (usurps?) the throne. (Hrothulf, of dubious morality in *Beowulf*, is the great hero-king Hrolf Kraki in Icelandic Saga.)
532 G, S	Second Swedish-Geatish feud begins.

533 G, S	Death of the Swedish king Ohthere (Ottar Vendel-Crow, buried at Vendel in Uppland, Sweden). His brother Ónela seizes the throne while his sons Eanmund and Eadgils seek refuge in the Geatish court. Ónela attacks the Geats and kills their young king Heardred; Beowulf (by Ónela's permission?) becomes king of the Geats. In the battle Eanmund is killed by Weohstan, Ónela's champion. Weohstan is the father of Wiglaf, who is Beowulf's only surviving relative and his most loyal companion. (Eadgils' desire to avenge his brother's death would cause his enmity not only toward Weohstan but, in case of Weohstan's death, toward his son Wiglaf as well—and if Wiglaf becomes king of the Geats after Beowulf this could serve as an excuse for the Swedes to attack yet again.)
535 G, S	Beowulf supports Eadgils in war against Ónela.
575 S	Eadgils is laid in a mound at Old Uppsala.
(583) G	This date is a poetic fiction: note the date of Beowulf's birth. *Beowulf dies in battle with a fire dragon*. Wiglaf probably succeeds him as king of the Geats. Third Swedish-Geatish feud begins?
[625]	[A cenotaph ship containing rich treasures analogous to those described in *Beowulf* is buried in a mound at Sutton Hoo in East Anglia.]

IV.

Harry Jay Solo

The field of Old English offers graduate students special opportunities for professional growth. With an eye toward exploiting these opportunities, I have set the following goals for my Old English seminars: Having completed two courses, students should be able (1) to read Old English prose at sight; (2) to recognize the more common Old English grammatical forms; (3) to make reasonable guesses about the meaning of Old English words with Modern English reflexes; (4) to translate Old English poetry with the aid of a dictionary; (5) to teach the four major codices of Old English poetry; (6) to make observations relating Old English grammar, language, and literature to those of more familiar periods; (7) to locate and assess the scholarship, information sources, and reference tools relevant to the field; (8) to read Old English poetry aloud and scan Old English verse; (9) to construct arguments regarding the meaning of Old English words; (10) to edit a simple Old English prose text from manuscript or facsimile; (11) to interpret the apparatus of the scholarly editions of Old English texts.

The business of learning the language occupies the first five weeks of classes. During this time we study Old English grammar systematically, using Moore and Knott's *Elements of Old English.* I like this text because it clearly describes the articulatory phonetics of the Old English sound system and meaningfully integrates a learnable presentation of the Old English paradigms with a description of the major Old English sound changes. We spend a considerable amount of time at first parsing forms presented in isolation and manipulating sound changes, both of which I expect my students to be able to do in the midterm exam. While dealing with the paradigms, we observe in passing what the study of Old English grammar can tell us about various peculiarities of Modern English, such as the relation of the singular and plural of the noun "foot" or of the verbs "to lie" and "to lay."

As we work through the grammar, we also read prose texts from Cassidy and Ringler's revision of *Bright's Old English Grammar and Reader*. My aim here is to develop the ability to sight-read, and accordingly only sight passages appear on the midterm exam. This relieves my students of the temptation to memorize translations of the assigned readings and thus frees them to work on real reading skills. I advise my students to attack each day's reading using a method described by William G. Moulton in his *Linguistic Guide to Language Learning* whereby different parts of the text are read with varying degrees of care. I further advise them to work quickly, to allow themselves to make mistakes, and to trust their memories. In examining the prose—both the assigned readings and sight passages, which I introduce from the first class on—we observe the correspondence (or noncorrespondence) of forms in the reading to the ideal forms in the paradigms we are learning and the relation of the meanings of selected Old English vocabulary items to their Modern English reflexes; these observations help my students get into the habit of reading *through* a text for its underlying language and also introduce them to the notion of semantic drift. By the midterm exam, almost everyone in the class has control of the Old English paradigms and rudimentary sight-reading skills. We all breathe a sigh of relief.

For a variety of reasons, few of us remember our graduate seminar reports with much fondness. Yet the seminar report has enormous potential for fostering certain kinds of professional growth. I have developed a procedure for organizing reports in my seminars that has proved effective. At the class following the midterm exam, I outline for my students four objectives that the report exercise aims to accomplish. I tell them that in doing the reports they should learn (1) to locate quickly and systematically material essential to studying an Old English poem; (2) to communicate orally the major trends of a body of Old English scholarship within a strictly limited space of time to interested colleagues; (3) to stimulate the thinking of students engaged in studying an Old English poem by raising challenging questions; and (4) to coordinate scholarly and pedagogical efforts with other scholars and teachers. I then divide the class into groups of three or four and assign each group a poem to report on. The report consists of three parts. Each report group produces an annotated bibliography of scholarship on its poem and then gives oral presentations in two successive classes, the first a fifteen- to eighteen-minute talk on the major points of interest in the scholarship on the poem, the second a twelve- to fifteen-minute talk designed to provoke discussion from the class at large.

The reports on *Beowulf*—I usually assign the poem to two groups each semester—present special problems and often produce particularly interesting results. Because there is such a mass of scholarship on the poem, each group must find a way to limit its field of research. Some choose to focus on a single scene (e.g., Grendel's mere) or a thematic strand (e.g., the use of treasure). Others work with a critical approach (e.g., historical criticism) or a period of time (e.g., scholarship from 1970 to 1975). These different definitions of field yield a variety of insights into the poem that in turn lends considerable diversity to the oral presentations. We have had reports on the function of the Finnsburg episode, the poet's use of interlace structure and manipulation of descriptive detail, and the difficulty of assessing the historical and cultural context of the poem, among other topics. Taken together, the three parts of the assignment result in a very efficient and intensive development of a variety of scholarly, critical, and pedagogical tools.

Reports in the second semester—each student gives two or three, depending on class size—focus on either some particular part of *Beowulf* (e.g., Hrothgar's sermon, the "digressions") or some ancillary field (e.g., metrical theory, archaeology, oral-formulaic theory) as it applies to the poem. Although less closely structured than the first semester reports, these follow the same principles that govern the earlier presentations. Extensive consultation with me before and after each report, a focus on relatively broad topics rather than on individual pieces of scholarship, and a clearly defined sense of the potential usefulness of each talk ensure that these exercises will continue to enrich the seminar.

During the second half of the first seminar, my students prepare translations of Old English poetry—about two hundred lines a week—which I expect them to know for the final exam. In the second semester course, we read about five hundred lines a week, one hundred or so intensively. I ask the students to examine the intensive passage for problems in grammar, text, vocabulary, and general meaning, to practice the first half of it aloud until they can read it with comfort, and to scan the first ten lines according to a version of Sievers' system. We spend the first forty-five minutes of each three-hour seminar reading aloud to each other, comparing notes on scansion, and translating from the intensive passage. By the end of the semester, the students have a good sense of what the poetry sounds like, how it is put together, and the difficulties the advanced student can expect to encounter when attempting to discover its precise meaning.

The students gain additional sophistication in dealing with the texts through a series of exercises assigned early in the second semester. One exercise requires them to transcribe, edit, and translate about fifteen lines of prose from manuscript facsimile. Another has them expand the apparatus of variant readings for about forty lines of Klaeber's edition of *Beowulf*. These exercises give the students a feeling for the sorts of decisions editors make in producing a modern edition of a medieval text and the sort of information they can get from such an edition. They also give students a sense of the problematic nature of the witnesses to early English literature.

One last exercise introduces the students to Old English lexicography. I ask them to look up one or more words (this year's list: *blac, nicor, stapol*) in the four major dictionaries of Old English (Bosworth-Toller, Grein, Holthausen, Clark Hall) and the *OED* and to make notes on each dictionary's treatment of its entries, paying particular attention to (1) the kind of information available, (2) the evidence on which the lexicographer bases definitions, (3) the accessibility of different kinds of information and evidence, (4) peculiarities of format, and (5) the different situations in which one dictionary or another might be preferred. Following the suggestion of a former student, I also ask them to consider how they might use these dictionaries— and any other resources they can think of—to make meaningful distinctions among the terms used in *Beowulf* to designate the head (*heafod-, hafela-, helm*), the heart (*ferhþ-, breost-, hreþer-, heorte*), and the spirit (*mod-, sawol-, -sefa, gast-*). This exercise sensitizes the students to some of the subtleties of the Old English poetic vocabulary and frees them from dependence on editors' glossaries.

Class discussion plays an increasingly important part in my Old English seminars as the year progresses. The business of language learning leaves little time for anything but brief questions and responses during the first weeks of class. By the second half of the first semester, my students have begun to acquire some confidence in the field, and the hour or so of discussion that follows each seminar report has at times produced remarkably sharp argument and insight. By the second semester, the students are generally ready for extended, intensive interchange, and I try to reserve from one third to one half of each seminar meeting for discussion. I provide only minimal guidance for this part of the class, sometimes posing broad questions designed to steer the conversation away from monotonously general thematic analysis—What other works in literature is *Beowulf* like? How does the *Beowulf* poet signal meaning in his poem? What details in a given episode seem puzzling, superfluous, or out of place?—sometimes refraining from giving any direction at all.

Some readers will remark that in discussing the teaching of *Beowulf* I have said much about teaching and precious little about *Beowulf* itself. This has been altogether intentional. When my seminars work, the students, not the instructor, provide the ideas that give each class its substance. Seeing these ideas develop is, to my mind, the greatest reward teaching has to offer.

TEACHING THE BACKGROUNDS

HISTORY, RELIGION, CULTURE

Fred C. Robinson

History

The scholar of *Beowulf* is concerned with three distinct chronological periods that bear on an understanding of the poem. First, there is the time and place of the poem's action, the late fifth and early sixth centuries in Northern Europe. Then there is the period on the island of England centuries later when an English poet, looking back over the dark, estranging expanses of time, composed a heroic poem about his distant ancestors on the continent. Finally, there is the late Anglo-Saxon period, around A.D. 1000, when scribes copied the poem *Beowulf* onto the manuscript that, among the many manuscripts of the poem that probably once existed, happens to survive today. Especially important for the student to remember is the time between the period of the poem's action and the period when it was composed, for this separation makes *Beowulf* a profoundly retrospective, archaistic poem. The gap between the time of composition and the time of the scribe's last recording of the poem is important mainly for a scholarly understanding of the state of the text rather than for an understanding of the poem itself. It is a gap to be noted by the teacher and the scholar but not dwelled on by students lest they lose their focus on that more important contrast of historical periods, the age of Beowulf and his people as opposed to the age of the *Beowulf* poet and his people.

How much detail about these periods do students need to master? Unless they are studying *Beowulf* as a vehicle for learning history rather than as a poem to be understood and enjoyed for itself, historical details are probably not as important as a general sense of each period. We are not sure just how precisely the poet knew details about the period. Francis B. Gummere believed that to the Anglo-Saxon poet "the figures of his continental legends, even when historical, had no chronology" (191). According to this view, the *Beowulf* poet would have conceived of all the characters as having lived simply long, long ago, with no thought given to their specific and respective dates. Not all would agree with Gummere, but it is probably true that no strict chronology was sought by the poet for the characters of his narrative. As for the details of the period when the poem was composed, these will be impossible to establish before and unless we can establish the precise date of the poem's composition. And the date of composition now seems more maddeningly uncertain than ever, Ashley Crandell Amos having demonstrated that traditional reliance on linguistic dating of Old English poems has been generally misguided (*Linguistic Means*), and the symposium papers on *The Dating of* Beowulf, edited by Colin Chase, having shown that scholars of the highest authority can reach no agreement on even an approximate date of composition. Indeed, some of these papers (notably that by Kevin Kiernan) move the date of composition forward so close to the date of the scribe's copying that we might have to say that there are, for students at least, but two historical periods that require consideration: Northern Europe around the turn of the sixth century and Anglo-Saxon England in general. Such a broad conception of the historical background of poet and audience might seem inadequate for professional scholars, but for students it is preferable to a distracting immersion in the minutiae of scholarly debate over linguistic forms and paleographical details.

The Historical Background of the Poem's Action

According to contemporary historical accounts, a Scandinavian king named Hygelac lost his life between A.D. 521 and 526 in the course of a military expedition against West Germanic peoples (Franks, Frisians, and Hetware) living in the realm of Theodoric, King of the Austrasian Franks. This Hygelac is mentioned often in the poem *Beowulf* as the king whom Beowulf served loyally for many years, accompanied on his expedition against the Franks, and ultimately followed on the throne. Extrapolating from the date of this historical event described in the poem, we can determine that Beowulf would have been born around A.D. 495, become King of the Geatas in 533, and died in the last quarter of the sixth century. Hygelac's fatal raid is described four times in the poem, and the repetition and elaboration of the event give it symbolic resonance, as if it is meant to represent fate working through history, a tragic error that presages the doom of the nation. This artistic use of a historical event is representative of the poet's consistent use of the past as both the subject and the medium of his poetry and supports Morton Bloomfield's contention that *Beowulf* "belongs to the category of *historical* works, and in its reciting the tradition of society was being carried on" ("Understanding Old English Poetry" 70).

The Danish kingdom during the reign of Hrothgar is the setting of the poem after the prologue about Scyld Scefing. There are no reliable historical documents from this period, but a variety of medieval Scandinavian sources in prose and poetry discuss Kings Scyld, Healfdene, and Hrothgar as well as the younger generation of Danes whom Beowulf meets in Heorot, such as Hrethric and Hrothulf. The legendary history concerning these characters interacts importantly with hints and allusions of the *Beowulf* poet and helps us complete the sense of what Wealhtheow says when she anxiously insists that Hrothulf will not forget his debt of gratitude toward the reigning king's family when Hrothgar's sons need support (1180–87). "By rather complicated, but quite unforced, fitting together of various Scandinavian authorities, we find that Hrothulf deposed and slew his cousin Hrethric" (Chambers 26). Attention to historical sources, then, reveals the tragic irony resident in Wealhtheow's speech and explains the *Beowulf* poet's (as well as the *Widsith* poet's) implicit statements that peace between Hrothgar and his nephew Hrothulf was but temporary. Scholars who, following Kenneth Sisam (*The Structure of* Beowulf 80–82), refuse to accept the dark implications here would seem determined to turn a deaf ear to the tone and words of the poem. Anyone who does not hear anxiety in Wealhtheow's speech about how Hrothulf will act toward her offspring must think that Mark Antony genuinely believes Caesar's murderers to be honorable men. In the legendary history of Denmark Hrothulf, not Hrethric, takes the Danish throne after Hrothgar, and Saxo Grammaticus notes that this happened only after Hrothulf slew Røricus (= Hrethric). Wealhtheow had good reason to be anxious.

Much of the circumstantial detail in the poem is shown by parallel sources from the Continent to be part of the legendary history of Scandinavia and not the English poet's invention. Hrothgar (and later Hrothulf) ruled from a royal settlement whose present location can with fair confidence be fixed as the modern Danish village of Leire, the actual location of Heorot. The strife between Danes and Heathobards, which Beowulf predicts so astutely in lines 2020–69, was well known to Saxo Grammaticus and other medieval chroniclers on the Continent, and these sources confirm the accuracy of Beowulf's prescient speculation as to the unhappy results of Freawaru's marriage to Ingeld. Modern readers of *Beowulf* must be aware that what happens in the Danish episode of *Beowulf* is part of traditional lore and that the lore at times spells out the full meaning of the actions in the poem. But a detailed study of early Danish history is hardly necessary for the student whose primary concern is *Beowulf*, since editors and translators of the poem place the crucial historical facts at the reader's disposal in notes and commentary. Those who are curious about fuller details of the Danish background can turn to Chambers' excellent syntheses in Beowulf: *An Introduction to the Study of the Poem.*

There seems to be widespread agreement now that Beowulf's tribe, the Geatas, are to be identified with the Götar, a people who lived in the southern portion of Sweden and who gave their name to the modern Swedish city of Göteborg, among other places. Early historians like Ptolemy (second century A.D.) and Procopius (sixth century A.D.) identify the Götar as a large and independent power, but in later reports they appear to have declined into a dependency of the Swedish nation. The *Beowulf* poet tells us that the Geatas are a flourishing power with Hygelac as their king, and another Anglo-Saxon source supplies the same information. The *Liber Monstrorum*, a Latin work of early English origin, tells us that Hygelac was King of the Geatas and that his body lies near the mouth of the Rhine, a detail that tallies with the *Beowulf* poet's description of Hygelac's death in the realm of Theodoric. Historical sources have nothing to say about a Beowulf being king of the Geatas, and the likelihood is that his is a fictional story inserted in the midst of a more sober historical narrative about a verifiable nation of Geatas who lived near the Swedes at the time of the action of the poem.

In *Beowulf* we read of much strife between the Geatas and the Swedes, and Scandinavian records verify both the conflicts of the Swedes at this time and the names of their rulers—Ohthere, Onela, Eadgils, and others. The records are not specific about the role the Geatas play in these wars or about their ultimate fate, but the speakers in the poem are very specific about the fate of the Geatas: Wiglaf, the messenger, and the woman mourning at Beowulf's funeral all agree that the nation faces disaster once King Beowulf is dead. Knowing the dismal future that history holds for the Geatas enables us to complete the poem's tragic meaning: heroic splendor and the values of the pre-Christian world are unavailing before the destructive forces of a brutal age; Beowulf's awesome achievement in protecting his people must end with his death, after which the forces of history so carefully delineated in the poem will turn inexorably against the nation whose moment of grandeur the poem has celebrated. Such knowledge as the Anglo-Saxons had of Geatish history would appear to have borne out this representation of events by the poet. As we have seen, the Anglo-Saxon author of the *Liber Monstrorum* affirms that Hygelac, King of the Geatas, was leading his army against powerful neighboring realms at the time when Beowulf also says he was doing so. But later, when the Latin history of Orosius was translated into Old English, during the period 890–99, the scholarly Anglo-Saxon who prepared the prefatory description of Europe "as it was known in the second half of the ninth century" (Bately 166) appears to know nothing of a Geatish realm, although in other respects his knowledge of Scandinavian lands and people is full and precise. Evidently the Geatas experienced a decline after the time of Hygelac and Beowulf and were absorbed into Sweden—as if in fulfillment of the prophecy in *Beowulf* 2922–3007 that the Swedes and other enemies would fall upon the Geatish nation as soon as they heard that King Beowulf had fallen.

Kenneth Sisam, in an influential argument in *The Structure of* Beowulf (51–59), has pointed out that some Scandinavian sources indicate an awareness of the Geatas "as a distinct people" well after the period when *Beowulf* seems to indicate that they were overrun by the Swedes. From this Sisam reasons that no tragic fate awaited the Geatas following Beowulf's fall and that hence the poem has a brighter ending than scholars had assumed. But for readers of *Beowulf*, late Scandinavian sources and even the facts of Scandinavian history are irrelevant: the history that matters for *Beowulf* is the history that the poet knew and used in the poem. Records surviving from Anglo-Saxon England, as we have seen, do not show any awareness of a flourishing nation of Geatas after the time of Beowulf. Moreover, the poet is more explicit about the fate of the Geatas than Sisam has allowed. Just before the messenger utters his long and circumstantial description of how the Geatas will be overcome by their enemies, the poet is careful to announce, in his own authorial voice, that the things the messenger is going to say are true: "he spoke to them all truthfully" (2899). Again, at the close of the speech, the authorial voice intrudes to declare, "nor did he much lie in his words or his prophecies" (3029–30)—that is, he spoke only the truth. (I use the translation by Donaldson, who renders *wyrda ne worda*, rightly I think, as "words or . . . prophecies.") Near the end of the poem the dire prophecies are repeated by the woman leading the funeral dirge, who laments that evil days, the horror of warfare, killings, and captivity await the nation now that the king is dead (3153–54). It is significant that this prediction is assigned by the poet to a woman, for in Germanic society (as Tacitus makes clear in his *Germania*) women were credited with special powers of prophecy, a belief exemplified by the *Beowulf* poet himself when he has Wealhtheow express such accurate forebodings about future trouble from Hrothulf. Whatever late Scandinavian chroniclers may say, then, the *Beowulf* poet clearly assumed that history held a bleak future for the Geatas, and he used this assumed downfall of his hero's nation as an important part of his narrative strategy. If modern historians construct from sources at their disposal a different fate for the Geatas, their revisionism may have historical interest, but it has no bearing on our reading of *Beowulf*, just as it would have no bearing on our reading of *Macbeth* if modern historians should determine from documentary evidence that Duncan died of natural causes. The protagonist of Shakespeare's play would still be a regicide, and the play would still be a tragedy. Modern revisions of history are not retroactive to the old poets' uses of the history they knew.

The World of the Poet and His Audience

In order to understand *Paradise Lost* it is not enough to know about the biblical history out of which the poem was made; one needs to know something about John Milton's historical context in seventeenth-century England as well. The reader of *Beowulf*, for similar reasons, needs to have some sense of the thought world inhabited by the Anglo-Saxon poet and his audience. What attitudes and ideas did they share concerning paganism, kingship, runes, cremation, battle boasts, oaths of allegiance, vows of revenge, and other subjects that figure prominently in *Beowulf*? Here once again we are vexed by the problem of the poem's indeterminable date. Are we to concern ourselves with England of the early seventh century, when H. M. Chadwick thought the poem came into being (*The Heroic Age* 56), or with a vastly different England of the eleventh century, when Kevin Kiernan thinks the poem was composed (Beowulf *and the* Beowulf *Manuscript*)? For present purposes it seems best, once again, to evade the question by limiting our attention to more general aspects of the period and eschewing details of history. All but a few partisans of extremely early or extremely late dating would in any event accept the limits A.D. 750 to 950 for the time of *Beowulf*'s composition, and most of the generalizations offered here would hold true for even this broad stretch of time.

For readers of *Beowulf*, the most important source of information about the values prevailing at the time the poem was composed is the poet himself, insofar as he declares his views. When in lines 178–88 he laments the horror and hopelessness of pagan worship, we may be sure he is expressing an attitude that his audience shared with him, whether they lived in the eighth, ninth, or tenth centuries. Sermons, penitentials, and other writings of the Anglo-Saxons, early and late, condemn all pagan practices. The poet's praise of loyalty to kin (e.g., 2600–01), his admiration for good kings and loyal subjects (e.g., 11, 20–25, 3174–77), his sense of the importance of being as good as one's word (758–60) are attitudes that accord with those expressed in many Anglo-Saxon writings outside *Beowulf*.

On the other hand, certain practices and speeches of characters in the poem would definitely not agree with the values of Christian Anglo-Saxons. Beowulf's speech to Hrothgar declaring that the best thing a person can do in this life is to achieve fame (1387–89) would jar rudely with the ideal of Christian humility, as would Beowulf's concern that he be given a splendid funeral and a prominent resting place that will proclaim his name and renown to the seafarers passing by (2802–08, 3140). ("Let one not seek the empty renown of a famous name on earth," said Augustine, and many Anglo-Saxon homilists emphasize the vanity of worldly fame.) The description of Beowulf's cremation (as well as that of the dead warriors in the Finnsburg episode) may seem to the modern reader like mere vivid detail included to enhance the scenery, but to Christians living in the poet's time the implications of cremation were darkly ominous. Burning the dead is a pagan practice specifically forbidden to Christians, and Charlemagne's Saxon capitulary of 785 reveals just how determined Christian rulers were to prevent pagan cremations and burials:

> Whoever delivers the bodies of the dead to the flames, following the pagan rite, and reduces the bones to cinders, will be condemned to death. . . . We ordain that the bodies of Christian Saxons are to be borne to our church's cemeteries and not to the tumuli of the pagans. . . .
>
> (Riché, *Daily Life in the World of Charlemagne* 181–82)

Similarly, the sermons and penitentials of the Anglo-Saxons inveigh repeatedly against the pagan practice of observing omens, and this suggests that when the poet has Beowulf's first expedition launched with a reading of the omens (204), he is reminding his audience that the heroic society described in the poem is pagan.

Some aspects of Beowulfian society that modern readers might suspect to be at variance with the poet's Christian values, however, may not have been. Vengeance is urgently recommended as a noble course of action by Beowulf in lines 1384–85, and vengeance is practiced and praised elsewhere in the poem. Alien though this behavior is to strict Christian doctrine, Dorothy Whitelock, in her valuable study *The Audience of* Beowulf (13–19), has shown that Christianity did not bring an end to vengeance taking in Anglo-Saxon society, that such behavior came to be accepted as a necessity and received the express approval of the clergy as well as of the laity. Since runes originated in pagan Germanic times and have been associated with divination, the runes engraved on the sword hilt Beowulf gives to Hrothgar may be thought to carry alarming connotations of paganism. But while rune writing would be historically appropriate for Beowulf's pre-Christian society, the Christian Anglo-Saxon scribes and rune masters had adapted this writing system so completely to Christian uses that mention of runes in the poem would hardly bring gasps of horror from a contemporary audience. Even the audience's attitude toward paganism itself should not be conceived as simply one of horrified disgust. In an important essay called "The Pagan Coloring in *Beowulf*," Larry D. Benson traces the growth and complication of Anglo-Saxon attitudes toward Germanic pagans as the English mission to the Continent brought increasing contacts between Christian Anglo-Saxons and their non-Christian cousins in Europe. Compassion rather than revulsion was often the dominant sentiment Anglo-Saxons felt toward the as yet unconverted, and occasionally they even expressed admiration for those who, without benefit of Christianity, still managed to comport themselves in a manner sometimes superior to that of the Christian English. Recent studies have shown further how the poet of *Beowulf* may have drawn on the pagan Viking society dwelling in parts of England as he formed his conception of the Germanic heroic age. The skillful essays by R. I. Page and Roberta Frank in *The Dating of* Beowulf (ed. Colin Chase) reveal how such intercultural contacts might have taken place. Yet other scholars have emphasized the possible influence on *Beowulf* of the traditional Irish tolerance of a pagan past. None of this should be construed as meaning that the *Beowulf* poet may have had a nostalgic preference for paganism over Christianity; such a preference would have been as abhorrent to him as it was to the Anglo-Saxon churchmen who, from the beginning to the end of the period, denounced those who reverted to paganism or who aped the pagan customs of the Vikings resident in England. But we should also not assume that Anglo-Saxons were insensitive to the fact that pagans were civilized people capable of goodness despite their tragic ignorance of Christianity.

Beyond these general aspects of the thought world of Anglo-Saxon England, we should like to have specific knowledge of the cultural environment from which *Beowulf* emerged. Was the poet a churchman or a layman? For what audience was the poem intended? Did poet and audience conceive of the poem as relating primarily to contemporary Christian doctrine or to the themes and attitudes of the old heroic tradition? Scholars' answers to these questions show a rich disparity of opinion, of which the following three views may be representative.

First, some see *Beowulf* as essentially a secular English poem written for an audience knowledgeable about Christianity but not concerned exclusively with religion. Dorothy Whitelock in *The Audience of* Beowulf gives authoritative expression to the view that the poem was composed for a lay audience of the privileged class that, though not steeped in Christian doctrine, was familiar with the basic tenets of Christianity. In an important essay building on her work, Patrick Wormald argues that the secularized, aristocratic monasteries of which Alcuin, Bede, and other ecclesiastics complain were the institutions most likely to have provided the intended audience of the poem, and he shows that many if not all the basic elements of *Beowulf* are explicable in terms of such a context for the poem. A second view, that *Beowulf* was intended to be read primarily as a Christian document and in terms of Christian allegory, is represented most fully by W. F. Bolton's *Alcuin and* Beowulf: *An Eighth-Century View*, where we are given a thoroughgoing exposition of the way in which the learned cleric Alcuin would probably have read the poem. To some extent Alcuin's reading of literature, as Bolton presents it, seems to resemble that of D. W. Robertson, Jr., who feels that Christian instruction must be present in all serious literature of the Middle Ages and that where such instruction is not apparent in the literal narrative it must be present in allegorical form. Finally, Alain Renoir, in a series of wide-ranging literary-comparative studies (most recently "Oral-Formulaic Context: Implications for the Comparative Criticism of Medieval Texts"), urges that *Beowulf* should be read in the context of western European heroic-age literature at large. In a way an oral-formulaic sophistication of the earlier contention of H. M. Chadwick that *Beowulf* needs to be judged alongside epic poetry from around the world, Renoir's studies constitute a needed reminder that we must see the poem in a transnational, generic context as well as in its historical context.

No amount of irenic scholarly diplomacy will succeed in reconciling completely the approaches of Wormald, Bolton, Renoir, and the many other interpreters of *Beowulf*, but fair-minded students will probably find something persuasive in all of them. Readers coming to *Beowulf* for the first time should be made aware of the existence of competing conceptualizations of the poem in its time and should be encouraged to measure each approach against their own experience of the text. Those who wish to make their own synthesis of the poem and its cultural context can learn about the historical background of Anglo-Saxon England by sampling the works listed in the chapter "The Instructor's Library," such as those by Page, David Hill, and Whitelock.

Religion

As is clear from the historical context of the poem, two distinct religious systems are operative in *Beowulf*. The characters in the story are obviously pagan, but the poet narrating the story is manifestly Christian. The Germanic tribes on the Continent in the fifth and sixth centuries had not yet come into contact with Christianity, as any Anglo-Saxon would have known. In lines 175–88 the poet tells us that the Danes to whose aid Beowulf comes prayed to heathen gods for assistance and would be damned for their ignorance. The Geatas' omen reading and Beowulf's cremation, as we have just seen, are other indications that the poet is careful to portray his characters as what they historically were: pre-Christian. On the other hand, he does not shock his audience by naming the pagan gods and portraying his characters engaged in the particular abominations that scandalized Christians throughout the Anglo-Saxon period. If he had shown his characters invoking Thor, casting spells, exposing unwanted children, or practicing ritual sacrifice, he could probably not have engaged sufficient audience sympathy for his story to win a hearing. Beowulf and Hrothgar accordingly refer to the deity with words like "god," "lord," or "the all-powerful one." They do not use designations that would be appropriate only for Christians, such as "Christ," "Savior," or "Redeemer," and they never refer to angels, the Virgin Mary, the Holy Ghost, the saints, and other specifically Christian subjects that Anglo-Saxon poets regularly treat in poems that have Christian settings. This deliberate blurring in the mode of religious reference allows the characters of *Beowulf* to attain some dignity and even nobility in the eyes of the Christian audience without belying their pre-Christian status.

When he speaks in his own voice, the poet alludes to the Bible, to salvation and damnation, to the devil, and to other Christian topics, but even then he is usually not specific and emphatic in his allusions to Christianity. His biblical references are limited to the pre-Mosaic Old Testament, and his allusions to the deity are muted and general. By making them so, he avoids emphasizing the contrast between his own religion and that of his characters. This dictional restraint in no way implies that the poet's Christian belief is primitive or half-hearted; it is a matter of literary skill and tact used to unite rather than divide the audience and its ancestry.

Commentators on *Beowulf* usually allow Alcuin to represent Anglo-Saxon Christianity in its confrontation with *Beowulf*. In a letter to monks of Lindisfarne in A.D. 797 reprimanding them for listening to ancient pagan tales rather than to Bible readings when they supped, the stern churchman from York says,

> Let the word of God be read at the meal of the clergy. There it is proper to hear a reader, not a harp-player; to hear sermons of the church fathers, not songs of the laity. What has Ingeld to do with Christ? The house is narrow; it cannot hold both. The King of Heaven will have nothing to do with so-called kings who are heathen and damned, for that King reigns in Heaven eternally, while the heathen one is damned and laments in Hell.   (2: 183)

This uncompromising, Augustinian view of Christian salvation was no doubt widely held among Anglo-Saxon ecclesiastics, and Alcuin's specific reference to Ingeld, a character who figures in the poem *Beowulf*, as being the kind of subject in which devout Anglo-Saxons should take no interest, gives cause for wonder that a poem like *Beowulf* should have survived at all in such an inhospitable intellectual climate. But we should perhaps not think of the religious views of all Christian Anglo-Saxons as being uniformly identical with those of Alcuin. Benson's demonstration that a saintly man like Boniface could admire the virtues of Germanic heathens should be recalled, as should Charles Donahue's essays "*Beowulf*, Ireland, and the Natural Good" and "*Beowulf* and Christian Tradition: A Reconsideration from a Celtic Stance," where we learn that Irish thinkers contemporary with the *Beowulf* poet took a much more hopeful view of the destiny of pagans who, though deprived of revelation, behaved well according to an instinctive sense of what is good in human conduct. Morton W. Bloomfield has observed that the poet's limitation of his biblical references to pre-Mosaic times implies a kind of analogy between patriarchs like Abraham (who lived before the revelation of the law to Moses as well as before New Testament revelation) and the virtuous pagans of the Germanic world ("Patristics and Old English Literature: Notes on Some Poems"). Both Abraham and Beowulf led their lives as well as they could without Judeo-Christian revelation; if the one gained salvation, is it not possible that the other might? If such questionings seem overbold for a medieval poet, we might recall that *Beowulf* was composed in "the privacy of the vernacular," as Thomas D. Hill, in a different connection, has interestingly termed Old English poetic language ("The Fall of Angels and Man in the Old English *Genesis B*"). That is, serious theological reasoning was normally conducted in Latin and was subject to the scrutiny of Christian scholars throughout the Western world. But when one wrote poetry in a vernacular like Old English, one was addressing a much more intimate audience, an audience prepared for the relaxed explorations of local poetry rather than the rigors of theological debate in an international language. Residents in the aristocratic and secularized monasteries where Wormald conjectures that *Beowulf* had its origin and its audience would be naturally inclined to speculate wistfully over the destiny of their pagan ancestors despite the stern orthodoxy to which Alcuin summons them in his Latin epistle.

Culture

Among the questions often raised by scholars concerning the cultural background of *Beowulf* are: Was the text orally composed, or was it composed in writing, which implies the possibility of long reflection and revision? Was the poet's method and matter influenced by Celtic literature? Did he know and use Vergil? Important though these questions are, discussion of them would probably do little to improve students' comprehension and appreciation of the poem in a literature class. Exponents of oral composition, who are fewer in number and increasingly on the defensive in recent years, have never succeeded in proving their case that *Beowulf* is the result of more or less instinctive oral improvisation rather than a highly conscious literary composition, but neither have the skeptics been able to disprove it conclusively. Le Gentil's response to disputes over the possible oral origin of *Roland* may suffice for the general reader of *Beowulf*: "Since it is so sure, it hardly matters whether this [poet's] intelligence is more instinctive than conscious" (*The Song of Roland*, trans. Francis F. Beer 101). The question of Celtic influence, too, remains unresolved: only loose parallels have been adduced as internal evidence, and speculation over possible cultural contacts constitutes almost the only explanation as to how the Celtic themes would have reached the *Beowulf* poet. Similarly loose parallels have been cited to prove Vergilian influence, but few scholars have found them convincing. The most interesting discussion is the most recent: Theodore Andersson, *Early Epic Scenery*, finds suggestive similarities in the modes of narration in the two poems. But scholars at large do not regard the connection between *The Aeneid* and *Beowulf* as proved.

Instead of reviewing scholarly investigations of the cultural background of *Beowulf*, the general reader may find it useful to examine a few of the instances where a theme or subject in *Beowulf* had markedly different cultural significance for the poet and his audience than it has for the modern student of the poem. Consideration of six such topics will help readers free themselves from their own cultural preconceptions and project themselves into the imaginative world of *Beowulf*: love and friendship, shame culture and guilt culture, vengeance, descriptions of artifacts and nature, gift giving, and fate.

Our first instance of a cultural conflict between Anglo-Saxon and modern worlds is not precisely a subject dealt with in *Beowulf* but one that is conspicuously missing from it. Although women as well as men figure importantly in the narrative and although a husband's love (or the cooling of his love) is mentioned once (2065–66), romantic passion between the sexes is absent from *Beowulf*, as it is absent from most Old English poetry, while feelings of friendship and loyalty between men are surprisingly intense. C. S. Lewis in *The Allegory of Love* has characterized the Germanic attitude toward love and friendship in the Middle Ages:

> "Love," in our sense of the word, is as absent from the literature of the Dark Ages as from that of classical antiquity. . . . The deepest of worldly emotions in this period is the love of man for man, the mutual love of warriors who die together fighting against odds, and the affection between vassal and lord. We shall never understand this last, if we think of it in the light of our own moderated and impersonal loyalties. . . . The feeling is more passionate and less ideal than our

patriotism. . . . Of romance, of reverence for women, of the idealizing imagination exercised about sex, there is hardly a hint. The centre of gravity is elsewhere—in the hopes and fears of religion, or in the clean and happy fidelities of the feudal hall. But, as we have seen, these male affections—though wholly free from the taint that hangs about "friendship" in the ancient world—were themselves lover-like; in their intensity, their wilful exclusion of other values, and their uncertainty, they provided an exercise of the spirit not wholly unlike that which later ages have found in "love." (9–10)

Lewis may overdramatize the distinction between medieval and modern attitudes, but the distinction is there and must be remembered when we read of Beowulf's farewell from Hrothgar (1870–80) or of his expression of affection for Hygelac (2149–51). We should also remember Lewis' words when we read the description of Beowulf at the end of the poem. Readers have often assumed that since the hero has no heir and since no wife is mentioned we are to understand that he remained solitary and celibate throughout his life. It is quite possible, however, that the poet simply felt that Beowulf's marital status was of insufficient interest to warrant mention in the poem.

In *The Greeks and the Irrational* (17–18) E. R. Dodds adopts the anthropologists' terms shame culture and guilt culture to explain an important difference between the outlook of the heroic age and a later day. The highest good in a society like that of Homer or Beowulf is public esteem and the greatest evil is public disgrace. *Dom bið selest* according to an Old English maxim, which one might translate "Favorable judgment by others is the best thing there is." Beowulf says as much in lines 1386–89. The public dispute with Unferth, the obsession with fame, the hero's concern for his memorial after his death, all should be viewed in the light of the fact that Beowulf lived in a shame culture. The Christian society of the poet and his audience, on the other hand, is a guilt culture, where the highest good is the enjoyment of a quiet conscience. In the poem *Beowulf*, then, we have a shame culture as viewed through the eyes of a guilt culture, and at one point the contrast between the two comes to the surface. When Beowulf asks himself whether the dragon's attacks can be the result of some unrecognized wrongdoing on his part, the poet observes, "His breast within was troubled with dark thoughts, *which was not usual with him*" (2331–32). The heroic world is a world of action and of public recognition for deeds performed, not of brooding and soul searching.

One form of public esteem sought by Germanic man is revealed in the ritual of revenge. Each man sought to demonstrate that injury done to him or to any of his people would have to be remedied or vengeance would be taken. Francis Bacon defined revenge as "a kind of wild justice," but in the ancient Germanic world it was an exceedingly precise and elaborate kind of justice. Traditional laws prescribed that if a person is killed or injured by another, then the injuring party must offer to the victim's lord an amount of compensation precisely calibrated according to the predetermined worth of the victim. Otherwise life will be taken in talion for life. This system of organized retribution protected the weak against injury and the strong against loss of esteem. When the system breaks down, the result is extreme anguish—as when the Danes have to suffer Grendel's depredations without restitution (154–58) or when Hrethel must see his son die unavenged (2442–43). In these instances the survivors must bitterly accept their bereavement with no outlet for grief.

Another feature of Beowulfian society that is related to the importance of public esteem is the giving of gifts. Scene after scene in the royal halls shows king and retainer giving and receiving gold, weapons, horses, accoutrements, grants of land, and other items of great value. Early in the poem (20–25) the poet remarks how important it is for young kings to be generous with gifts, and much of Hrothgar's long speech to Beowulf in lines 1700–84 is devoted to the importance of generosity. In large part this emphasis is a function of a culture oriented toward fame and shame. Receiving a splendid gift is a visible sign of a man's worth, and since visible recognition is the central good in this society, the deserving men must receive rewards. It is the act of giving and receiving that is important more than the actual possession of the gift. Often in *Beowulf* a gift received is promptly presented to another person, as when Queen Wealhtheow gives Beowulf a splendid torque and he, on his return to Geatland, promptly gives it to the Geatish royal family. Gift taking also had social and ceremonial significance, being an overt symbol of the social contract implicit in the heroic world. When a man receives a gift from his lord or queen, for example, he solemnizes his allegiance to the dispenser of the gift. For a man to accept a gift and then fail his benefactor in time of need would not merely be ingratitude; it would be a violation of the social code. Beyond these symbolic aspects of gift giving, moreover, the *Beowulf* poet seems to imply an even more elemental good in openhandedness, as if it were a measure of one's well-being. There is warmth and joy in the scenes of gift giving and a reassuring sense that social harmony is attainable. Negative examples like the niggardly Heremod, on the other hand, suggest that stinginess is a sign of almost pathological unhappiness. The *Beowulf* poet would have found it fitting that the modern English word "misery" is derived from "miser."

Any reader of *Beowulf* will be struck by the poet's frequent and enthusiastic descriptions of artifacts: sword hilts, saddles, shields, jewelry, and helmets are all carefully depicted, and the building of Heorot is described as if it were the crowning achievement of Hrothgar's kingship. While it is true that archaeological discoveries like Sutton Hoo have revealed remarkable craftsmanship among Anglo-Saxon smiths, jewelers, and metalworkers, one might think nonetheless that so much attention to artifacts in *Beowulf* bespeaks an almost childish preoccupation with material objects. But this impression would result from a conflict in medieval and modern cultural values. Rousseau and the English Romantic writers have taught us to mistrust the artificial products of a calculating mind and to put our trust in nature— an external nature that is benign and instructive and a human nature that is inherently good. But to medieval people and the poet of *Beowulf* nature is chaotic and menacing. The few descriptions we get of nature are almost entirely of storms, fire, and the frightening mere. Grendel emerges from fens that are swarming with natural and reptilian life. Each artifact that the *Beowulf* poet describes is reassurance that mankind can control the natural world, can constrain its brute substance into pattern and order. The Anglo-Saxons would have understood Alfred North Whitehead's observation that "art is the imposing of a pattern on experience, and our aesthetic enjoyment is recognition of the pattern." The zoomorphic capital letters in Anglo-Saxon manuscripts are perfect examples of this mind-set. The illuminator forces vegetation, animals, and fantastic creatures to assume the abstract patterns and shapes that are beautiful and meaningful to human beings. The conduct of human beings is formalized into banqueting rituals, social forms, traditions, and patterns of allegiance, thus bringing human nature as well as external nature into reassuring patterns. It is in the light of this desire for rational order as a defense against the anarchy of nature that we should read the description of artifacts in *Beowulf*. Each celebration of a damascened sword or a well-constructed helmet recapitulates in miniature that moment early in the poem when Hrothgar builds Heorot—when a good king brings order to a people and a place by walling out the beasts and fens and darkness and constructing a place of control and assembly whose "light shone over many lands."

The common Old English word for "fate" is *wyrd*, a word that is still used by Shakespeare when he refers to the "weird sisters" (i.e., the sisters of fate) in *Macbeth*. *Wyrd* is mentioned repeatedly in *Beowulf* as the force determining lives, and some scholars have thought that behind these usages lurks the old pagan idea of the Germanic goddess of fate. The plural of *wyrd* is used by other writers to translate Latin *Parcae*, the name of the Roman mythological goddesses of fate, so clearly *wyrd* did have this association, but most scholars think that in *Beowulf* the term refers to fate in a more abstract sense. In his translation of Boethius' *Consolation of Philosophy* King Alfred reasons from a Christian viewpoint that *wyrd* is the accomplishment of God's providence. That is, *wyrd* is subject to God, it is what God determines shall be. In *Beowulf*, *wyrd* and God are mentioned as parallel and simultaneous forces at times, which would seem to support the Boethian reading of the concept in the poem. But quite possibly the term is to be understood according to context. To the characters in the poem, their lives seem to be governed by a stern and implacable fate. Both the poet and his audience knew that that fate, *wyrd*, was simply the accomplishment of God's will, but they also knew that to Beowulf and his contemporaries, who were deprived of Christian revelation, *wyrd* represented something more obscure and disquieting.

These aspects of the world of *Beowulf* that have meanings different from those our modern culture would lead us to expect are only representative of a larger number of such subjects requiring modern readers to question their cultural assumptions as they read the poem. Understanding literature from another time and land is an exercise in projecting ourselves imaginatively into other people's minds and lives and language. It is this exercise that constitutes one of the greatest rewards of literary study, as one thinks one's way into a different time and a different world from one's own. The world of *Beowulf* is worth the effort.

PARALLELS, USEFUL ANALOGUES, AND ELUSIVE SOURCES

Constance B. Hieatt

Literary parallels and analogues serve many classroom functions, such as alleviating the tedium of immersion in Old English grammar, providing stimulating materials for term papers or seminar reports, giving the instructor exempla to use in clarifying points, or, simply, assisting to bridge a cultural gap that has little to do with the theoretical decline of religion in our time ("theoretical" in view of the worldwide resurgence of fundamentalism) and the general ignorance of history among young North Americans. As T. A. Shippey has reminded us, students find a "boast" uncouth and scenes of violence disturbing. A preliminary reading of *Brunanburh* may be instructive in introducing an Anglo-Saxon poet's enjoyment in describing a field flowing with blood. Far from being tragic, the fact that "five young kings lay on the battlefield" is celebrated joyously, just as Byrhtnoth thanked God for granting him his day's work at Maldon.

The Christian context should be noted: readers may observe that the Christ of the Anglo-Saxons was not a Sunday school teacher's gentle Jesus meek and mild but *The Dream of the Rood's* "young warrior—who was God almighty." *Maldon* is also especially useful in introducing such concepts as the retainers' duty to avenge a fallen lord or die in the attempt, the relationship of the "boast" to the lord's generosity, and the retainer's duty of "earning his mead" in battle. *The Dream of the Rood* and *The Wanderer* illuminate the concept of the mead hall as a symbol of human felicity, whether heavenly or earthly and transitory. The difficult voyages of *The Wanderer* and *The Seafarer* put Beowulf's "easy" voyage to Denmark in sharp relief, and both poems express various heroic attitudes similar to sentiments voiced in *Beowulf*. The *Seafarer*'s statement that a man should work to earn the praise of those who live after him is, for example, exactly what Beowulf tells Hrothgar in urging him to seek vengeance for Aeschere's death. That such statements are made in explicitly Christian settings in the shorter poems may help dispel suspicion that similar sentiments in *Beowulf* are pagan and at variance with the "Christian coloring" of the poem.

Many of the same points can be demonstrated in Old English prose. Bede's account of the conversion of Edwin gives us a memorable version of the transitory joys of the mead hall (*Ecclesiastical History* 2.13) and also provides an example of a loyal retainer who sacrifices his own life to save his lord (2.9). The *Anglo-Saxon Chronicle*'s account of Cynewulf and Cyneheard, like *Maldon*, tells of retainers who would rather die than fail to avenge their lord, a situation parallel to that of Hengest and his men in *Beowulf*'s Finn episode. Wulfstan's *Sermo Lupi* emphasizes throughout the dire results of sins against lords and kinsmen and the breaking of faith (*treow*), the sins emphasized in the portrayal of most of the evildoers in *Beowulf*, including the ten pledge breakers (*treowlogan*) who fail to come to the hero's aid in his last battle.

Less obvious parallels in Old English literature include *The Wife's Lament* and *Wulf and Eadwacer*, where, if we can agree that there is a female narrator in both cases, women appear to be depicted as the victims of hostility between the men in their lives, like *Beowulf*'s Hildeburh, in a situation for which the causes are just as arguable as those in the shorter poems. Of lesser literary appeal but useful precisely because of their gnomic quality are *Maxims I* and *Maxims II*, excerpts from which can provide easy and instructive reading for beginners in Old English. Both series speak of the transitory and cyclical nature of a world in which only God is unchangeable; both emphasize that an individual's destiny after death is hidden to mortal men and women. This view of life (and death) may have some application to our interpretation of Beowulf's funeral pyre, as well as the puzzlement of Scyld Scefing's councillors.

Both sets of *Maxims* state that people should (shall, ought to, must, are destined to) take their proper places and fulfill their duties in a basically orderly world, as do the elements ("fire shall burn wood") and the dumb beasts ("the boar shall be in the forest"). Thus *Maxims I* says a queen shall be cheerful, keep secrets, be generous in giving out treasure, serve her lord first with the mead cup, and give her lord good advice—as Wealhtheow does in *Beowulf*. Brothers should be companions, not kill each other as Cain did Abel, which event gives a primary symbol for disorder in *Maxims I* as in *Beowulf*. *Maxims II* emphasizes the nobleman's duty, including valor (*ellen*) and keeping faith (*treow*). It informs us that just as the fish shall propagate its kind in the water, the dragon shall take pride in treasure in the barrow, and as birds sport in the air, the *þyrs* 'monster' shall dwell alone in the fen. Thus we see that dragons are a fact of life and that Grendel, a *þyrs* (*Beowulf* 426), lives as he should, isolated from mankind and in a fen. The *Maxims* also give us clear indications that the audience they addressed was primarily aristocratic and military. The treasures described are mostly weapons, and the most humble social duty stated is that of the sailor's wife to be true to her spouse in his absence and comfort him with fresh garments when he returns.

In some respects the world of Icelandic saga is not quite like that of the Anglo-Saxon poet's audience. It is not aristocratic in the same sense, although certainly hierarchical: the great leaders, like heroes of Homer's age, often plow their own fields and tend their own herds, activities never attributed to Beowulf or Hrothgar. But sagas are a stimulating and enlightening alternative, or supplement, to Old English works as an introduction to some aspects of the cultural milieu of *Beowulf*. *Egil's Saga* depicts Viking ferocity in a way that may cast light on how and why Scyld Scefing harried his neighbors and Hygelac undertook his fatal expedition, and, like many other sagas, it tells some of the circumstances under which men served foreign kings. It gives an unforgettable picture of a warrior rewarded (and consoled) by a king's gift of a gold arm ring, and it celebrates a hero who is a great poet as well as an utterly ruthless warrior, reminding us that a poet in Hrothgar's Heorot was probably also a warrior.

Njal's Saga is incomparably effective in eliciting a reader's sympathy for the problems of men and women in a society where loyalties to kin and/or lord and master entail the duty of vengeance, which leads to feuds as apparently impossible to settle with blood money as Grendel's feud with the Danes and as destructive to large clans as the feud between the Swedes and the Geats threatens to be to the Geatish nation. It shows Christians who are just as ruthless and vengeful as anyone in *Beowulf*'s pagan world— although the prime villain, Mord Valgardsson, is stubbornly unconvertible— and strong-willed women who give plenty of guidance, good and bad, to their men.

Carol Clover has demonstrated how the entire body of saga literature can illuminate scenes in *Beowulf* in "The Germanic Context of the Unferth Episode," but the sagas usually thought of as analogues are ones that use the same characters. Of course, many names mentioned in *Beowulf* also appear in other Old English works. Literary analogues in this sense include *Widsith* and *Deor*, especially the former because of the information it gives us about Breca, Finn, Hnaef, Offa, Hama, and above all the battle of Hrothulf and Hrothgar against Ingeld at Heorot. Both poems mention Eormanric, and *Deor* gives an important account of Weland. *Deor*, at least, is worth the time of a class of beginners, but not because it will give them information about two names mentioned in passing in *Beowulf*: the notes and/or glossaries of names in most editions of the poem provide background of this kind.

The Finnsburg fragment is also worth assigning for itself—as the only surviving "heroic lay" in Old English, and a very effective one at that—but also for the light it sheds on the Finn episode of *Beowulf*, both in giving some information about how the trouble there started and in providing a contrast to the *Beowulf* poet's concentration on the plight of Hildeburh. Of course it still does not tell us enough to make the situation really clear. Donald K. Fry's *Finnesburh Fragment and Episode* is now the first place to send students in search of background (and interpretive) material, but they should also be aware of the material in Chambers' *Beowulf: An Introduction to the Study of the Poem*. Advanced students should be able to find more recent contributions to the controversies that continue to rage around this episode, but a beginner may be more stimulated by Jill Paton Walsh's reconstruction of the story in her children's novel *Hengest's Tale*.

Those interested in research on the Ingeld episode will also find Chambers helpful, but a cautionary note must be sounded: the scenario given in part 1, section 5, suggesting we are to understand that Hrothgar and his brother Halga had killed Ingeld's father, Froda, is not borne out by all the evidence. The full picture, in all its hopeless confusion, is given by the excerpts in Garmonsway and Simpson's *Beowulf and Its Analogues* from *Langfeðgatal*, Skjǫldunga saga, Saxo Grammaticus, Sven Aageson, the *Series Runica Regum Daniae Altera*, and *Hrólfs saga kraka*. Unfortunately, the references are in two widely separated sections of this volume, some appearing under "Froda" and "Ingeld" in section 5 and others under "Healfdene" in section 2. It takes an experienced and intrepid researcher to make much sense of this collection of extracts.

Sigemund is an example of a more limited subject for which anyone may find Garmonsway and Simpson helpful. Still, there are two problems here: first, one of the excerpts refers to "Hermoðr" as a parallel heroic figure, as do those collected under the heading "Heremod." *Beowulf*'s Heremod is no such heroic figure and is contrasted, not coupled, with Sigemund; it is hard to see what a neophyte could make of this reference. A second problem is that the Norse versions casting Sigurd rather than his father Sigmund as the dragon killer are of considerably later origin than *Beowulf*, whatever date we finally assign to the Old English poem. Theodore Andersson's *The Legend of Brynhild* argues that Sigurd was originally a minor figure who was greatly elaborated and changed by the time the extant versions of tales about him were written. If so, a dragon-killing episode originally attributed to Sigmund might have been transferred to his son. Thus, researchers who think the Norse analogues closer to "the truth" may be misled.

We must also recall that the sagas are all of later date when we turn to the two most important analogues to the exploits of Beowulf himself, *Grettir's Saga* (c. 1325) and *King Hrolf's Saga* (*Hrólfs saga kraka*, c. 1400). The latter is the closest analogue in that its setting is the court of the Danish king Hrolf, *Beowulf's* Hrothulf, and its most prominent hero, aside from Hrolf and his father, Helgi, is Bothvar Bjarki, whose cognomen "Bjarki" means "little bear." The name is thus cognate with "Beowulf," presuming it to be a kenning meaning "enemy of the bee"—that is, bear. Other parallels include the fact that, like Beowulf, Bothvar comes to the aid of a Danish king plagued by a monster and assists the Swedish king Athils (Eadgils) against his rival Ali (Onela). In origin, he must be the same hero.

But the differences between *Beowulf* and *King Hrolf's Saga* are as notable as their similarities. Not only is the "bear" (and "bear's son") hero aiding Hrothgar's successor (to think of Hrothulf in the terms apparently intended by the *Beowulf* poet) rather than Hrothgar, but the details of his triumph come perilously close to being a parody of Beowulf's achievements. These details are evidently comic in intention as well as in effect. First, there is the almost slapstick comedy of the scene in which the hero, having arrived at court in Hrolf's absence, protects the abject coward Hott from the king's retainers. Hott is *not* shown as deserving our sympathy, nor are Bothvar's motives entirely altruistic. After he has slain the monster, who has wings and thus resembles a dragon more than a *þyrs*, and has given Hott a strengthening draught of monster blood, Bothvar contrives, by an elaborate and farcical charade, to make Hott appear to be the monster slayer.

Thus the slaying of the monster in the saga seems almost incidental to the story of how Bothvar rehabilitated Hott, who is celebrated in Norse analogues as a hero in no way inferior to Bothvar himself (see Gwyn Jones's full treatment of the saga and its analogues in *Kings, Beasts, and Heroes*). Further, *King Hrolf's Saga* is not a work centered on the deeds of "Bjarki" but an account of a by-then-legendary heroic age presided over by Hrolf, whom Norse writers thought of as an ideal king. As such, the saga has the sort of structure we are used to in works of the Arthurian and Charlemagne cycles in which the histories of other traditional heroes are made subsidiary to the story of the rise and fall of an ideal kingdom and its exemplary king.

Bothvar Bjarki, like Beowulf and Grettir Asmundsson, is a character of a distinctively different sort from most of those he associates with in that he is a manifestation of the internationally known folktale hero of the tale type known as the "Bear's Son," now classified, because of the content of later folktales of this pattern, as "The Three Stolen Princesses." Note that one of the Norse analogues to *Beowulf*, *Samsons saga fagra*, does involve a stolen princess. Students who wish to untangle folktale skeins that enmesh Beowulf, Bothvar, and Grettir should be referred to Aarne-Thompson tale types 301 and 650A; some of the features characteristic of heroic versions have been summarized by A. Margaret Arent in "The Heroic Pattern: Old Germanic Helmets, *Beowulf*, and *Grettis saga.*"

Although the hero of *Grettir's Saga* does not have a name that implies kinship with bears, he demonstrates that he is the equal of a bear in an early section of the saga where he deals with, successively, a group of twelve berserks ("bearshirts"), a bear, and a man named Bjorn 'bear.' Of his two later exploits that parallel Beowulf's battles with Grendel and his mother, the fight with Glam is most worth drawing to students' attention in detail because of the many striking parallels, including some on the verbal level. The later fight with a monster in a cave behind a waterfall does not have all the distinctive features of the episode in *Beowulf* that occur in some of the other analogues: it lacks the appearance of light and the hero's need for a prayer or vow to God before he can overcome his opponent, a feature to be discerned, if without explicit prayer, in *Beowulf* 1553–56. But a reading of the saga as a whole can be recommended as demonstrating an equally impressive, but entirely different, use of the same folk materials.

Analyzing a larger group of "Bear's Son" analogues can lead readers of *Beowulf* to observe what the poet retained of the many traditional features of the plot and to consider their usefulness to him. The traditional nature of the material may go some way toward explaining the sudden introduction of the hero's "Unpromising Youth" and the difficulty he has in subduing Grendel's mother. It can surely be argued that the partial retention of the motif of the desertion of the hero's companions, after they mistake his foe's blood on the water for his, gives an excellent setting for Beowulf's dramatic return to Heorot, and that Grendel's head and the sword hilt function as the recognition tokens found in many later versions of the tale type.

Translations of most of the sagas mentioned here will be found in the Works Cited; for others, see Donald K. Fry's bibliography *Norse Sagas Translated into English*. Not all relevant sagas are available in complete translations, but more will no doubt appear in the next few years. For the parallels in *Orms þattr*, see the complete translation in Simpson's *The Northmen Talk*: the excerpts in Garmonsway and Simpson's *Beowulf and Its Analogues* are insufficient to establish the hero as a "Bear's Son" figure. (He fits that category because his father is said to be a shape changer and he has the standard Unpromising Youth.)

Folklore patterns are not the only identifiable sources of *Beowulf*, which draws on a vast background of Germanic, Christian, and classical legends and traditions. Almost none of these, however, survives in any form we can demonstrate to have been certainly known by the poet. Only the Bible is indubitable: Genesis 4.1–12 is the ultimate (although not necessarily immediate) source of the references to Cain. There are other possible biblical

echoes, but none are incontestible, even the account of the Flood (1688–
93). Among other possible sources for particular passages, the close similarity
of the description of Grendel's mere (1357–76) to a passage in *Blickling
Homily* 17, deriving from the apocryphal *Vision of St. Paul*, suggests influence one way or the other or a mutual source.

The *Aeneid* has sometimes been thought to be a source or influence (e.g.,
Haber), but even the case for "influence" remains unproved. The *Iliad* and
Odyssey have also been suggested as sources (e.g., Klaeber cxviii), but they
are even less likely, although they have considerable interest as analogues.
Albert B. Lord has pointed out extensive parallels between the fight with
Grendel and Odysseus' blinding of Polyphemus and between Unferth's challenge and that given Odysseus by Euryalus in Phaiacia ("Beowulf and Odysseus"). Such coincidences are to be ascribed to long-standing, orally transmitted
traditions, as must echoes in other bodies of literature, myth, and legend,
such as those identified by Martin Puhvel in Beowulf *and Celtic Tradition*.
Other interesting analogues that may modify views of *Beowulf* continue to
be brought to light as scholars look further afield: an interesting recent
example is Earl R. Anderson's identification of more-or-less contemporary
Armenian accounts of swimming feats resembling "Beowulf's Retreat from
Frisia."

BEOWULF: ORAL TRADITION BEHIND THE MANUSCRIPT

John Miles Foley

The Scop. Although the opening three lines of *Beowulf* constitute as brief and general a proem as we are likely to encounter, they nonetheless tell us much about both the action to follow and the mode of its presentation.

> Hwæt, we Gar-Dena   in geardagum,
> þeodcyninga   þrym gefrunon,
> hu ða æþelingas   ellen fremedon!

> Lo, we have heard of the glory of the Spear-Danes in days past,
> Of the chieftain-kings, how these princes performed valor!

The tale is to be one of glory (*þrym*) and valor (*ellen*); the remembered accomplishments of Danish heroes are to be retold, the heroes themselves revivified in the time of the telling. And this apotheosis will take place under the aegis of the oral poetic tradition: "We have *heard*" the story before, and now, to fill out the ellipsis of tradition, we shall hear it again. Clearly, as even a first reading of the proem must indicate, at least some of the materials of the poem *Beowulf* are both oral and traditional.

This rough sketch of a singer, or *scop*, practicing his craft is elaborated by cognate descriptions throughout the poem, one of the most intriguing of which is the passage (867b–74a) that introduces the episodes of Sigemund and Heremod, type and antitype of the Germanic hero whom Beowulf is in the process of becoming.

At times the king's thane, a man covered with glory,
Mindful of tales, he who remembered a great number
Of the old sagas, found another word bound in truth;
In turn the man began to recite the story of Beowulf wisely,
And to utter with skill a fitting tale, to exchange words.

On the way back from the monsters' mere all who view the bloody tracks celebrate the past night's deeds, and the oral singer offers his own praise by setting Beowulf alongside his traditional brethren in the Germanic family of kings and heroes. As others have shown (Creed, " 'wel-hwelc gecwæþ,' " and Opland, "Beowulf on the Poet" and Anglo-Saxon Oral Poetry 202–05), we have in this vignette of the king's thane a poetic description of a singer practicing his craft. In drawing an implicit parallel with the dragon slayer Sigemund and an implicit contrast with Heremod, a sorrow to his people, the poet heaps the kudos of tradition on the hero of our poem. It is, in short, by "exchanging words" or telling the story of Beowulf at one heroic remove that the singer weaves together a characterization of the hero. In fact, we may note that this narrative nexus is paradigmatic of the whole skein of episodes and digressions in the poem: when our own "king's thane," the Beowulf poet, turns to another related story, we may assume that the analogous tale is, like those of Sigemund and Heremod, "bound in truth" to the main frame of the poem. Not only the epic as a whole, then, but also its parts are in this way eulogistic of the heroic tradition in general and of Beowulf in particular. To tell and retell the tales, to reformulate their parts, is to reincarnate the heroes whose exploits they commemorate: such is the epic tradition, oral or written.

Oral Traditional Theory and Structure. Of course, poetic accounts of cultural events or patterns are idealized descriptions and, no matter how evocative, cannot serve as ethnographic data. Not even Bede's much-discussed chapter on Caedmon's miraculous gift of oral composition (see *A History of the English Church and People* 250–53; Magoun, "Bede's Story of Caedman"; and Fry, "Caedmon as a Formulaic Poet" and "The Memory of Caedmon") can provide the kind of evidence we would require to pronounce our *Beowulf* an oral poem. So it may not be surprising that for many years passages such as the two treated above were understood primarily as imaginative cameos and that the notion of oral tradition was either ignored or cast comfortably into the mists of the irrecoverable past. But with the emergence of studies of Homeric Greek and Serbo-Croatian by Milman Parry and Albert Lord, and especially with the application of Parry-Lord oral theory to Old English poetry by Magoun and others, a much-argued transformation of attitude began (on the history of the field, see Foley, "Oral Literature" and "The Oral Theory in Context"). Just as the Sutton Hoo find made it impossible to pass off the Beowulfian descriptions of treasure and funeral practices as poetic embroidery on the real cultural fabric of Anglo-Saxon society, so the new school of oral-formulaic research soon made it necessary to consider the role of oral tradition in the composition and transmission of the poem.

Parry took his first steps in 1928 with his doctoral theses, two lengthy textual analyses of the *Iliad* and *Odyssey*. Defining the verbal formula as "an expression regularly used, under the same metrical conditions, to express an essential idea" (*The Making of Homeric Verse* 13) and demonstrating the recurrence and usefulness of formulaic diction, he was able to show that Homer composed in a special and artificial poetic language, an idiom that could have evolved only over generations under the active sponsorship of a tradition of bards. A few years later his more famous "Studies" articles argued that this tradition of verse making must have been oral, that Homer and Homer's forebears were singers who employed the same poetic language to compose in performance. In 1933–35 Parry traveled to Yugoslavia to prove his textual hypothesis in the living laboratory of Serbo-Croatian oral epic; by collecting and studying unambiguously oral narrative, he reasoned, one could learn by analogy about Homeric compositional techniques.

After Parry's death in 1935, his research was carried on and greatly enhanced by his collaborator and cofieldworker, Albert Lord. In 1953–54 Lord published the first two volumes of the series Serbo-Croatian Heroic Songs, original language texts and English translations of material recorded in Yugoslavia and preserved in the Milman Parry Collection at Harvard University (a series now grown to six volumes; see Lord and Bynum, and Bynum). In 1960 Lord's comparative study *The Singer of Tales* appeared, offering a comprehensive account of oral epic composition in Yugoslavia, and made the case for Homeric and medieval oral literature through an analogy with a living and observable oral tradition. Together with the writings of Magoun ("Oral-Formulaic Character" and "The Theme of Beasts of Battle"), Stanley B. Greenfield ("The Formulaic Expression of the Theme of 'Exile' "), and others, Lord's book ushered in a multidisciplinary new field that now includes literatures as diverse as Old French, Old Irish, Vedic Sanskrit, Chinese, Japanese, a great many African traditions, and black American folk preaching, among dozens more (Foley, "Oral Literature" and *The Oral-Formulaic Theory*).

The same burst of intellectual energy also instituted a polemic that continues to this day. The dialectic thus engendered may be formulated, in imitation of the old Homeric Question, as the Oral Traditional Question: given the existence of oral traditions somewhere in the background of extant texts in various literatures, are the texts that actually survive in manuscript themselves truly oral? Hard on the heels of this much-debated conundrum comes another: what are the implications of oral tradition for the interpretation of these extant poems, in the present case for *Beowulf*? These are immensely difficult problems, of course, and they cannot be profitably treated at any length in this format. Suffice it to say that there have been clever and even brilliant contributions on both sides of the question; witness, for example, Larry Benson's compelling demonstration ("The Literary Character of Anglo-Saxon Formulaic Poetry") that supposedly literate poets also composed formulaically and Alain Renoir's equally convincing description ("Oral-Formulaic Context") of the new and promising comparative context that oral-formulaic criticism encourages.

Outstanding and influential attacks on or modifications of the original oral-formulaic position with special reference to its use in Old English poetics include Claes Schaar, "On a New Theory of Old English Poetic Diction"; Robert D. Stevick, "The Oral-Formulaic Analysis of Old English Verse"; Michael Curschmann, "Oral Poetry in Medieval English, French, and German Literature"; Alan Jabbour, "Memorial Transmission in Old English Poetry"; William Whallon, *Formula, Character, and Context*; Ann Chalmers Watts, *The Lyre and the Harp*; and Geoffrey R. Russom, "Artful Avoidance of the Useful Phrase in *Beowulf, The Battle of Maldon*, and *Fates of the Apostles.*" The latest full-scale study is Jeff Opland's *Anglo-Saxon Oral Poetry*.

Our concern here, however, is with the effect of oral theory on the interpretation and teaching of *Beowulf*, and for this purpose we must concentrate on what is demonstrable if ambiguous—the oral traditional structure of the poem. Whether we consider Cotton Vitellius A. XV a performance record that is some manuscript copies removed from the transcription of a *scop*'s song or a literary text executed in writing with its ultimate roots in oral tradition, the structure of *Beowulf* is in part traditional at the level of both diction and narrative design.

The Formula. This tradition is perhaps most evident in terms of what Parry and others have called the "formula." In translating oral theory directly from ancient Greek and Serbo-Croatian, unfortunately omitting to make allowances for the idiosyncrasies of the Old English alliterative line (Foley, "Tradition-Dependent and -Independent Features in Oral Literature"), Magoun distinguished the formula or verbatim repetition from the "formulaic system," which Parry had defined as "a group of phrases which have the same metrical value and which are enough alike in thought and words to leave no doubt that the poet who used them knew them not only as single formulas, but also as formulas of a certain type" (*The Making of Homeric Verse* 275). In later writings, especially the works of Donald K. Fry ("Old English Formulas and Systems" and "Caedmon as a Formulaic Poet"), the system has been described as a generative template that in the process of composition yields a theoretically infinite number of formulaic phrases.

However one construes and defines units within the patterned phraseology, we can easily explain its usefulness as a poetic language by pointing out a striking similarity among the Homeric Greek, Serbo-Croatian, and Old English words for "word": Greek ἔπος (*épos*); Serbo-Croatian *reč*; Old English *word*. In these three traditional poetries, *word* may designate what we mean by our modern term for a single lexical element, or it may refer to a larger, more extensive unit, sometimes with a metrical definition, such as a half line or hemistich, a whole line, a speech, a scene, or even a whole poem. On being directly questioned as to the nature of a "word in a song" (*reč u pjesmi*), many Yugoslav singers respond with a whole line or some multiple of a line. The point is that the "building blocks" of traditional narrative can be perceived as units of utterance larger than our typographical words, metrically or narratively bound units that are available to the poet in tale-telling. Johannes Kail conceived of a traditional word-hoard (*Phrasenvorrat*) in 1889, and Eduard Sievers assembled a *Formelverzeichnis* for the Old Saxon *Heliand* in 1878, but the demonstration of the morphology and usefulness of these metrical and narrative "words" is the contribution of Parry, Lord, Magoun, and their followers.

We may understand how the scop's "words" work at the level of diction with two brief examples. Beowulf's speeches, for instance, are almost always introduced with the same whole-line formula: *Beowulf maþelode,   bearn Ecgþeowes* 'Beowulf spoke,   son of Ecgtheow.' In the Old English poetic tradition, however, whole-line phrases like this one are more the exception than the rule. More frequently, the formula expresses its essential idea in a half line or verse, and we may discern a generative system underlying a group of related verses. One example is the formulaic system _X_ under wolcnum (_X_ under the clouds), where the solid underlining indicates the constant part of the expression and the broken underlining the variable element. Phrases or metrical "words" that belong to this system include (Bessinger, *Concordance to the Anglo-Saxon Poetic Records*):

weox under wolcnum	grew up under the clouds
wan under wolcnum	dark under the clouds
Wod under wolcnum	advanced under the clouds
wæter under wolcnum	water under the clouds
weold under wolcnum	ruled under the clouds

The formulaic structure of the diction may be defined in other ways as well, by emphasizing the syntactic (Cassidy, "How Free Was the Anglo-Saxon Scop?") or metrical (Foley, "Formula and Theme in Old English Poetry") patterns, to mention two possibilities. But whatever method of taxonomy is chosen, it is evident that the *Beowulf* poet is composing in a traditional idiom; even if we conceive of him as a fully literate craftsman no longer a member of the oral tradition, we must deal critically with the special nature of his oral traditional phraseology.

But of what importance is the fact that *Beowulf* was composed in a formulaic language? Not a few critics of Old English and ancient Greek poetry have seen patterned diction as a constraint on creativity, a set of prefabricated forms that must stifle the poetic inspiration. Why is Beowulf, for instance, called only Ecgtheow's son? Would not an alternate epithet help to relieve the linguistic ennui induced by too much repetition? Here we encounter the most essential issue in oral poetics—the problem of meaning. Parry argued that an epithet, whether "swift-footed" Achilles or Hrothgar's characterization as "protector of the Scieldings," is useful to a poet composing in performance; presumably at least, it remains so for some time after the advent of writing. Parry also assigned the epithet a generic level of meaning, maintaining that the traditional element's most important responsibility was not to the immediate and fleeting narrative moment but to the continuity of the tradition as a whole. The denomination "Ecgtheow's son," for example, echoes not simply a standard filial relation but an entire mythic history, operating on the word-hoard as a patronymic metaphor. To varying extents and in various ways, all formulaic diction follows this metonymic rule of thumb: the familiar metrical "words" conjure a network of essential ideas, so that a poet and audience steeped in the telling of tales—and, to a lesser degree, the modern reader alive to traditional method—will experience the present poem against the backdrop of the poetic tradition.

The Theme. Much the same can be said of oral traditional structure at the level of typical narrative scenes or *themes*, which Lord defines as "the groups of ideas regularly used in telling a tale in the formulaic style of traditional song" (*The Singer of Tales* 68). As Lord first showed in "Composition by Theme in Homer and Southslavic Epos" and as has been illustrated subsequently in Old English poetry (summary in Foley, "The Oral Theory in Context" 79–91, 116–22), oral traditional narrative contains recurrent and multiform scenic units, such as arming for battle, speaking a boast, or fighting a monster. Although thematic patterns may vary in their details from one occurrence to the next according to the demands of the immediate situation, just as the formulaic system modulates under different conditions, the general sequence of ideas and at least some of the phraseology remain relatively consistent. Greenfield's "Exile," Magoun's "Beast of Battle," and David Crowne's "Hero on the Beach" are the most thoroughly documented themes in Old English verse, but there are many others, and some themes have been shown to have analogues in other traditions (e.g., Renoir, "Oral-Formulaic Theme Survival: A Possible Instance in the *Nibelungenlied*").

For an audience acquainted with the Old English word-hoard, such families of narrative patterns will engender a host of connotations and expectations. An obvious example in *Beowulf* is the theme of the sea voyage. As Lee C. Ramsey and I ("*Beowulf* and Traditional Narrative Song") have pointed out, the two actual episodes of seafaring to Hrothgar's court in Denmark and back home to Hygelac's domain are complemented by a third voyage: the ship-burial of Scyld Scefing at the poem's opening. Just as do the bona fide expeditions, the funeral depends on a basic sequence of elements: (a) the hero and his men go to the ship; (b) the ship waits, moored; (c) the hero's comrades carry treasure aboard; (d) departure, voyage, and arrival; (e) mooring the ship. Although all five elements are fleshed out in expected form during Beowulf's sea voyages, they undergo subtle changes in the description of Scyld's burial, as in the mode of the hero's leadership. Additionally, instead of the customary thematic closure involving the sighting of land and tying up of the vessel, the poet tells us that Scyld's was a journey into the unknown, that its destination is beyond mortal ken (50b–52):

> Men do not know
> to say truthfully, hall-counselors,
> heroes under the heavens, who received that burden.

Scyld's last rites are in this way a sea voyage. By synecdoche, the theme or "narrative word" uses the connotative power of reference to the word-hoard to create and then to modify an expectation. By virtue of the thematic pattern of sea journey that underlies this last and sorrowful voyage, the funeral reverberates with traditional meaning.

Pedagogical Applications. In seeking to recover the lost ambience of oral tradition that at some point provided a crucially important context for *Beowulf*, I customarily begin by reading passages aloud in metrical cadence and encouraging students first to listen and then to perform small selections themselves. There are also a number of fine recordings of *Beowulf* and other Old English poetry in the original language (e.g., discs and cassettes by Bessinger, Creed and Raffel, and Malone). Even if the students are to study *Beowulf* strictly in translation, I find it very useful to furnish them with a copy of the first page of the manuscript and a transcription while they listen to a performance of the lines there inscribed; this tactic helps to introduce the initially somewhat strange concept of oral tradition and makes later discussion of the implications of the concept more fruitful.

Study of those implications must start, in my opinion, with explanations of the formula and theme suited to the level of the course. Occasional references to these units in other poetries assist in illustrating the morphology of traditional units. At all points I stress the nature of "words" in oral tradition, sometimes composing or recomposing a passage in Old English (cf. Creed; "The Making of an Anglo-Saxon Poem") or Serbo-Croatian or ancient Greek through the compositional device of *wordum wrixlan* 'exchanging words.' What requires special emphasis is the poetic status of phrases, speeches, scenes, and entire poems as units of utterance, each with its structure and grammar. Students should be urged to think in terms of patterns rather than the inflexibility of typographical accuracy, in terms of traditional rather than modern units of expression.

From examples and descriptions of metrical and narrative "words" I turn to the bearing of oral traditional structure on the interpretation of *Beowulf*. I open by giving examples of the poem's formulaic diction, concentrating on the connotative force of epithets and other formulas of various kinds. Once students grasp the idea of a stereotypical phraseology that generates meaning not by its freshness of expression but by echoic reference to the word-hoard of tradition, it becomes easier and more productive to deal with the issues of characterization, cultural values, unity, and so on. In my experience it has proved most rewarding to focus on a number of heroic epithets and set phrases at the start, using (or asking advanced students to use for themselves) the Bessinger-Smith concordance to locate occurrences of formulas. Again, whether in Old English or in translation, it is a relatively simple matter, as well as a rewarding exercise, to sensitize a class to the presence and aesthetic implications of formulaic diction.

Although we have as yet no corresponding concordance of scenic units, thematic "words" can be studied in a similar fashion. I introduce the concept through the Sea Voyage multiform and continue on with examples of the Exile, Beasts of Battle, and Hero on the Beach patterns, furnishing handouts of relevant passages from other Old English poems for advanced classes. As with the formula, the first stage of investigation consists of sketching the morphology of a given theme: how does it adapt to different narrative environments and what are its essential ideas? For elementary courses I provide a schema and consider exemplary passages in translation; for graduate seminars I ask the students to construct their own morphologies after considering instances of a theme in the original language. With some notion of a multiform in hand, a class can then begin to assess the limits of expectation, connotation, unity, and design. Even if some critics would not term the monster fights three occurrences of a single typical scene, I find it pedagogically valid to use the concept to highlight the ritualistic aspects of heroic battle and to explain how in a traditional work variations played on a known theme take on a resonance unknown in modern literary works. In this connection, I am beginning to teach a computer to provide formulaic and thematic contexts for Old English, Homeric Greek, and Serbo-Croatian poems, so that the student or scholar reading any given passage will automatically be provided with parallel phraseology and narrative patterns as he or she proceeds through a text (Foley, "Editing Oral Texts").

Finally, depending on the level and particular aims of the course involved, I may ask students to gain a broader underpinning in oral tradition by consulting Lord's fundamental comparative study *The Singer of Tales* and a series of reserve books and articles, most prominently Parry's "Studies," my histories of formulaic theory in Old English ("The Oral Theory in Context" 51–91, 103–22, and *The Oral-Formulaic Theory*), some important shorter works (e.g., Creed, "The Making of an Anglo-Saxon Poem"; Benson, "The Literary Character of Anglo-Saxon Formulaic Poetry"; Lord, "Perspectives on Recent Work on Oral Literature"; Renoir, "Oral-Formulaic Context") and selections from anthologies on oral literature (Stolz and Shannon, *Oral Literature and the Formula*; Duggan, *Oral Literature*; Foley, *Oral Traditional Literature*). To complement these readings I play field recordings of oral epic from the Milman Parry Collection and from my own field work in Yugoslavia (see "Research on Oral Traditional Expression in Šumadija"), the latter of which I would be pleased to share with anyone interested. *Modern Greek Oral Heroic Poetry*, recorded in situ by James Notopoulos, helps to provide a fruitful comparative context and to offer the class another living analogue in oral tradition.

When teaching *Beowulf*, a daunting but fascinating task, I try to encourage among beginning as well as graduate students an open-minded and pluralistic approach. All of the methods described in this volume have their value and are best applied collectively. In recommending the approach through oral tradition, I would emphasize once again that one need not espouse this or that belief about the actual orality of our received text of the poem; adamant inflexibility on that score will only prove counterproductive in the present state of knowledge. What we must recognize, however, is the oral traditional heritage of *Beowulf*, and as responsible teachers and scholars we must strive to explain the aesthetic implications of that structure to our classes. In aspiring to that pedagogical fidelity, we may begin to revivify a text now more read than heard and in the process raise once more the sounds of *ellen* and the echoes of *þrym* at the traditional heart of this epic Anglo-Saxon poem.

SPECIAL APPROACHES

THE NEW RHETORIC: WRITING AS AN INSTRUMENT FOR TEACHING *BEOWULF*

Myra Berman

In spring 1980 I taught *Beowulf* in translation in an introductory-level "theme" course with an enrollment of fifty undergraduate nonmajors, mostly freshmen. The aim of the course was to define heroism by reading such diverse texts as *Beowulf, Sir Gawain and the Green Knight, Billy Budd,* and *Lord Jim.* A second aim was to develop a way in which "freely written" journals could be used to engage student interest in unfamiliar and challenging literature.

Free writing, as defined by Ken Macrorie (*Telling Writing*), is designed to overcome blank-page anxiety by encouraging writing-as-speech. I hoped to use it to encourage not just spontaneous but also critical thinking: to enable students both to discover texts as individual readers and to deal specifically with those texts in a workshop atmosphere.

I began the semester with four one-hour classes devoted to free-writing exercises. These introductory classes were essential, for most students trained to write conventional essays must be taught that writing need not always be formal and painstaking. We sat in a circle, produced ten-minute "pinballings" in which we wrote down whatever came into our minds, and then read these to each other and compared them. By the end of the fourth session most students had relaxed enough to write naturally and spontaneously and, more important, to talk to each other about what they had written.

My unit on *Beowulf* consisted of seven hour-long sessions:

Session 1 was devoted to an introductory lecture, in which I discussed the form and function of Anglo-Saxon poetry, as well as the historical and geographical elements in *Beowulf*.

139

Session 2 was a discussion of some values of Anglo-Saxon society as compared with our own, particularly religious attitudes and the importance of community. At the end of this session I assigned the first journal entry, a free writing in which the students were asked to react to the character of Beowulf: "Cite incidents to support each adjective you use to describe him. Try to see Beowulf through the eyes of the poet and the other characters. Then go beyond his actions and consider his motives."

Session 3 concentrated on the results of this writing assignment. The format, followed throughout this unit, consisted of two or three students reading their entries (usually two to five pages in length) while the rest of us listened carefully and noted those issues and ideas we wished to discuss. The initial entries, for example, stressed Beowulf's qualities as a warrior: his external appearance, his prowess and fortitude, and his almost detached military attitude toward his own men and the Danes. The students wrote about those incidents I'd hoped they would notice: the Unferth episode, the watchman's assessment of Beowulf, Hrothgar's reception of the hero, Beowulf's tactics in fighting Grendel, and Beowulf's total allegiance to Hrothgar as king and treasure giver as demonstrated by his willingness to avenge Aeschere's murder. Toward the end of this session, one student noted that we'd discussed Beowulf the warrior without ever characterizing Beowulf the king, so we decided to examine kingship at our next "seminar." I assigned the following journal entry: "Characterize Hrothgar, Hygelac, and Beowulf as kings. Take a close look at Hrothgar's speech to Beowulf, and try to build an interpretation of the poet's notions of kingship, old age, and wisdom." In this way the journal entries provided the text for class discussion—which in turn provided the topics for subsequent journal entries. This format, too, continued throughout the course.

Session 4 involved reading journal entries in which students noted how the young Beowulf's relation with Hrothgar in the first part of the poem parallels the old Beowulf's relation with Wiglaf at the end of the poem. They saw similarities between Hrothgar and Beowulf as wise but aging kings; they saw major differences in the way each man defined his responsibilities to himself and to his people. Several students were struck with the symmetry of both the characters and the incidents. They were even more struck by their failure to notice that blatant symmetry. I think this was the moment when the students realized that they all had the ability to analyze literature— that if they looked deeply enough below the surface, they could discover meanings on their own, at their own pace, stimulated by their own curiosities and interests. Most of them just needed an initial push. Occasionally, though, they required an insistent shove, as with the purpose of the digressions, which all of them had managed to ignore even while writing of the poem's symmetry. I therefore raised the issue at an appropriate point in discussion, and when none of the students could explain the function of the Finnsburg episode or the story of Sigemund, I asked them to write about it for our next class. Their third entry was "Write about how one or two of the 'less essential parts' of this poem fit into the whole."

Session 5 was devoted to a discussion of the digressions. Most students dealt with Sigemund, Finnsburg, Heremod, or the last survivor monologue. They had been able to find their own explanations as to how these particular digressions related to the main narrative. Most of the students realized that they were thinking superficially when they labeled these incidents as "boring and unimportant." Finnsburg bored them only because they hadn't taken the time to try to understand its purpose; the journal writing led to understanding, which led to appreciation. Since I was now satisfied with the students' ability to analyze digressions, I allowed them to return to the question of unity, especially as depicted by the placement of the three monster fights. They decided that their next assignment should be, "What was Beowulf fighting against in each of the three encounters? Why does he fight the dragon? If you were Beowulf would you have fought the dragon? Or would you have behaved as Hrothgar did and hope that a young Beowulf would rescue you and your people? Does Beowulf win or lose the dragon fight?"

Session 6 demonstrated how thoroughly engaged most of these students were. They wrote lengthy entries that focused on Beowulf's final battle. They cursed the slave although they realized that even if he hadn't awakened the dragon someone else would have. They condemned the deserters, claiming that they, the students, surely would have followed Beowulf. They praised Wiglaf, although they all wished he had spoken less and acted more quickly. But mostly they admired and pitied Beowulf. In their writings they tried to determine how much his sense of responsibility as king and his pride as warrior had affected his heroic behavior. By the end of this session we were all satisfied. But since our goal was to define heroism, I felt compelled to assign one final entry: "Name a modern hero/heroine and explain why he/she is heroic? How does this person compare with Beowulf?"

Session 7 consisted mostly of arguments among the students, since they could not agree on anyone else's choice of hero. One student's hero was another student's enemy. Anwar Sadat was the only figure comparable to this Anglo-Saxon hero whom none of them had cared about or understood three weeks earlier. This attitude persisted through the semester: no character equaled Beowulf—the mildest, gentlest, most human of heroes.

In integrating reading, writing, and talking I was trying to create an atmosphere in which self-teaching—primarily through the act of writing—could flourish. At some point during the *Beowulf* unit I realized that such a method would succeed only if I constantly demonstrated open-mindedness and respect for students' capabilities and beliefs. Specifically, I had to allow the journals to work by encouraging students to express and explore their own ideas. I did so by refusing to present answers, by assuring the students that they could find these answers for themselves. This was not always easy, for it involved relinquishing my role of authority figure while maintaining a subtle but strong control.

I renounced the traditional forms of authority by stepping down from the lectern and joining the circle. I could direct and focus this class in several ways: by assigning topics for journal entries until students had developed their own tactics for unraveling texts; by writing my own entries and "volunteering" to read when there was an issue I felt had to be raised; by challenging every unsupported statement a student made and insisting on a written reevaluation; by restricting writings and discussions to the issues at hand; by making sure that no single voice, including my own, dominated the discussions.

One disadvantage inherent in such a student-centered approach is that self-teaching takes longer. The seven hours I spent on *Beowulf* could undoubtedly have been reduced to three or four had I imparted information to the students. Since that first semester, I have learned to minimize the inefficiency by increasing (in subtle ways) my direction over journal assignments, which determine the content of class discussions. I stress the subtlety because it is essential to balance teacher control with student self-teaching. I know I must manipulate my students, but I must do so from my position in the circle.

One final point, especially important for those of us who teach medieval literature: we have the particular problem of asking students to read material they automatically perceive as irrelevant, anachronistic, often ludicrous. We enter our classrooms hoping that students will respond to beautiful, profound poetry or, in lieu of such a response, that our own enthusiasm for the material will be contagious. Sometimes the literature succeeds and sometimes our personalities engage the students' interest, but all too often both means fail. Part of the success of this method stems from the fact that neither the literature nor the teacher bears sole responsibility for stimulating students. My students voluntarily accept the challenge of "responsibility"—of being ready and able to respond—to a literary work, and they feel this way largely because of their journals. Here is one student's assessment of our unit on *Beowulf*:

> The class began with a book most of us were not at all enthusiastic about reading. We were asked to read *Beowulf* and then write freely

about its contents in a journal. These journals made it possible for me to get through the book. I wrote about how confused I was, and eventually I was able to figure out why, and then I could organize my thoughts. By the time I finished writing, I had been able to grasp some understanding of what I'd read. I usually found myself reading some of the book, writing whatever came to mind, and then discovering some meaning in that particular section. *Beowulf* would have been so discouraging if we hadn't been able to write our journals. Instead, it was interesting and exciting. I learned that I can understand, even enjoy, the most difficult book just by thinking about it in my writing. My only complaint is that I can't stop dreaming about that damned dragon.

Though they may not recall Hygelac or Wealhtheow for long, these students will not forget Beowulf the warrior-king and his heroism. They will read about modern heroes and compare them to Beowulf, whom they perceived as an exceptional man attempting to cope with real problems. Some thought he failed, others thought he succeeded, but all admired his struggle. And because they came to understand him through both emotional and intellectual engagement, they had no trouble recognizing universal values and ideals in this difficult and challenging poem.

VISUAL MATERIALS FOR TEACHING *BEOWULF*

Donald K. Fry

Most students picture medieval stories in terms of movies they have seen. Unfortunately for the Anglo-Saxonist, most such movies draw on standing Renaissance buildings, fifteenth-century French costume and armor, and Walter Scott's language. Students tend to see *Beowulf* in plate armor posturing romantically in front of a crenellated castle. The Anglo-Saxonist therefore needs to induce a visual reorientation from plate and stone to chain mail and wood. For such purposes, one picture may beat a thousand words, well, one thousand Modern English words anyway.

I begin all Old English courses with a slide lecture or two, later illustrate specific points with individual pictures, and occasionally bring reproductions and even original objects to class at appropriate moments. Slide lectures, or even talks from pictures in books or postcards, can fill in the necessary visual backgrounds. They can also provide a quick introduction to Germanic artistry; a few close-ups of the Sutton Hoo jewelry quickly dispel any notions of crudity. One glance at the last leaf of the *Beowulf* manuscript conveys to students the chancy nature of literary survival, as well as the flimsiness of our evidence of the past.

Objects and pictures can illuminate specific points in the text, such as the Coastguard's first glance at Beowulf's helmet:

> Eoforlic scionon
> ofer hleorbergan   gehroden golde,
> fah ond fyrheard,—   ferhwearde heold
> guþmod grimmon.

Boar-images adorned with gold, decorated and fire-hard, shined
over the cheek-protectors; the war-minded-one held life-guard over
the fierce-ones.   (Klaeber, lines 303b–06a; trans. mine)

Students can deal with this imagery better if they see a picture of boar
helmets from Benty Grange or the Torslunda plate. With a full-size repro-
duction of the Sutton Hoo helmet, the instructor can point out the gilded
boarhead terminals on each eyebrow, literally above the face mask or "cheek-
protector." One can physically demonstrate the puns in *ferh-wearde*, both
"life-" and "swine-guard," and in *grimmon* 'fierce-ones,' punning on *grim*
'mask, visor.' But the instructor should warn students of the seductiveness
of visual analogues; vastly different helmets might explain the features just
as well. Pictures also help to explain the construction of halls and the dragon
mound, material details of daily life (lyres, armor, horns, etc.), and the
geography of the episodes.

Many sources provide pictures and objects for the scholar's or the library's
collections. The University of Toronto Media Centre (121 St. George St.)
has an excellent videotape or 16mm film on the Sutton Hoo Ship Burial, for
sale or rental. One other visual rendering of *Beowulf*, hardly accurate historically but doubtless of interest to many students (and teachers), is the
Australian animated film *Grendel Grendel Grendel*. Adapted from the novel
Grendel by John Gardner, the film is designed, written, and directed by
Alexander Stitt, with voices of the characters rendered by Peter Ustinov
and others. Running time is ninety minutes.

Most coin dealers specializing in "Ancients" can supply Anglo-Saxon pen-
nies or *stycas*. Many hobby shops carry plastic model kits of Viking ships,
usually rather souped-up in details; and some offer more austere wooden
models. The British Library sells a cardboard kit of the Sutton Hoo helmet
and silver facsimiles of two of the Byzantine bowls, as well as forty-one
Sutton Hoo slides and various Anglo-Saxon postcards for reasonable prices.
(Write to British Library Publications, 46 Bloomsbury St., London WC1B
3QQ, for a catalog.) I obtain many fine illustrations free by saving postcards
sent by friends and by clipping pictures from advertisements or dust jackets.

Formal slide lectures convey a great deal of information in a short space,
but they require equipment and preparation time. For single pictures to
illustrate a point, I use several methods. A small manual projector can show
a few slides on the classroom wall or even on the ceiling. Students can view
one slide at a time by passing around a hand viewer. I often mount single
pictures on black cardboard in a plastic sleeve. For small classes, students
can cluster around an illustration in a book.

Most colleges have a photographic service that will produce slides from
books for a reasonable fee, but I save money and hand-tailor the presentation

by making my own slides. Anyone who can take a picture can do such photocopying with simple equipment. You need a single-lens reflex camera, two photoflood lights, either an invertible elevating tripod or a copystand, and a close-up lens attachment: copyrings, supplemental lenses, a bellows, or a macro lens. Any camera dealer can teach you how to use this equipment, and Kodak issues easily understood booklets on the subject. I will furnish simple instructions on request. For photographic klutzes, Kodak also makes a gadget called the Ektagraphic Visualmaker Camera Outfit, which automatically defines the area copied, the focus, and the lighting; you just stand it on the picture and click it.

Scholars may have to relax their usual standards a little in choosing pictures for *Beowulf* courses; for example, the Oseberg ship dates much later than the poem's events but may represent the poet's idea of a splendid vessel. Furthermore, the least likely sources often contain the best color pictures and reconstructions. David Wilson's admirable *Archaeology of Anglo-Saxon England* has duller pictures than his popular *The Northern World*, and my favorite slides tend to come from children's books. Roy Gallant's *National Geographic Picture Atlas of Our Universe* (10) has a dandy painting of Germanic cosmology—hokey, but students like it. More important, they understand it.

The following pages give a personal selection of pictures I find useful for *Beowulf* courses, keyed to a bibliography of handy sources. For most items, I list multiple examples, generally in color but some in black-and-white. For me, one Anglo-Saxon word is worth a thousand pictures, but the pictures do illuminate the words and the world of *Beowulf*.

Sources for pictures (* = most useful):

*	A.	Almgren, B. *The Viking.*
	B.	Anker, P. *The Art of Scandinavia.* Vol. 1.
	C.	Backes, M., and R. Dölling. *Art of the Dark Ages.*
	D.	Branston, B. *Lost Gods of England.*
*	E.	Bruce-Mitford, R. L. S. *Aspects of Anglo-Saxon Archaeology.*
*	F.	———. *The Sutton Hoo Ship-Burial: A Handbook.*
*	G.	———. *The Sutton Hoo Ship-Burial.* Vol. 1.
*	H.	Davidson, H. R. E. *Scandinavian Mythology.*
*	J.	Dixon, P. *Barbarian Europe.*
	K.	Gibbs-Smith, C. H. *The Bayeux Tapestry.*
*	L.	Graham-Campbell, J. *The Viking World.*
*	M.	———, and D. Kydd. *The Vikings.*
	N.	Green, C. *Sutton Hoo.*

P.   Grohskopf, B. *The Treasure of Sutton Hoo.*

Q.   Jessupp, R. *Age by Age.*

R.   Jones, G. *History of the Vikings.*

S.   ———. *Kings, Beasts, and Heroes.*

T.   Kidson, P. *The Medieval World.*

U.   Kirkby, M. H. *The Vikings.*

W.   Kotker, N. *The Horizon Book of the Middle Ages.*

X.   Magnusson, M. *Viking Expansion Westwards.*

Y.   ———. *Vikings!*

Z.   Mitchell, S. *Medieval Manuscript Painting.*

AA. Oxenstierna, E. *The Norsemen.*

AB. ———. *The World of the Norsemen.*

* AC. Rice, D. T. *The Dawn of European Civilization.*

AD. Simpson, J. *The Viking World.*

AE. Stenton, F. M. *The Bayeux Tapestry.*

AF. Unstead, R. J. *Invaded Island.* Vol. 1.

AG. Wilson, D. M. *The Archaeology of Anglo-Saxon England.*

* AH. ———. *The Northern World.*

AJ. ———, and O. Klindt-Jensen. *Viking Art.*

(Abbreviations: p. = page, fig. = figure, front. = frontispiece, pl. = plate.)

Sutton Hoo site: *F* front.; *G* figs. 92, 107; *P* p. 16; *Q* p. 59; *AF* p. 38.

Sutton Hoo plan: *E* pl. 17; *F* fig. 3; *G* fig. 111; *N* fig. 9.

Sutton Hoo helmet: *E* figs. 27–30, pls. 47–49; *G* pl. K; *J* p. 94; *AG* pl. 8.

Sutton Hoo sword: *E* pl. 8; *F* fig. 9, pl. D; *G* pl. G; *N* pl. 24; *P* p. 97.

Sutton Hoo clasps: *C* pl. 45; *F* pl. F, pl. 34; *G* pl. F; *H* p. 73; *N* pl. 25; *P* p. 72; *T* pl. 1; *AC* p. 246.

Sutton Hoo buckle: *F* pl. E; *G* pl. E; *N* pl. 20.

Sutton Hoo purse: *C* p. 46; *F* pl. G; *N* front.; *S* pl. 5; *T* pl. 1; *AC* p. 246.

Sutton Hoo coins: *D* fig. 54; *F* pl. 27; *G* pl. A; *N* pl. 21.

Sutton Hoo shield: *H* p. 59; *N* pl. 11–12; *P* pp. 86, 90–91; *AG* pl. 7.

Sutton Hoo dragon: *H* p. 59; *S* pl. 4.

Sutton Hoo horns: *P* p. 93.

Sutton Hoo spoons: *F* pl. 25a; *G* fig. 437; *N* pl. 19.

Sutton Hoo hanging bowl: *F* pl. 8; *P* p. 83.

Sutton Hoo lyre: *D* fig. 39; *E* pl. 40–42, 44; *F* pl. 10–11.

Sutton Hoo whetstone: *E* fig. 9, pl. 1; *F* fig. 5, pl. A; *G* fig. 432; *J* p. 94; *AH* p. 73.

Sutton Hoo stand: *E* fig. 1; *F* fig. 4; *G* fig. 433.

Shield wall: *K* pl. 37; *W* pp. 10–11, 44; *AE* figs. 62–63.

Vendel warrior: *A* p. 230.

Vendel arms: *S* pl. 16.

Vendel helmets: *D* fig. 84; *J* p. 119; *U* p. 34; *AB* pl. 48; *AC* p. 221; *AD* p. 110.

Valsgärde helmets: *L* p. 15; *AH* p. 129.

Agilulf helmet: *J* p. 74; *W* p. 15; *AC* p. 163.

Benty Grange helmet: *D* figs. 93–94; *E* pls. 63–67; *H* p. 99.

Torslunda plates: *B* pls. 86–89; *E* pls. 58–59; *AD* p. 138.

Norse weapons: *R* pl. 6; *AD* p. 120; *AH* p. 139.

Mailshirt: *K* pl. 29; *AE* pl. 40; *AF* p. 51.

Snartemo hilt: *B* pl. 18; *S* pl. 1; *AB* pls. 32–33; *AC* p. 229; *AH* p. 133.

Seax: *D* fig. 21; *AG* pl. 4a.

Spears: *A* p. 225; *AD* p. 112.

Odin: *B* pl. 154; *H* p. 29.

Thor: *B* pl. 154; *H* p. 65; *R* pl. 23; *X* front.; *Y* p. 12; *AD* p. 163; *AF* p. 49.

Frey: *B* pl. 98; *H* p. 55; *M* fig. 40; *R* pl. 22; *AD* p. 165.

Loki: *H* p. 121.

Valkyries: *H* pp. 46–47; *AA* fig. 115; *AD* pp. 54, 172; *AH* p. 142; *AJ* pls. 24c–24e.

Dragon slaying: *Z* pl. 67.

Nydam ship: *D* fig. 17; *J* p. 47; *AC* p. 224; *AF* pp. 26–27.

Gokstad ship: *A* pp. 9, 246; *M* fig. 6; *R* pl. 14, fig. 25; *X* facing p. 64; *Y* p. 35; *AA*
figs. 5, 101; *AB* pl. 56b; *AC* p. 225; *AD* p. 66.

Oseberg ship: *A* pp. 257–58; *B* pls. 34–35; *D* fig. 18; *H* pp. 83, 86; *J* p. 121; *Y* p. 23;
AA fig. 88; *AC* p. 225; *AD* p. 70; *AJ* pl. 4.

Bayeux ships: *G* fig. 320; *J* p. 136; *K* pl. 41; *L* p. 63; *AE* pl. 8.

Halls: *J* pp. 61, 111.

Trelleborg fortress: *B* fig. 34, pls. 58–59; *H* p. 17; *L* p. 206; *U* p. 127; *AB* pl. 63; *AD*
pp. 122–23, 125; *AF* p. 45.

Cheddar: *J* p. 114; *Q* p. 55; *AG* fig. 2.20, pl. 11.

Kings enthroned: *K* pl. 11; *W* p. 43; *Y* p. 307; *AC* p. 258; *AE* pl. v; *AF* p. 67.

Banquets: *K* pl. 44; *AE* pl. ix.

Franks casket: *D* figs. 1–5, 74; *H* pp. 60, 73; *AA* figs. 14–15; *AH* pp. 30–31.

Sigemund carving: *B* pls. 220, 222, 224; *H* p. 95; *R* pl. 28; *S* pl. 6; *AC* p. 237; *AD*
p. 115; *AH* p. 26.

Neck rings: *B* pls. 19–20, 75, 77; *C* pp. 56–57; *H* p. 99; *J* p. 118; *M* fig. 58; *S* pl. 5;
U p. 33; *AB* pls. 29b, 43–44; *AC* p. 231; *AH* p. 133.

Arm rings: *A* p. 198; *L* p. 111; *M* figs. 18, 53, 59, 81; *X* p. 13; *AA* fig. 67; *AB* pl.
39b.

Kingston brooch: *C* p. 44; *AC* p. 247; *AH* p. 76.

Finglesham buckle: *E* pl. 53b; *H* p. 106; *AD* p. 139.

Jewelry mold: *A* p. 142; *L* p. 187; *R* pl. 18; *U* p. 166; *AH* p. 20.

Maps: *A* p. 163; *E* fig. 8; *L* p. 11; *M* fig. 2; *P* p. 116; Klaeber p. viii; Fry *Finnsburh* p. x.

Beowulf manuscript: *S* endpapers; Zupitza-Davis passim; Kiernan passim.

Hickes transcript: Fry *Finnsburh* front.

James Campbell's *The Anglo-Saxons*, which arrived too late for analysis above, contains many excellent, colorful pictures.

WOMEN IN *BEOWULF*

Alexandra Hennessey Olsen

As may be exemplified by the introduction to E. Talbot Donaldson's translation, traditional interpretations and pedagogical approaches have stressed that *Beowulf* is a heroic poem, focusing on a male hero as he matures from youth to age and promoting masculine values. The traditional critical interpretation views *Beowulf* as a two-part poem focusing on such themes as the youth and age of the hero and the beginnings and ends of dynasties (see Tolkien, "*Beowulf*: The Monsters and the Critics"). The women of the poem have been considered largely irrelevant to the main action thereof, and, consequently, students interested in studying the roles of women in literature believe that *Beowulf* is not worth studying. A serious problem results because, to borrow Alain Renoir's comment about the use of translations in the classroom, "the future of this part of our tradition may well depend on our making certain that what . . . [students] see does not automatically steer them away from the Middle Ages in general and Old English in particular" ("The Ugly and the Unfaithful" 168). Students interested in women need not automatically be deflected from Old English studies. As F. M. Stenton has said, "there is no doubt that Old English society allowed to women, not only private influence, but also the widest liberty of intervention in public affairs" ("The Historical Bearing of Place-Name Studies" 1). Recent research has reinforced Stenton's opinion that the women depicted in documents extant from the Old English period possessed "an impressive independence and influence" (Dietrich 32; see also Judd). The problem therefore lies not in the literature but in our limited approaches to it as teachers.

150

The solution to the problem may be found in recent attempts to reexamine Anglo-Saxon life for ways to read and teach *Beowulf*. Many critics argue that art—including literature—is "the product of a particular cultural milieu, sometimes embodying a society's most deeply held convictions, sometimes questioning these values, sometimes disguising an artist's own ambivalence with regard to these matters, but never disengaged from the claims of time or social order" (Diamond and Edwards ix). A brief review of recent scholarship suggests that interest in the Old English poetic depiction of women is rising (see, e.g., Kliman). Elaine Tuttle Hansen has pointed out that although "the romantic attractions of women were of no literary interest, poets were nevertheless far from disregarding other qualities belonging to the female half of their world" (117). Renoir has reinterpreted *Genesis B*, arguing that "Eve may have fallen because she was intelligent enough to follow a logical argument" and suggesting that "if mediaeval studies had been initiated by female scholars nurtured on the early Germanic tradition rather than by male scholars nurtured on French and monastic traditions, it might conceivably be that the official teaching today would assert that the Middle Ages unexceptionally assumed the intellectual superiority of women" ("Eve's IQ Rating"). Most important for the study of *Beowulf*, Jane C. Nitzsche has argued that the poem has been misinterpreted by critics who ignore the importance of Grendel's mother.

In contrast to Tolkien and those who have followed his lead, some scholars have suggested that *Beowulf* has three sections (see Nitzsche; H. L. Rogers, "Beowulf's Three Great Fights"; and Kathryn Hume, "The Theme and Structure of *Beowulf*"). One advantage of reading *Beowulf* as a tripartite poem is that so doing gives appropriate weight to the middle, which depicts both human women and Grendel's mother.

Nitzsche points out that, like Grendel and the dragon, Grendel's mother is "described in human and social terms. She is specifically called a *wif unhyre* 'terrible woman' . . . and an *ides āglǣcwif* 'the lady, the valiant warrior-woman'. . . . In addition, as if the poet wished to stress her maternal role, she is characterized usually as Grendel's *mōdor* 'mother' or 'kinswoman' " (288). In order to understand the women of the poem, one must understand the word *ides*, since Wealhtheow, Hildeburh, and Modthryth, as well as Grendel's mother, are so described. Helen Damico has studied the word and has argued that it represents the dual role of the valkyrie—benevolent and malevolent—in Germanic legend. She concludes that the *ides aglǣcwif* should be compared to "the *idisi* of the Merseburg charm and the *dísir* of ON [Old Norse] literature" (152) because Grendel's mother is "an abstract rendering of the battle-demon" (153). In contrast, Modthryth "is a specific personage" who also represents "a baleful valkyrie figure," and the "sympathetic queens" represent the valkyrie in her beneficent aspects (153, 163).

Because Grendel's mother is depicted as a woman, we are automatically expected to compare her to the human women of the poem. According to Nitzsche, the section of the poem dealing with Grendel's mother has two parts; in the second, "Hygd and Freawaru contrast with the *wif* as queen or cup-passer as Hildeburh and Wealhtheow contrasted with Grendel's dam as mother in the first" (296). Grendel's mother is introduced after a long passage that depicts two mothers, Wealhtheow and Hildeburh, concerned about the fates of their children. In the Finn episode, Hildeburh mourns the loss of her son and brother in battle, and immediately thereafter Wealhtheow worries about the fate of *hyre byre* 'her sons' (1188b). It is linguistically appropriate that Wealhtheow should worry about her *byre*, because the noun is related to the verb *beran* 'to bear' and refers to sons perceived from the mother's point of view; the use of *byre* thus reinforces the picture of Wealhtheow's maternal concern. I should like to suggest that it is significant that the poet makes no mention of the existence of Grendel's mother until after the passage in which he depicts two mothers, one sorrowing for a lost son and the other worrying about possible future danger to the sons she bore; by describing three sorrowing mothers, the poet gives us the point of view of Grendel's mother before he describes her effect on the men with whom we normally sympathize. Grendel's mother is *yrmþe gemunde* 'mindful of misery' (1259b), and the poet manipulates our sympathies so that we see her more as a woman deprived of her protectors than as a monster.

The exact emphasis that one places on the actions of Grendel's mother varies depending on one's perceptions of two related terms, *freoðuwebbe* 'peace-weaver' (1942a) and *friðusibb* 'peace-bond' (2017a). Nitzsche suggests that "the role of woman in *Beowulf* primarily depends upon 'peace-making,' either biologically through her marital ties with foreign kings as a peace-pledge or mother of sons, or socially and psychologically as a cup-passing and peace-weaving queen within a hall" (289). Larry K. Sklute, however, has argued that *freoðuwebbe* does not refer to the historical practice of making a royal marriage to "settle the enmity between warring tribes" (537). He points out that the word is not used in the passages of *Beowulf* that describe such a marriage and that it is used in *Elene* to describe an angel who bears a message from God. Nitzsche argues that *freoðuwebbe* is a passive epithet and that the *Beowulf* poet stresses "that a kinswoman or mother must passively accept and not actively avenge the loss of her son" (291). In contrast, Sklute assumes that it is a more active epithet: "The compound 'freoðuwebbe' expresses the duty of the king's wife (or of the King's messenger in *Elene*), to construct bonds of allegiance between the outsider and the king and his court. If it reflects anything of the social system of the Anglo-Saxons, it is that of the diplomat"(540).

If one agrees with Nitzsche that the woman's role in Anglo-Saxon society was passive, then one will agree with her contention that the "masculine aggression" of Grendel's mother contrasts to "the feminine passivity of both Hildeburh and Wealhtheow" (291–92). In addition, one will tend to agree with Hansen's contention that the women of *Beowulf* provide "a poetic voice for all lonely and innocent victims of fate, and an apt symbol . . . of the weakness inherent in the human condition" (117). If, however, one agrees with Sklute that women in Anglo-Saxon society played an active role comparable to that of diplomats, one is not so surprised to find Grendel's mother assuming an active role in the poem.

Dietrich argues that "the disparity of modern treatments underscores the necessity of going directly to the primary sources. In some cases this involves stripping away the accretions of another writer's bias or orientation, and asking new questions of very old records" (33). One useful way to go "directly to the primary sources" is to study texts from other Germanic cultures, as scholars like Damico have done, although one should bear in mind Jeff Opland's warning that scholars have assumed "too readily that there was absolute uniformity within the various Germanic . . . traditions" (*Anglo-Saxon Oral Poetry* 19). In the Icelandic sagas, a woman does not usually seek vengeance personally; in *Laxdaela Saga*, Aud, who wears breeches and goes, sword in hand, to avenge herself on the man who divorced her, is exceptional. Nevertheless, the role that the women play cannot be considered passive. In *Laxdaela Saga*, the women remember the death of their kinsmen and goad the male members of their family to seek vengeance. Thorgerd, for example, reminds her sons of their duty as avengers and later accompanies them when they seek vengeance for Kjartan, overruling their objections: "They tried to dissuade her, saying that this was no journey for a woman. But she insisted on going—'For I know you well enough, my sons, to realize that you will need spurring on.' So they let her have her way" (Magnusson and Pálsson 185).

Grendel's mother is called by nouns normally reserved for males—for example, *secg* 'man, warrior' (1379a) and *wrecend* 'avenger' (1256b)—and she is referred to by masculine pronouns; her portrayal therefore links her to women like Aud and Thorgerd, each of whom adopts the role of a warrior. Some women depicted in Old Norse poetry also act like warriors. In *The Waking of Angantyr*, Hervor goes alone at night to her father's grave to ask his ghost for the sword Tyrfing in order to avenge his death; she takes the sword even though her father prophesies that so doing will "doom" her son

(Terry 252). Similarly, in *Atlakvitha*, Gudrun, who avenges her brothers' murders by killing her husband Atli and his retainers, gains the approval of the Eddic poet:

> The tale has been told.   Never since that time
> has a woman wrought   such revenge for her brothers;
> three great kings   Gudrun the fair
> sent to their deaths   before she died.   (Terry 216)

The active roles played by Thorgerd, Aud, Hervor, and Gudrun resemble that of Grendel's mother, both when she invades Heorot and when she drags Beowulf *to hofe sinum* 'to her hall' (1507b) and tries to kill him *hire bearn wrecan* 'in order to avenge her son' (1546b). Note also the role of Hildegyth in the Old English *Waldere*. In one of the extant fragments, Hildegyth *hyrde hyne georne* 'encouraged him [Waldere] greatly' (Dobbie, *The Anglo-Saxon Minor Poems* 4, Magoun and Smyser, *Walter of Aquitaine* 1) as Thorgerd encourages her sons while they fight Bolli. In contrast is Hildegund in the Latin *Poem of Walter*, who is called "the timid girl" (Magoun and Smyser 36) and who is not present during the battle. Unlike Hildegund, who reflects monastic values, the women of *Beowulf* reflect heroic values.

Whatever the exact emphasis they choose to place on the role of women in *Beowulf*, all the critics cited herein agree on the importance of women in the poem. Teachers should make that importance equally clear in the classroom. When I teach *Beowulf* in the original (to a class of graduate and advanced undergraduate students), I assign various scholarly and historical essays. I place two anthologies of *Beowulf* studies (Lewis E. Nicholson's *An Anthology of* Beowulf *Criticism* and Donald K. Fry's *The* Beowulf *Poet*) on library reserve. Among the essays that I assign are Renoir's "Point of View and Design for Terror" to accompany Grendel's approach to Heorot and Robert E. Kaske's "*Sapientia et Fortitudo* as the Controlling Theme of *Beowulf*" to accompany Hrothgar's sermon. Because the recent research on women has not been anthologized, I lend copies of the articles to the students. Wealhtheow is introduced in line 612b, and at that point I assign Stenton's "The Historical Bearing of Place-Name Studies" and Dietrich's "An Introduction to Women in Anglo-Saxon Society." Since Wealhtheow is described as *goldhroden* 'gold-adorned' (614a), I assign Damico's study "The Valkyrie Reflex in Old English Literature." I assign Nitzsche and Sklute to accompany lines 1255b–1569b, the passage describing the attack made by Grendel's mother on Heorot and Beowulf's fight with her. In addition, class discussions of linguistic matters include the meaning of *ides* 'semi-divine lady' and the normally masculine referent of *wrecend* 'avenger.'

Most of the students who read *Beowulf* in the original have had a term of introductory Old English. When I teach both courses, I plan them as a unit and assign works in the introductory course in order to provide a reading context for *Beowulf*. (I use Cassidy and Ringler's *Bright's Old English Grammar and Reader*, which contains major Old English texts.) Because of the amount of linguistic material to be mastered, I assign little secondary reading in the course. The first section involves studying the grammar and the brief readings provided therein by the editors, and the length of this section varies depending on the students; the second section involves reading texts. For prose, I assign the tale of Cynewulf and Cyneheard, which provides a good introduction to heroic values, and Bede's story of Caedmon. For poetry, I assign *The Dream of the Rood*, *The Battle of Maldon*, *The Wanderer*, and *The Wife's Lament*. Because the *Lament* depicts "the sufferings of a woman when for various reasons the social order has failed to support and protect her" (Hansen 112), I assign Hansen to accompany it. Then I assign some riddles and sections from *Maxims II*, including lines 43b–45a about the *ides*. I also give a handout of lines 63b–65b, 81a–92b, and 94b–106b of *Maxims I*, which are a "poetic enumeration of the virtues, privileges, and duties of Anglo-Saxon femininity" (Hansen 111). The last poem read in the course is *Judith*, which provides a useful introduction to the women of *Beowulf*. Because of the time constraint, I usually assign it in shortened form (lines 1a–235b). I recommend that students read Damico and Nitzsche, because Damico argues that Judith is a valkyrielike warrior-woman who is analogous to both Wealhtheow and Grendel's mother, and Nitzsche (295–96) views Judith's encounter with Holofernes as similar to that between Beowulf and Grendel's mother.

It is more difficult to teach *Beowulf* in translation than in the original because translations necessarily obscure both the meaning of a word like *ides* and the fact that a noun like *wrecend* normally refers to a man. I never assign secondary reading in an undergraduate class, because the articles are too highly specialized for the students. I find it useful, however, to summarize some of the important articles, because the students are interested to learn that *Beowulf* is not merely of antiquarian value but is indeed a work that merits serious modern scholarly investigation. In the medieval and Renaissance section of the University of Denver's Freshman Coordinated Humanities Program, I arrange the reading list in order to teach changes in the concepts of the hero, of tragedy, and of women. I begin with Cynewulf and Cyneheard (Whitelock, *English Historical Documents* 162–63) and then assign Icelandic works that depict men of heroic stature and women who are active, assertive members of society, *Laxdaela Saga* (Magnusson and Pálsson) and *The Waking of Angantyr* and *Atlakvitha* (Terry). Although they are of later date than the Old English works, they reflect an older form of

Germanic society and were unaffected by monastic writings that viewed women as inferior to men. As a contrast, I next assign *The Poem of Walter* (Magoun and Smyser 4–37) to show what happens when heroic material is written from a monastic point of view. I conclude the early medieval portion of the course with short Old English poems, including *The Wife's Lament* and *Judith* (Raffel, *Poems from the Old English*; Robert K. Gordon, *Anglo-Saxon Poetry* could be used if one prefers prose translations) and *Beowulf*.

The anthology that my English department uses for the sophomore survey course is Hazelton Spencer, *British Literature*, volume 1, which includes only works (like *The Battle of Maldon*) that do not provide a good context for teaching about the women in *Beowulf*. I therefore assign Raffel in order to teach *The Wife's Lament* and *Judith*. In addition, I provide a handout of passages about women from *Laxdaela Saga* (principally those portions of chs. 53–55 and 60 in the translation of Magnusson and Pálsson that describe the way in which Thorgerd and Gudrun each urge their sons to seek vengeance) and sections of *Atlakvitha* and *The Waking of Angantyr* (Patricia Terry, *Poems of the Vikings*) that illustrate the Norse idea of the warrior-woman.

It seems to me that the pedagogical approaches represented by Spencer's anthology, which omit women from Old English literature, do a great disservice to our discipline. Students come to believe that this literature is of no interest to modern women and thus develop a mistaken idea of the shape of English letters. If one uses modern scholarship about women in Anglo-Saxon society and Old English literature, one can increase the number of courses in which *Beowulf* can be taught and therefore introduce more students to the poem. Specifically, *Beowulf* can be incorporated in a course called "Literary Images of Women's Lives." Although some instructors include medieval works in such courses (Susan Schibanoff, "The Crooked Rib"), too many courses match the description given by the University of Denver: "The development of women's lives in 19th- and 20th-century American fiction." Such courses may be broadened by beginning with *Beowulf* and *Judith* and including works by authors like Chaucer, Shakespeare, and Defoe. It seems to me that often the students who take an English course or two to satisfy their humanities requirement are those who most need to be introduced to the tradition of Western letters but who are least likely to take any course that advertises itself as outmoded, outdated, and irrelevant. By including *Beowulf* in a course in literary images of women's lives, one is able to obey Renoir's injunction "to do what must be done to find ways of saving the tradition of letters" ("*Vox Clamantis*" 16).

TEACHING *BEOWULF* AS PERFORMANCE

John D. Niles

Students encountering *Beowulf* in Old English for the first time labor to read it as a text. They study it as they might have studied their *Aeneid* or any other monument of the world's early literature: with a glossary and with detailed textual and interpretive notes, supplemented by the instructor as needed. In its original and primary mode of being, however, *Beowulf* was not a text to be painstakingly pieced together. It was a fluent sequence of words. Like any dramatic or semidramatic performance, it was a communicative event shared for a few hours between a listening audience and a speaker or singer proficient in the arts of verbal mimesis. It existed in a living context, not in isolation, particularly not in isolation on the page.

In teaching *Beowulf* to a mixed group of graduates and undergraduates, I encourage students to keep in mind this concept of the poem as a performance. When we read the text aloud, as we regularly do, I ask my students to imagine that they are hearing it performed in an Anglo-Saxon hall or monastery. There is no mystique about this approach. We do not dress in tunics or sip mead. We simply listen to the words and their alliterative music, we absorb the rhythms of the verse, and we are attentive to the inflections and pauses of a natural speaking voice.

When students take the text home with them, I again ask them to read the text as a means of listening to it, in their mind's ear, however foreign it may sound to them at first. When they use their glossaries and notes, I ask them to be aware that they are studying the poem as it was never studied in Anglo-Saxon times. What they are studying is not the poem but only a written trace of the poet's words. They are reading footprints in the sand after the bird has flown. Once they have studied the footprints in scrupulous detail with the detachment of scientific observers, I ask them to close their eyes for a while and imagine the bird in flight.

Although such a procedure may at first seem frivolous, it is actually less so than to read the poem as if it had been meant to be read in an armchair or cunningly dismembered in a university classroom. Our understanding of *Beowulf* will be on a sound footing to the extent that we can discover how the poem was heard by an audience of Anglo-Saxons. Debate over the fine points of Old English meter, for example, will help our understanding only to the extent that it will help us read the poem aloud smoothly. Smoothness does not imply mechanical perfection. One of the defining characteristics of oral poetry is that it does not scan, as anyone knows who has transcribed a tape-recorded song that was not learned by rote. The many textual emendations to *Beowulf* that have been adopted *metri causa* can be dispensed with when one considers the text as the record of a performance.

Neither do the poem's narrative anomalies survive a reading of the poem as performance. What is anomalous to a reader is often unnoticed by a listener. In traditional narrative poetry that is performed aloud, each scene has its own integrity regardless of what is said or left unsaid elsewhere. The story is time-bound. Each scene is self-consistent and is to be interpreted only with reference to itself and the controlling themes of the story. When the *Beowulf* poet introduces the idea of a curse on the dragon's treasure, for example, he is not obligated to go on to specify that the curse had an effect. Scholars who worry about the curse are reading the text, not hearing it. In performance, the curse has our attention for a moment, and then the poet goes on to other things. The curse is forgotten; in effect, it has ceased to exist. To cite another example: when Beowulf returns to his homeland and recounts his Danish adventures to Hygelac, the poet is not obligated to repeat the earlier account with verbatim consistency. He introduces new details and speaks of Freawaru and her role at the feast, of Ingeld and the Heathobards, of Grendel's dragonskin glove, and of Hrothgar's abilities as a singer and harpist. Instead of troubling over these inconsistencies, students who approach *Beowulf* as performance will recognize them as freedoms of the sort that any storyteller will take.

A skilled storyteller will know how to assume the voice of different actors. Unferth's whining voice and Beowulf's emphatic voice, we may imagine, would be clearly distinguished in performance. Hrothgar's dignified voice would be vested with authority, especially in his long homiletic speech after the hero has killed Grendel's mother (1700–84). Just before the address, the narrator calls attention to the quiet in the hall: *swigedon ealle* 'they all fell silent' (1699b). In oral performance this aside serves as a signpost telling listeners to prick up their ears. The audience is invited to partake of the same silence that reigns in Heorot, as it were. The narrator's voice then begins to merge with Hrothgar's. Each member of the listening audience is encouraged to take the king's wisdom to heart. "You take heed by this," Hrothgar and the narrator say. "In the wisdom of my old age I have spoken these words about you!" (1722b–24a). In oral performance, Hrothgar's address has an immediacy beyond what is possible for most readers encountering a mute text on the page.

The fitt divisions can have a key role in hearing the poem as well. Few editors draw attention to these divisions, all of which are marked by Roman numerals in the manuscript, yet they are significant if, as I suspect, they are traces of the singer's pauses or guidelines for pauses. Their placement can influence the poem's effect on listeners by letting certain messages or images reverberate in silence.

An example is the division between lines 2693 and 2694 (numeral XXXVII). Here, with a sense of timing that can only be called masterful, the narrative is suspended just after the dragon's jaws have closed around Beowulf's neck. The hero's blood wells forth in waves, and until the singer resumes his story the dragon seems triumphant. Another suspenseful pause occurs at division XII (between lines 790 and 791). As Beowulf holds Grendel fast in a grip of superhuman strength, the monster lets forth an unearthly howl that resounds from wall to wall and leaves the Danes in terror. Here too the action is suspended with the plot unresolved. Other pauses promote a horrific detail. At division XXIV (between lines 1650 and 1651), four of the Geats have just brought Grendel's severed head to Heorot. As they carry the grisly token in to the bench where Hrothgar and Wealhtheow are sitting, "the men looked on" (*weras on sawon*). The poet adds no further comment. Also frequent is the pause that sets off an emphatic moral or gnomic judgment. Examples are the silences that follow the "Christian Excursus" of lines 178b–88 (*Wa bið . . . wel bið . . . !*) and Wiglaf's ringing condemnation of the cowardly Geats: "Death is better for any man than a life of shame!" (2890b–91). One of the most significant fitt divisions falls soon after the hero's laconic last words. The narrator first looks forward to the flames of the impending funeral, then comments on the destiny of Beowulf's spirit: "From his breast his soul departed to seek out the judgment reserved for the righteous" (2819b–20). The fitt division that follows permits a silence, heavy with regret and sorrow, that encompasses the sense of exaltation one feels in the presence of the blessed dead. If the divisions do represent pauses, the poet thus raises and lowers the curtain of his little theater with some awareness of dramatic effects.

In these and many other ways, the poem becomes more nearly its true self when encountered through the ear rather than through the eye. Teachers and students who believe in a cloistered *Beowulf* poet writing out his text for a select group of readers will have little use for the approach I am recommending. For them the text will suffice. Those who adopt the more likely view that poems of this kind had a central role in the enculturation of Anglo-Saxon princes, thanes, and perhaps some churchmen, will find their appreciation of *Beowulf* enhanced when they make an effort to hear it as it once was heard, in its austere grandeur, by people who were so close to the poem as to need no text to mediate it.

FORGERIES AND FACSIMILES:
PALEOGRAPHY WITHOUT TEARS

Jess B. Bessinger, Jr.

When my students visit London they like to stalk Grendel and his mother in the monsters' current habitat, in Bloomsbury. Once I was at the British Museum with a student who had never seen the *Beowulf* manuscript. She bent over the glass case to peer closely—the book treasures in that room, which contains also precious versions of the Magna Carta and the King James Bible, are not brightly illuminated.

"I didn't expect it to seem so small," she said. "Zupitza seems larger, I suppose, because of the wide Oxford margins and the binding. Oh, it's the A-scribe—the folio they have open is in the first scribe's hand." Her eye picked up the alliterative patterns; she began to read aloud to herself, as scribes and readers of the Dark and Middle Ages would have done, part of Hrothgar's speech to Beowulf about Grendel's mere. She attracted a small but attentive group of listeners, perhaps as much because of the delighted wonder in her voice as for the Anglo-Saxon sounds. Few members of her accidental oral audience had been trained, as she had, to copy (that is, to forge) Anglo-Saxon facsimiles and thus at least haltingly to comprehend some things about the original manuscripts.

Most students outside England have no opportunity to read Old English manuscripts in their original parchment or vellum, and no facsimile, however well represented in the Zupitza-Davis (1959) or Malone volumes or even photographically transformed in glowing autumnal impressionist colors like the frontispiece in Kiernan, can provide the access to paleography and codicology that an editor must command. Only "direct and prolonged access" to the manuscript can do that, as Kiernan asserts (xiii). This is true of the best and clearest manuscripts—at some point in the course, students ideally should look at facsimiles of the other three major Old English poetic codices and perhaps perform short exercises based on them—but it is especially true of a martyr-text like the *Beowulf* manuscript, a book damaged by age, dirt, scribal mishaps (pens blot, scribes nod), fire, water, the bookworm, and a good deal of human mishandling.

"Palaeography cannot be learnt from lectures, from books, nor even wholly by studying facsimiles. Even the best reproductions (collotype plates) give only one point of view. It is essential to go to the manuscripts themselves *and to transcribe them*; for there is a craft in correct transcription not to be learnt from books" (Denholm-Young 5). Still, even a beginner in Old English poetry needs to have enough knowledge of English insular hands to follow critical discussions of manuscript readings intelligently; weighty decisions rest on small details. Currently scholars are still debating the date of *Beowulf*, with a possible range extending from the seventh to the eleventh century (Chase, Kiernan). Some of the evidence they are debating can be found in facsimiles. All that is needed is a little encouragement to the student to study these facsimiles, which is to say to read and transcribe them, using ordinary paper for vellum, ordinary washable black ink in the absence of a good carbon black and gall recipe, and an ordinary Osmiroid or other commercial italic pen instead of a goose quill.

My students pursue this exercise to different levels of achievement; I will discuss the most common level later. But making a copy of an ancient writing is either mere play or a mere drill unless something can be done with the copy. There are some twenty purely mechanical or subjective stylistic additions to or changes in the first sentence of *Beowulf* in Klaeber's edition. Not counting lineation and the imposition of an arbitrary medial caesura between each verse pair, one notes punctuation, hyphenation, individual decisions about capitalization, macrons for vowel quantity, and changes of word spacings that are not in the manuscript or any facsimile of it. After the first page or two, this kind of mechanical modernization would seem tedious to most students. What they really want and need to do is to edit the manuscript, or a part of it, and to make important decisions along with trivial ones. Language, prosody, and deep matters of poetry go with editing. A first-year Beowulfian may not get far, but the first steps count.

Before my beginners look at facsimiles, their patience is tested with what some might think cruel and unnecessary treatment: they are forced to confront the tyranny of modern poetic typographical format. A poem is supposed to look a certain way. It is discomforting that Old English poetic facsimiles do not resemble poems. But any modern poem is equally at the mercy of conventions, editors, and critics. Let students become at ease with the notion that Old English and modern orthographic rules, or the lack of them, are each the equivalent of the Mikado's arbitrary game: "On a cloth untrue / With a twisted cue / And elliptical billiard balls."

Modern editorial rules for the printing of any poetry, including of course Old English poetry, are conventional and determinative. One learns quickly from facsimiles (or manuscripts) to note details like capitalization and the lack of it, words divided or joined falsely or significantly (students may be made aware of Stevick's *Beowulf: An Edition with Manuscript Spacing Notation*), abbreviations and contractions, long and short *s*, odd and occasional punctuation, the Tironian sign for "and," and the like. For paleographic perspective, students can be assigned first readings in a handbook like Denholm-Young's, which contains a short history of ancient and medieval paleography with collotype plates of English and Latin handwriting. Some will enjoy looking at a recent popular guide, *British Literary Manuscripts, Series I: from 800 to 1800*, and some may find it amusing to introduce Old English scribal traits into, say, F. J. Child's ballad no. 169, the B-text (*The English and Scottish Popular Ballads*, vol. 3):

"Johnie Armstrong"	*Beowulf*
SAID JOHN FIGHT ON MY MER	HWÆT WE GARDE
ry menall. i am a lit	na. inȝear dagum. þeod cyninȝa
tle hurt bt I am not slaī.	þrym ȝe frunon huða æþelingas el-
I will lay me do forto bleed	len
a while then ile rife &	fre medon. Oft scyld sccfing sceaþena
fightwith you a gain	þreatum monegū mæȝþum meodo
	setla
	of teah eȝsode eorl syððan ærest wearð

The ballad's "do" needs expansion to "down," as the *eorl* 'nobleman' in *Beowulf* 6 must be emended to *eorlas* 'noblemen' or *Eorle* 'Heruli' or whatever; the *f* in the ballad's "rife" is masquerading as a long *s*. Or let someone make an arbitrary scribal transcription from Tennyson's *The Princess*, which will lead the class into a classic Beowulfian controversy. Let the transcriber be a little careless with minims and ligatures this time.

> sweetis everysound sweeter thy voice but everysound is sweet myriads of rivulets hurrying through the lawn themoan of doves inimmemorial elmsthe mur mur ing ofinnumerable bees

Myriads of minims meandering down the page might lead to a quick look at *Beowulf* 1382 in facsimile, where editors are still having trouble with, and arguments about, a minim or two. A minim is of course merely a single downstroke made by the quill, but in sequence minims may be puzzling and pregnant. Does our poem here have *wundini golde* or *wundmi golde*, the first word to be either retained or emended to *wundnum* or *wundun* (for *wunden*) and the phrase so made to mean "with twisted gold"? But the editor's choice here, working one minim at a time, may date the poem sometime before about A.D. 750 or sometime in the eleventh century. The most interesting discussions of this matter will be digestible for any students not made nervous by minims; Chase and Kiernan will lead them into engrossing side explorations from the dating of the poem to questions of politics, religion, language, style, and the history of poetry.

Students are now ready to forge manuscripts. Teaching amateur scribes their trade is a good exercise for the teacher of *Beowulf*, who must contrive to guide students through several categories of new knowledge more or less simultaneously: elementary paleography, with a survey of ordinary Old English orthographic phenomena; the distinguishing and reproducing (by hand, later on a typewriter or word processor) of the special characters (though exotic forms like thorn and wynn will cause less trouble to beginners than some forms of *a* and *e*); the prosody of *Beowulf*, a polemical science and to some an impenetrable mystery even beyond the end of the first semester; and at last to where we began, with the problem of making the original folio look agreeable on a modern page. Some students find the usual modern Old English printed page a bit too conventional and try to find alternative arrangements for the Old English lines. For instance, the wide-spaced caesura between verse pairs would disappear if some of my students had their way. It serves no purpose, they argue, since the verse pairs are recognizable via prosody, and a caesura often violates modern syntactic sense with an obtrusive space in lines like, *Đæm eafera wæs æfter cenned* 'To him an heir was [caesura] later born.'

At any rate, students arrive at such considerations through the transcription of facsimiles. I give them a dittograph that looks something like the following; they go on eventually to make a hundred-line "edition" from their own *Beowulf*-facsimile transcription after comparison with several modern editions. On the final examination they normally encounter a facsimile or a diplomatic transcript of one to edit and scan.

Beowulf: Paleographic & Metrical Exercise I

Starting with the Zupitza-Davis facsimile, make an Osmiroid transcription of *Bwf* 32–42; from this, by identifying alliterative verse pairs, write out a tentative raw poetic edition without capitals, punctuation, etc., and with contractions expanded, then test your raw edition by scanning it. On a third page present your finished edition.

To repeat, your exercise should consist of three pages: your copy of Zupitza-Davis, your scansion verifying the verse pairs as recognizable Old English poetry, and your new edition of the lines. For scansion, I suggest you mark your lineated raw text with measure bars, supra-segmental stress marks, and initial rests if called for. Identify the verse types with marginal Sievers letters. That is, you may try to scan the poem by combining and simplifying the theories of Sievers and Pope. For the first two verse pairs you should have something like this:

B | ⌣ þǽr ǽt | hýðĕ stód | hríngeð | stéfnǎ   A

A | ísiǧ aňd | útfús | ǽðélingĕs | fǽr   E

With this assignment sheet, I provide a checklist of metrical rules, options, suggestions, and potential headaches. These are arbitrary, based on my sense of Sievers and Pope. Other teachers will wish to improve on this kind of exercise, and many will quarrel with details in it. Of course many will teach another scansion, often their own. All would agree, I hope, that some introduction to prosody must accompany an introduction to paleography, since in Old English the two are inseparable.

The pleasures and challenges that arise from their study lead straight to the original manuscript, currently preserved in a glass case in Bloomsbury. How pleasant to contemplate it and know that you have at home a forgery of it—a misrepresentation without malice, "a source of innocent merriment," in fact, especially since the choice of a broad nib incongruously replaced the first scribe's thinner, more delicate Caroline hand with the thicker Anglo-Saxon minuscule of the second scribe. A facsimile of such a forgery appears on the cover of the paperback version of this volume. It was made by this year's best and busiest student scribe.

THE WORDS

Stephen A. Barney

Your audience, both few and unfit, at least offers the challenge of variety: the surly graduate student meeting an ancient requirement called Philology, which your colleagues won't abolish lest they seem less scholarly than thou; the fey freshman whose Aunt Melinda said he must take Old English (she thought it meant Chaucer); the poet, suspecting as he hears in early classes about Bede and Grimm's law that Ezra Pound misled him; the panphilological woman whose grandmother taught philosophy at Bryn Mawr, fitting you in between advanced Greek and introductory Arabic, contemptuous of your learning; the passive English major whose faculty adviser, yourself, recommended the course; the linguist, required by his department to wax diachronic awhile, stunned by your Victorian idea of grammar; the earnest English major (such once was I) who wishes to read it from the beginning; the dear souls who took Chaucer and want to be medieval; the not insubstantial mass—there he sits, in the front row—of those who, because you are charming and devoted and inspiring, want to take whatever you teach. What can you give this pied muddle of mind?

A great deal, and much of it will be surprising. We are lucky in the rich diversity of topics we can treat in our tiny field, those six little volumes of poems, that shelf of prose. Most students want to take a course that repeats a course that they have had before: we all resist change, and few things are as painful and humiliating as learning something new. Initially our task is to keep Old English from looking too new. We can, first of all, assure the students that they will get an A: unique among English courses, Old English requires only sustained application, a mere diligence. Even a good graduate student, during a semester in which he is trying to impress Helen Vendler with his sensitivity to Yeats's drama or to overwhelm Stephen Orgel with his command of Renaissance magical lore, can breathe in the quiet tedia of our accretive course with relief. You don't have to be clever, just learn the words and figure out the syntax. No big essay.

But the teacher must be bold, must allow a wild profusion of materials to ensnare the diverse intransigencies of the customers. You must delight in disorder and leave loose ends for the sake of higher ends. You must condone, even foster, the amateurism you will meet (your colleagues will never know). Let the linguists discover their latent urge to do a close reading of *The Wanderer.* Perhaps the refined Keats man will keep in the closet his dark masochistic craving to reckon up all the cases in *Beowulf* of type C verses whose second halves are filled by the preterite endings of weak class II verbs. That man, a schoolteacher taking a year off to get his master's, perhaps he will use the Russian he learned in the army to compare the oral bases of Old English epic and Russian folktales. And her—is she a nun?—she will observe that Wiglaf is an anachronistically ninth-century sort of theologian. This one, a politician bent only on passing his Ph.D. orals, doubts the date of the Ruthwell cross or concludes that the Sutton Hoo spoons are really eggcups. That one, a frustrated rabbi, suspects that Sisam was right after all and plunges into comparative koine studies. This angry tennis player wants to write poems as a safe backup career: to her, some of von Schaubert's emendations seem feckless. Bede calls *that* a conversion? asks a psych major. Surely, they say, the ones with any spirit, surely Sievers was wrong (and they are wrong). So they are becoming—this is the Platonic land of Becoming. who is perfect in these arts? who wants to be?—literary critics, linguists, religious historians, anthropologists, archaeologists, Teutonists, meterites, an oral formulaity.

One of them, call him Vico, plunging rapidly into *Beowulf*, having looked up *Hwæt* and *Gār-Denum* in the back of his Klaeber, comes on *gēardagum.* Vico looks it up. *Gēar-dagas*, says Klaeber, are "D A Y S of Y O R E." Now "spaced small capitals indicate direct modern representatives," whereas non-spaced small capitals are merely related words; therefore "days" and "yore" are direct reflexes of *dagas* and *gēar-.* Vico's eye stumbles up a little to *gēar* 'Y E A R' and *geāra* 'of Y O R E,' which Klaeber says is the genitive plural of *gēar.* Here beginneth game.

Tired and jaded as we are, we must make the grand assumption that something about this process intrigues Vico. I don't know why it should. One can survive with the attitude of Ken Baumbach of San Diego, who wrote to *Newsweek* on 9 August 1982 that such questions as "How did the Norman Conquest affect the English language?" are "not only ludicrous and irrelevant to surviving in the world (or college), they were also not taught at the high school I went to." One can survive with certain basic knowledge—how to eat, sleep, get a mortgage, procreate, surf—with never a thought about our prime human instrument, our language. But Vico and you and I, we are intrigued. Our eyes roll to the ceiling, our stomachs rumble, our feet jiggle: we are distracted, we are curious.

Vico has more than curiosity; he has a memory. The next day you begin class as usual, shouting "Hwæt!" and you elicit a translation of the opening lines of *Beowulf*. Vico raises his hand. He may ask:

1. Why doesn't *gēardagum* mean "in yores of days"?
2. Would you run over it again why /yuh/ and /guh/ alliterate?
3. Remember that word *yesteryear* in *The Lone Ranger*? Can we translate *in gēardagum* as "in yesteryear"? Is *yester-* related to *year*?
4. Remember that line *þæt waes geāra iū* last semester [i.e., *Dream of the Rood* 28, cf. *Wanderer* 22], "that was long ago." Does that *iū* (= *geō*) mean "yore" too, or what? Does *ago* come from *iū*?
5. Hey, is *year* the same as *yore*?
6. What does it mean in the glossary that *yore* is from the genitive plural of *year*?
7. If *year* and *yore* are both from *gēar*, why are they different now?
8. Are *year* and *yore* related to one of those Grimm's law things too?
9. Why does he put the long mark on the *e* in *gēar* and on the *a* in *geāra*?
10. I can see [in fact, Vico cannot yet see] how *year* comes from *gēar*, but how does *yore* come from *geāra*?

Your first reaction may be that Vico is more trouble than he is worth. He does not wear cufflinks, he eschews the comb, his posture . . . , his voice. . . . Furthermore, you cannot answer his question. If you try your usual ploy ("Well, what do *you* think of Vico's question, Susan?") the class may react badly, the question so obviously demands facts beyond Susan's ken. In fact, your proper response is to juggle and bounce the question.

You juggle the question by telling what you know of the answer, sketching out whatever general principles seem to apply. You probably even know the answer to the first two-and-a-half questions. *Gēardagum* is not "yores of days" because in English, then and now, the first base of a compound specifies or qualifies or possesses the second base; the first base, like a genitive or an adjective, could be omitted. *Hogwash* is a kind of wash; a *washhog* would be a kind of hog. On /yuh/ and / guh/ it is probably enough to convince the students that the /k/ sounds in *keep* and *cool* differ—they are allophones of the same phoneme in complementary distribution—and that the g's in *Gār* and *gēar-* must have been treated as allophones, at least in earlier Old English (not in *Maldon*), at least for purposes of alliteration, just as we now would treat the different /g/ sounds of *gear* and *goon* as apt for alliteration. And sure, you can translate *in gēardagum* as "in yesteryear," but you should be aware that you will put your readers in mind, not of the Spear-Danes, but of the thundering hoofbeats of Silver.

For the rest, your ignorance will require more severe juggling. You may know (question 4) that *iū* is also spelled *geō*, that it means "ago," and (remembering your Chaucer) that *ago* is related to "go" (shortened from *agon* 'passed by') and not to *geō* or *gēar*. Thinking fast, you may recall another adverb or two that ends with -*a* (*fela*, *sōna*, *tela*), and you might guess (question 6) that these were once genitive plurals too (you would be wrong). You might speculate (question 7) that *year* and *yore* have their different vowel sounds now because the different placement of the macron (*gēar* v. *geāra*) indicates a falling diphthong in *gēar* and a rising diphthong in *geāra* and that the latter went the way of most long *a*'s in Middle English (south of the Humber), to a long *o* (like *stān* to *stōn*).

You can answer a few of Vico's questions, and you can juggle a few others, but mainly you have to bounce, that is, refer the students to resources outside the classroom. You cannot, if you wish to deserve the name of teacher, simply punt. For bouncing, you need to have at tongue tip the names of a few basic reference books. Own as many as you can afford, make certain that your library owns them all, and have them available, some on a reserve shelf. The basic books to own are *The American Heritage Dictionary of the English Language* (with Calvert Watkins' appendix, "Indo-European Roots"); Alistair Campbell's *Old English Grammar*; the *Oxford English Dictionary*; Holthausen's *Altenglisches etymologisches Wörterbuch* (which refers to Walde-Pokorny's *Vergleichendes Wörterbuch der indogermanischen Sprachen*); Jordan's *Handbuch der mittelenglischen Grammatik*; Bosworth-Toller's *Anglo-Saxon Dictionary*; Pokorny's *Indogermanisches etymologisches Wörterbuch* (an improved revision of Walde-Pokorny); and Brunner's *Altenglische Grammatik*. Encourage your students to buy *The American Heritage Dictionary* and (not of definitive authority, but good, delightful, and easy to use) Partridge's *Origins*. To these basic materials may be added Clark Hall's *Concise Anglo-Saxon Dictionary* (which usefully refers Old English words to the proper entry in the *OED*); Luick's *Historische Grammatik der englischen Sprache*; Wright's *Old English Grammar*; the new *Microfiche Concordance to Old English*, edited by Richard L. Venezky and Antonette di Paolo Healey; the Bessinger-Smith concordances to *Beowulf* and to the Anglo-Saxon poetic records; the etymological dictionaries of Klein and Onions (English), Holthausen and Feist (Gothic), Kluge (German), Walde-Hofmann and Ernout-Meillet (Latin), Hofmann and Frisk (Greek); and Buck's *Dictionary of Se-*

lected Synonyms in the Principal Indo-European Languages (entertaining). Further useful bibliography is best obtained from the bibliographies of these books.

Perfect Old English casteth out fear; but what of its teacher, who has small German and Latin and no Gothic and Greek at all, who doesn't know Sanskrit from macramé? That is, what about you and me, call us Casaubon? Casaubon is the resident medievalist, but his specialty is the *Pearl* poet and Old French lyric; he teaches Old English because he likes it and he learned it in graduate school. Is Casaubon expected to prowl through Feist's *Vergleichendes Wörterbuch der gotischen Sprache mit Einschluss des Krimgotischen und sonstiger zerstreuter Überreste des Gotischen* when, without benefit of clergy, he can only make out the title with a dictionary? The answer is, yes. For some time Casaubon will have, in fear and trembling, to fake it, but I think it a true principle that prolonged and assiduous faking will result in authentic competence. Besides, most of these hard books are dictionaries, which present the words Casaubon is after in a language (Old English) that he knows; furthermore, they repeat each other endlessly. The obvious strategy is to start with the easy ones (*OED*, Onions, Partridge, *American Heritage*, Campbell) and work out from there. Before teaching his first class in Old English, Casaubon would do well to work a couple of interesting words through these books. Ideally, he traces a word's history and form from a reconstructed proto-Indo-European root to Modern English.

Now Casaubon (perhaps having made up a sheet for his students, "How to Find Out about Old English Words") can send Vico to the library. Here are a few of the things Vico learns about *gēar* and *geāra*. The Indo-European root **ei-* has a sense, "go" (cf. Latin *eō* 'I go'). *Perhaps* this root is the basis of an extended form represented as **iēro-* (Pokorny) or **yēro-* (Watkins) meaning "season, period, year" (presumably because the "going" of time makes a "period"). From **yēro-* (in its o-grade form) derive the Greek words *hōros* 'year' and *hōra* 'period, year, hour, season' (our *hour*, by way of French, is from the Latin *hōra*, akin to the Greek—so "year" and "hour" are from the same root, brought to us through different language groups). Watkins connects the species of pickle *gherkin* with this root, but I cannot recommend Casaubon's setting his students the exercise, "What have pickles to do with time?"

The root **yēro-* appears in many Indo-European languages, and by regular sound changes it yields in primitive Germanic a neuter noun, **jǣrom* 'year.' This reconstructed word is the basis for words meaning "year" in several Germanic languages (German *Jahr*, Gothic *jēr*). From **jǣrom* to Old English *gēar* is easy: the *j* is practically the same as the *g*; the *ǣ* regularly goes to West Germanic *ā*, which goes to West Saxon *ǣ* (but to *ē* in other Old English dialects), and this *ǣ* is diphthongized after the palatal *g* to *ēa*; the *r*, the only sensible graph in this whole mess, remains the same; the -*om* ending drops away. In late West Saxon the *ēa* was smoothed to an open *ē*, and in the other dialects by 1100 the *ē* was narrowed to a long open *ē*, both regularly spelled "e." These Middle English long open *ē*'s were raised to the [i:] sound of "year" by the early eighteenth century. This vowel is often spelled "ea" in Modern English, a graph reintroduced into English by Anglo-Norman scribes.

Yester- and *geō* appear to be unrelated to *gēar* or *geāra*.

But when we come to *geāra* itself, we run into problems. Its development into "yore" is easy enough—you have juggled it already—but whence *geāra* comes, nobody knows. The other Germanic languages have no cognate adverb. Klaeber follows most of the authorities (Skeat, Bosworth-Toller, Wright, Holthausen, Campbell, Clark Hall, Klein, and, with a "perhaps," *The American Heritage Dictionary*) in saying that *geāra* is an adverb formed on the genitive plural of *gēar* (whose genitive plural is, indeed, spelled "geara"). Campbell says, "The adv. *ġeāra* is usually assumed to have the phonological *eā*, as its semantic development to 'formerly' has removed it from the influence of *ġēar* 'year' " (sec. 185, n. 2), and elsewhere he says *ġēara* (so spelled) is from the genitive plural of *ġēar* (sec. 666). On the other hand, the *OED* simply says (under "Yore") that *geāra* is "of obscure origin." The Sievers-Brunner grammar (sec. 317) includes *geāra* among a group of adverbs (like *fela, gīena, geostra, sōna, singala, tela*) with an -*a* ending (from primitive Germanic -*o*, from the Indo-European ablative ending -*ōd*). The Holthausen group assume that the genitive plural form *ġēara*, with a falling diphthong, became adverbial in sense, at some time was felt to be a separate word, and shifted its vowel to the rising diphthong *eā* (the difference is roughly that between the vowels of "yare" and "yard"), which accounts for the modern word "yore" (which would otherwise have been "year"). But the evidence for the formation of adverbs on genitive plurals of nouns is slim (Wright, sec. 557); it amounts to the observation, reasonable enough but of unsure significance, that *geāra* has to do with time and so does *gēar* and that the words look alike.

These uncertainties have induced wavering among recent editors other than Klaeber. In her *Beowulf*, Else von Schaubert lists *geāra* under the headword *gēar* as a genitive plural with adverbial meaning. Sweet-Whitelock's *Reader* and C. L. Wrenn's *Beowulf* list *geāra* separately, as an adverb, with no reference to *gēar*. Marckwardt and Rosier's *Old English* primer gives "*gēara/geāra*" as an adverb, with no reference to *gēar*. Pope in *Seven Old English Poems* comments on *ġeāra ġeō* that "The sense here develops in accordance with *ġēara* or *ġeāra*, genitive plural as an independent adverb." Bright's *Reader*, in its older (e.g., Bright-Hulbert, 1935) editions, lists *gēara* under *gēar* as genitive plural. Of the two times *geara* appears among Bright's texts, he spells it once *gēara* and once *geāra*. The new edition of Bright (Cassidy-Ringler) has a separate headword for *gēara* (so spelled) as an adverb, with no reference to *gēar*; however, the three times *geara* occurs in its texts, the editors move the macron back: *geāra*.

Vico has satisfactory answers to his questions 1, 2, 3, 4, 8, 9, and 10; to questions 5, 6, and 7 modern scholarship supplies no definitive answer. Vico may be wild with frustration, or he may be rather pleased with himself, out there on the frontiers of knowledge, finding inconsistency in a standard reader and more or less knowing its cause. Maybe Vico will go on to do some more work in the area, if not now, maybe twenty years from now.

An Old English course is practically the only place ordinary students of literature can brush up against the study of the history of words. Much recent criticism takes delight in playing with etymologies, but the ignorance displayed is an embarrassment to the profession. Old-fashioned philology cannot be the sole aim of a course in *Beowulf*, but it is fruitful and honorable to do a little of it along the way, to try to create a Vico when he does not spontaneously emerge. The suggestions that follow seem to work for me; some variation may work for you.

1. Have the students learn vocabulary. This method is used more in America than abroad. I was happy to be able to read Old English prose rapidly after a year's course because I had memorized a few hundred words. Memorizing individual words focuses attention on them and their mutual relations. Some teachers use my *Word-Hoard* as an aid to memorization and a stimulus to curiosity about words.

2. Assign a word for investigation. In a graduate course Morton Bloom-field assigned me the word "lordship"; I did well on "lord-," less well on "-ship." I learned an enormous amount quickly and wrote a five-page report on the history of the word.

3. Treat a word's meaning by way of the concordances. *Ofermōd* is the famous (and now trite) example; try perhaps *æglæca, trēow, drēam, blāc, mænan, tācen.*

4. Examine closely the words and forms in a short passage.

5. Do a library session on the dictionaries and grammars.

6. Especially for courses in which *Beowulf* is taught in translation, give a flashy treatment of a word or two in class ("tear" is a favorite for the prestidigitation by which you connect it with "lachrymose").

7. Juggle whenever your students' patience permits it; bounce a lot.

OLD ENGLISH PROSODY

Thomas Cable

Since few prosodists agree on the shape of the Old English verse form, the subject presents both difficulties and opportunities in the classroom. A too speedy excursion into the thicket of controversy, where types and subtypes assume alphabetical names and take on lives of their own, can leave the student bewildered. A slower and more deliberate approach can be a useful antidote to the more rigid and stringent aspects of philology.

Prosody, to be sure, has its stringent qualities too. As with the sound changes, there is a certain amount of information that must be learned. Memorizing and being able to apply Sievers' Five Types is essential for a start. It is better, in fact, to go directly to Sievers' Five Types than to ease into the subject by way of Gerard Manley Hopkins or *Christabel;* and most handbook summaries of the "strong stress tradition" from the seventh to the twentieth century are best avoided. Few of these give a clue why *lissa gelong* 'of joys dependent on' (2150a) is metrically suspect, and this kind of question is one of the first to ask, even in an introductory course.

There are two logical stages, then, in helping students to understand Old English prosody. In the first stage, one must be able to say why editors of *Beowulf* have long considered verses like *ræhte ongēan* 'reached toward' (747b) and *ðegn betstan* 'best thane' (1871b) to be unmetrical and why emendations of these verses have been proposed over the past century. But on the interpretation of the abstract pattern in terms of acoustic, perceptual, and musical reality, one can only say, undogmatically, that there are various possibilities, and in actual performance these possibilities differ remarkably. I encourage students to experiment with their readings after they understand

173

the abstract metrical pattern. My own theory of the meter of *Beowulf* leads to a performance that exaggerates the intervals of pitch, but in class I present this as one of several possibilities, with points in its favor and points against it.

Before going into the matter of performance in detail, however, it is worth reinforcing the idea that traditional summaries of Old English meter are often misleading. It might seem that the one sure first statement to make about Old English meter, following and simplifying Sievers' Five Types, is that each verse contains two main stresses, each full line four. But research during the past decade has shown that such a statement, though true, may express the inevitable result of a more basic metrical principle. One can invent "principles" that border on absurdity to illustrate the point; for example, "Each verse in the *Beowulf* meter must contain fewer than fifty-four syllables." A statement about meter can be incontestibly true and yet metrically irrelevant, indeed misleading, because it expresses derivative or accidental qualities of the metrical paradigm; and therefore it does not do what a paradigm of meter must do above all: exclude those sequences of words that are not metrical.

The clearest statement of this general principle of metrics that I know is Wimsatt and Beardsley's. I would recommend that their essay be part of the intellectual equipment of anyone who teaches meter for any period of English, though I would caution that it suffers the problem in summarizing Old English meter that I have described above; and because it is mainly about the meters of poetry in Modern English, I would not assign it in an Old English course. I would have the students read instead the excellent summaries in Pope's *Seven Old English Poems* or Cassidy and Ringler's *Bright's Old English Grammar and Reader*.

In metrical theory, as in linguistic theory, it is possible to account for the same facts with radically different mechanisms. Every theory of Old English meter differs from every other in certain details, and the details concern concepts such as arsis, thesis, foot, measure, rest, alliteration, long syllable, short syllable, resolution, suspension of resolution, anacrusis, secondary stress, light verse, heavy verse, expanded verse, hypermetric verse, on-verse, and off-verse. No metrical theory contains all of these concepts—some of them are incompatible—and therefore it is impossible to present even a simplified or composite description of Old English meter that would win general acceptance. The best that one can do is give an account fairly close to Sievers ("Zur Rhythmic," *Altgermanische Metrik*, or "Old Germanic Metrics") and then indicate how one might interpret these patterns rhythmically or melodically. This is what both Pope (*Seven Old English Poems*) and Cassidy and Ringler do. Their summaries of Sievers' system correspond exactly, and yet one should pay attention to Pope's comment that the division into feet obscures the true structure of the verse. Therefore, in addition to giving the familiar scheme for type A, ´ x | ´ x, Pope describes the "basic form" as *lift, drop, lift, drop*, without division; I find his analysis more satisfactory. The essential elements of Sievers' system, as presented by Cassidy and Ringler and by Pope, are:

		Cassidy and Ringler	Pope
Type A	*gomban gyldan* 'tribute to pay'	´ x | ´ x	lift, drop, lift, drop
Type B	*þǣr wæs hearpan swēg* 'there was harp's music'	x x ´ | x ´	drop, lift, drop, lift
Type C	*ofer hronrāde* 'over whale-road'	x x ´ | ´ x	drop, lift, lift, drop
Type D1	*lindhæbbende* 'shield-bearers'	´ | ´ ` x	lift, lift, half-lift, drop
Type D2	*blǣd wīde sprang* 'glory widely spread'	´ | ´ x `	lift, lift, drop, half-lift
Type E	*lofdǣdum sceal* 'by glorious deeds shall'	´ ` x | ´	lift, half-lift, drop, lift

These are the basic patterns for the "normal" verses in *Beowulf*. For the approximately 903 to 935 "hypermetric" verses in Old English, see Pope, *Seven Old English Poems* (99–158); Bliss (88–97); and Hieatt, "A New Theory." It is commonly thought that the Five Types apply with certain modifications to verses in Old Saxon, Old High German, and Old Norse, but these meters, though derived from a common source, are essentially different from the Old English meter, and it is misleading to apply a single paradigm, even with modifications, to all of them.

My own abstraction of Sievers' system follows Pope in avoiding the foot markers, but it focuses on a feature that has been largely ignored in this century. Sievers' basic distinction, preceding even the discrimination of types, was into *viergliedrige* and *fünfgliedrige Verse* 'four-member and five-member verses.' One can begin by saying that a normal Old English verse should contain four members. A member can be defined roughly as a lift, a drop, or a half-lift; or, more accurately, as a metrical unit (of one or more syllables) distinguished by a change of ictus (greater or less) from the metrical units that precede and follow within the same verse. My summary of Sievers' system, with certain modifications, would take the following form (where relative ictus between adjacent units, as indicated by the slanted lines, is the crucial feature):

Type A	gómbăn gýldăn	1 \ 2 / 3 \ 4
Type B	þǣr wăs héarpăn swég	1 / 2 \ 3 / 4

Type C	ófĕr hŕonrǎdě	1∕2∖3∖4
Type D1	líndhǽbbèndě	1∖2∖3∖4
Type D2	blǽd wǐdě spŕang	
Type E	lófdǽdǔm scéal	1∖2∖3∕4

The main exceptions to this paradigm are the apparent five-member verses known as D *, such as *sīde sænæssas*. I have argued (as Kaluza did seventy-five years ago) that D* verses are actually four-member verses with resolution of the first long syllable (*sǐdě*), but it is an argument rather too detailed to recapitulate here and not widely accepted.

A fourth account of the *Beowulf* meter should be mentioned, Bliss's, both because it makes important, original observations in its own right and because it purports to be "a triumphant vindication of Sievers." The features that Bliss abstracts from Sievers' system, however, are less central than those abstracted in the three summaries above. In modifying Sievers' Five Types to allow "light verses" and D and E verses without intermediate ictus, Bliss reduces the power of Sievers' system to exclude metrically corrupt verses. Without the offsetting constraints of Sievers' four-member idea, the paradigm becomes a long list of types and subtypes that in principle is open-ended. *Lissa gelong* is cataloged as an acceptable verse of the pattern 2E1a, $\stackrel{\smile}{}$ x | x $\stackrel{\smile}{}$. The general point then is a curious one: the best vindication of Sievers' system in this century is Pope's (*The Rhythm of* Beowulf, esp. the Appendix), which challenges Sievers. Bliss defends Sievers and presents a carefully constructed but ultimately different system.

This is not to say that Pope unwittingly confirms Sievers' system in trying to do something else. The distinction to make is between the abstract syllabic patterns of stress, length, and alliteration, which tell us if a verse is metrical, and the interpretation of these patterns in terms of composition and performance. Pope's interpretation of the rhythmical features of the Old English verse form takes the following shape:

Type A	gomban gyldan	
Type B	þǽr wæs hearpan swēg	
Type C	ofer hronrāde	
Type D1	lindhæbbende	
Type D2	blǽd wīde sprang	
Type E	lofdædum sceal	

Pope sees the rhythmic basis of every normal verse as consisting of two four-beat measures of 4/8 time. Rests can occur in all five types, but they are most important at the beginning of types B and C, which begin with one or more unstressed syllables. In these two types the rest, possibly filled by a stroke of the harp, gives the measure the initial downbeat that Pope sees as necessary. Pope's theory has been influential during the past forty years and has inspired similar rhythmical theories, including those by Creed ("A New Approach") and Hieatt ("A New Theory"). The objections to Pope's theory have mainly concerned its musicological implausibility. The conception of measure is peculiarly modern, and the music contemporary with Old English poetry and for centuries afterward had nothing comparable (see Cable, "The Meter and Melody" 12–17, Silver-Beck, and Luecke).

My own system focuses on pitch as the correlate of linguistic prominence to make the discriminations of metrical ictus that would be necessary in realizing the abstract pattern. The contours of pitch follow closely those of stress, though they exaggerate the intervals between intermediate levels of ictus and iron out differences of stress that are not metrically relevant (as in the preposition *ofer* in the verse *ofer hronrāde*) by assigning syllables bearing such patterns of stress to the same note:

Type A	gomban gyldan	
Type B	þǣr wæs hearpan swēg	
Type C	ofer hronrāde	
Type D1	lindhæbbende	
Type D2	blǣd wīde sprang	
Type E	lofdǣdum sceal	

What we know about melodic form in Gregorian chant during the Old English period supports the idea of composition and performance by melodic formulas such as these. Comparisons of form between Old English poetry and Latin chant have attained a specificity during the past ten years that makes the comparisons more instructive than was once thought. (See Treitler, "Homer and Gregory," " 'Centonate' Chante"; Luecke; Cable.) Despite certain of Luecke's methods that I would question, her assumptions and conclusions have a musicological plausibility that those of other rhythmical theories do not have. Among several objections that can be brought against my own theory the one that I find most telling is that in the fitting of syllables to notes, Old English poetry would have had to follow rules more rigorously and precisely than any extant notated texts of the period.

In closing, a few comments about the relation of metrical elements to linguistic elements might be useful in placing the various theories of Old English meter with respect to each other. A concept applicable to any metrical theory is that of *ictus*, if by ictus we understand the metrical prominence that is borne by certain syllables of a verse. Metrical ictus depends directly on linguistic prominence, which in turn is realized by various phonetic features, especially stress, time, and pitch. In Old English poetry the feature of time has two manifestations: as syllabic quantity, which is grammatically fixed, and as phrasal rhythm, which varies from theory to theory. One way of classifying the theories of Old English prosody is to say that each focuses on one of these phonetic features and organizes the others subordinately around it. Thus, the theories of Sievers and Bliss are primarily stress theories; those of Heusler, Pope, Creed, Foley, Hieatt, and Luecke are primarily rhythmical theories; my own is primarily a pitch theory.

This classification is not quite accurate, however, because stress and syllabic quantity must have priority over rhythm and melody. Stress and syllabic quantity can be inferred fairly certainly from the words themselves, but the punctuation and quasi-musical notation of the manuscripts are too sporadic and ambiguous to serve as a point of departure for either rhythm or melody. (See Clemoes, *Liturgical Influence*, and Thornley.) Therefore, all theories of Old English prosody must begin with an adequate system of stress-quantity meter, such as Sievers' ("Zur Rhythmik"). Many prosodists have found such a theory adequate as a basis for textual emendation but inadequate to account for the perceptual and aesthetic reality of the meter. Those who have pursued the matter have turned to rhythmic or melodic elements to enhance the stress patterns and set them apart from prose. An adequate theory of Old English prosody has yet to be formulated, whether stress-quantitative, stress-quantitative-rhythmic, or stress-quantitative-melodic. What is needed is a theory with the supporting evidence to incorporate both rhythmic and melodic features on a stress-quantitative base while avoiding the musicological anomalies of current theories.

Stated as such, the problem is comprehensible to a graduate or an undergraduate class, and even intellectually engaging. In the full scope of literary, linguistic, and cultural topics that one must cover in a *Beowulf* course, that of prosody is one of the smaller ones. But because it can be so precisely defined without being solved, it offers a certain expansiveness and pleasure that comes with the license to experiment within bounds.

PARTICIPANTS IN SURVEY OF *BEOWULF* INSTRUCTORS

Ashley C. Amos
University of Toronto

Richard Andersen
Engelsk Institutt
Bergen, Norway

W. Bryant Bachman, Jr.
University of Southwestern Louisiana

Stephen A. Barney
University of California, Irvine

James L. Barribeau
Cornell University

Frank Battaglia
College of Staten Island,
City University of New York

Joyce S. Beck
University of Texas, Arlington

Myra Berman
State University of New York, Stony Brook

Robert R. Black
The Citadel

Robert E. Boenig
Rutgers University, New Brunswick

Philip Bozek
Illinois Benedictine College

Elizabeth Buckmaster
Pennsylvania State University, Delaware County

W. F. Bolton
Rutgers University, New Brunswick

Thomas Cable
University of Texas, Austin

Michael D. Cherniss
University of Kansas

Howell Chickering
Amherst College

George Clark
Queen's University

Paul Clogan
North Texas State University

André Crépin
Paris-Sorbonne

Eugene J. Crook
Florida State University

Joseph P. Crowley
Auburn University, Montgomery

Terrie Curran
Providence College

Roger Dahood
University of Arizona

Alfred David
Indiana University, Bloomington

Diana M. DeLuca
Windward Community College

Susanne M. Dumbleton
Albany College of Pharmacy

James W. Earl
Fordham University

James A. Eby
James Madison University

Kenneth Florey
Southern Connecticut State College

John Miles Foley
University of Missouri, Columbia

Alan J. Frantzen
Loyola University, Chicago

Donald K. Fry
State University of New York, Stony
Brook

Thomas J. Garbáty
University of Michigan, Ann Arbor

Winnifred J. Geissler
Kansas State University

Sealy Gilles
Graduate Center, City University of
New York

Sandra A. Glass
Claremont University Center

Donald C. Green
California State College, Bakersfield

Elizabeth Greene
Queen's University

Louis B. Hall
University of Colorado, Denver

Elaine Tuttle Hansen
Haverford College

Hiroshi Hasegawa
Nihon University
Tokyo, Japan

Stanley R. Hauer
University of Southern Mississippi

Anne Hernández
University of California, Berkeley

Constance B. Hieatt
University of Western Ontario

Thomas D. Hill
Cornell University

Mamie Hofner
East Texas State University

Sue Ellen Holbrook
Franklin and Marshall College

Norma L. Hutman
Hartwick College

Edward B. Irving, Jr.
University of Pennsylvania

Theodora Jankowski
Norwich University

William C. Johnson
Stetson University

Stanley J. Kahrl
Ohio State University

Robert E. Kaske
Cornell University

Keith Keating
Nassau Community College

Calvin B. Kendall
University of Minnesota, Minneapolis

Kevin S. Kiernan
University of Kentucky

Robert L. Kindrick
Western Illinois University

Ann Mills King
Prince George's Community College

Hugh Kirkpatrick
North Texas State University

Lisa J. Kiser
Ohio State University

Bernice Kliman
Nassau Community College

Jeffrey A. Kurnit
Pace University, White Plains

Tim D. P. Lally
University of South Alabama

Ruth P. M. Lehmann
University of Texas, Austin

Theodore H. Leinbaugh
University of North Carolina, Chapel Hill

John B. Lord
Washington State University

Jane-Marie Luecke
Oklahoma State University

Alan C. Lupack
Wayne State College

John C. McGalliard
University of Wisconsin, Madison

Catherine A. McKenna
Queens College, City University of New York

Douglas J. McMillan
East Carolina University

Mary Elizabeth Meek
University of Pittsburgh

Henry Merritt
Cambridge Technical College
Cambridge, England

Anne Middleton
University of California, Berkeley

Elaine M. Miller
Seton Hall University

Miriam Y. Miller
University of New Orleans

John Nesselhof
Weib College

Marilyn Nellis
Clarkson College

John D. Niles
University of California, Berkeley

Lea T. Olsan
Northeast Louisiana University

Alexandra Hennessey Olsen
University of Denver

Marijane Osborn
University of California, Davis

Roger Owens
Whittier College

George S. Peek
Arkansas State University

Joyce E. Potter
East Tennessee State University

Robert J. Reddick
University of Texas, Arlington

Luke M. Reinsma
Gustavus Adolphus College

Gerald Richman
Mankato State University

Edward J. Rielly
St. Joseph's College
North Windham, Maine

S. M. Riley
Illinois State University

Richard Ringler
University of Wisconsin, Madison

Fred C. Robinson
Yale University

Sharon Robinson
Russell Sage College

E. C. Ronquist
Concordia University

Grant C. Roti
Housatonic Community College

Richard Schrader
Boston College

Douglas D. Short
North Carolina State University

Ruth S. Smith
Hofstra University

Harry Jay Solo
Princeton University

Charlotte Spivack
University of Massachusetts, Amherst

Henry J. Stauffenberg
University of Scranton

Robert D. Stevick
University of Washington

Melvin Storm
Emporia State University

Victor Strite
Baylor University

Paul Beekman Taylor
Université de Genève

Joseph F. Tuso
University of Science and Arts of
Oklahoma

Michael W. Twomey
Ithaca College

Alexander Weiss
Radford University

Elizabeth Walsh
University of San Diego

Andrew Welsh
Rutgers University, New Brunswick

Louise E. Wright
Community College of Philadelphia

WORKS CITED

Aarne, Antti, and Stith Thompson. *The Types of the Folktale*. 2nd ed. Folklore Fellows Communications, 184. Helsinki: Acad. Scientiarum Fennica, 1961.

Abraham, Lenore. "*Beowulf* in the Middle School." *Old English Newsletter* 11.2 (1978): 15–17.

Abrams, Meyer H., gen. ed. *The Norton Anthology of English Literature: Major Authors Edition*. 3rd ed. New York: Norton, 1957.

Albertson, Clinton. *Anglo-Saxon Saints and Heroes*. New York: Fordham Univ. Press, 1967.

Alcuin. *Monumenta Germaniae Historica: Epistolae Karolini Aevi*. Ed. Ernest Dümmler. Berlin, 1895.

Alexander, Michael, trans. *Beowulf: A Verse Translation*. Harmondsworth, Eng.: Penguin, 1973.

Alfred, William, trans. *Beowulf*. In *Medieval Epics*. New York: Random, 1963.

Almgren, B. *The Viking*. Gothenberg, Sweden: Cagner, 1966.

Amis, Kingsley. "Beowulf." In his *A Case of Samples: Poems, 1946–1956*. New York: Harcourt, 1957, 14.

Amos, Ashley Crandell. "The Dictionary of Old English: 1981 Progress Report." *Old English Newsletter* 15.2 (1982): 12–14.

———. *Linguistic Means of Determining the Dates of Old English Literary Texts*. Medieval Academy Books, 90. Cambridge: Medieval Academy of America, 1980.

Anderson, Earl R. "Beowulf's Retreat from Frisia: Analogues from the Fifth and Eighth Centuries." *English Language Notes* 19 (1981): 89–93.

Anderson, George K. "*Beowulf*, Chaucer and Their Backgrounds." In *Contemporary Literary Scholarship: A Critical Review*. Ed. Lewis Leary. New York: Appleton, 1958, 25–52.

———. *The Literature of the Anglo-Saxons*. Rev. ed. Princeton: Princeton Univ. Press, 1966.

Andersson, Theodore. *Early Epic Scenery*. Ithaca: Cornell Univ. Press, 1976.

———. *The Legend of Brynhild*. Ithaca: Cornell Univ. Press, 1980.

Anker, P. *The Art of Scandinavia*. Vol. 1. London: Hamlyn, 1970.

Arent, A. Margaret. "The Heroic Pattern: Old Germanic Helmets, *Beowulf*, and *Grettis Saga*." In *Old Norse Literature and Mythology: A Symposium*. Ed. Edgar C. Polomé. Austin: Univ. of Texas Press, 1969, 130–99.

Aubrey, James R. "Taming Beowulf's Monsters." *Old English Newsletter* 13.2 (1980): 23–24.

Backes, M., and R. Dölling. *Art of the Dark Ages*. New York: Abrams, 1969.

Baird, Joseph. "Grendel the Exile." *Neuphilologische Mitteilungen* 67 (1966): 375–81.

Barney, Stephen A., with David Stevens and Ellen Wertheimer. *Word-Hoard: An Introduction to Old English Vocabulary*. New Haven: Yale Univ. Press, 1977.

Bately, Janet, ed. *The Old English Orosius*. S.S. 6. London: Early English Text Society, 1980.

Beaty, John O. *Swords in the Dawn: A Story of the First Englishmen*. New York: Longman, 1937; London: Harrap, 1938.

Bede, the Venerable, Saint. *Ecclesiastical History of the English Nation*. Ed. and introd. Dom David Knowles. London: Dent, 1963.

———. *Ecclesiastical History of the English Nation, Based on the Version of Thomas Stapleton, 1565*. Ed. and trans. J. E. King. Loeb Classical Library, vols. 246, 248. Cambridge: Harvard Univ. Press, 1930.

———. *A History of the English Church and People*. Ed. and trans. Leo Sherley-Price. Rev. R. E. Latham. Harmondsworth, Eng.: Penguin, 1968.

Beer, Francis F., trans. *The Song of Roland*. Ed. Pierre Le Gentil. Cambridge: Harvard Univ. Press, 1969.

Benson, Larry D. "The Literary Character of Anglo-Saxon Formulaic Poetry." *PMLA* 81 (1966): 334–41.

———. "The Originality of *Beowulf*." *Harvard English Studies* 1 (1970): 1–43.

———. "The Pagan Coloring in *Beowulf*." In *Old English Poetry: Fifteen Essays*. Ed. Robert P. Creed. 193–213.

———. "Why Study the Middle Ages?" *Ralph: Studies in Medieval and Renaissance Teaching* 1982: 1–16.

Beowulf, Dragon-Slayer. Ed. Dennis O'Neil. Written by Michael Uslan. Illus. Ricardo Villamonte. 5 nos. New York: National Periodical Publications, 1975–1976.

Berger, Harry, Jr., and H. Marshall Leicester, Jr. "Social Structure as Doom: The Limits of Heroism in *Beowulf*." In *Old English Studies in Honour of John C. Pope*. Ed. Robert B. Burlin and Edward B. Irving, Jr. 37–79.

Berkhout, Carl, and Milton McC. Gatch, eds. *Anglo-Saxon Scholarship: The First Three Centuries*. Boston: Hall, 1982.

Bessinger, Jess B., Jr. "*Beowulf* and the Harp at Sutton Hoo." *University of Toronto Quarterly* 27 (1958): 148–68.

———. *A Short Dictionary of Anglo-Saxon Poetry in a Normalized Early West-Saxon Orthography*. Toronto: Univ. of Toronto Press, 1960.

———, ed. *A Concordance to* Beowulf. Programmed by Philip H. Smith, Jr. Ithaca: Cornell Univ. Press, 1969.

———, ed. *A Concordance to the Anglo-Saxon Poetic Records*. Programmed by Philip H. Smith, Jr. Index of compounds by Michael W. Twomey. Ithaca: Cornell Univ. Press, 1978.

———, and Robert P. Creed, eds. *Franciplegius: Medieval and Linguistic Studies in Honor of Francis Peabody Magoun, Jr*. New York: New York Univ. Press, 1965.

———, and Stanley J. Kahrl, eds. *Essential Articles for the Study of Old English Poetry*. Hamden, Conn.: Archon, 1968.

———, and Fred C. Robinson. "A Survey of Old English Teaching in America in 1966 [Tabulation of the Data from the Survey Questionnaires]." *Old English*

Newsletter 1.1 (1967): 1–4. "The Status of Old English in America Today [Commentary on the Results of the Survey]." *Old English Newsletter* 1.1 (1967): 5–8. "A Selection from Correspondents' Personal Comments on the Status and Value of Old English Studies in America Today." *Old English Newsletter* 1.1 (1967): 9–12.

Blair, Peter Hunter. *An Introduction to Anglo-Saxon England*. Cambridge: Cambridge Univ. Press, 1956.

———. *Roman Britain and Early England, 55 B.C.–A.D. 871*. Edinburgh: Nelson, 1963.

Bliss, A. J. *The Metre of* Beowulf. 2nd ed. Oxford: Blackwell, 1961.

Bloomfield, Morton W. "*Beowulf* and Christian Allegory: An Interpretation of Unferth." *Traditio* 7 (1951): 410–15. Rpt. in *An Anthology of* Beowulf *Criticism*. Ed. Lewis E. Nicholson. 155–64. Also rpt. in *The* Beowulf *Poet: A Collection of Critical Essays*. Ed. Donald K. Fry. 68–75.

———. "Patristics and Old English Literature: Notes on Some Poems." *Comparative Literature* 14 (1962): 36–43. Rpt. in *Studies in Old English Literature in Honor of Arthur G. Brodeur*. Ed. Stanley B. Greenfield. 36–43. Also rpt. in *An Anthology of* Beowulf *Criticism*. Ed. Lewis E. Nicholson. 367–72. Also rpt. in *Essential Articles for the Study of Old English Literature*. Ed. Jess B. Bessinger, Jr., and Stanley J. Kahrl. 63–73.

———. "Understanding Old English Poetry." *Annuale Mediaevale* 9 (1968): 5–25. Rpt. in his *Essays and Explorations: Studies in Ideas, Language, and Literature*. Cambridge: Harvard Univ. Press, 1970, 59–80.

Bolton, Whitney F. *Alcuin and* Beowulf: *An Eighth-Century View*. New Brunswick: Rutgers Univ. Press, 1978.

———. *An Old English Anthology*. London: Arnold, 1963.

Bonjour, Adrien. "*Beowulf* and the Beasts of Battle." *PMLA* 72 (1957): 563–73. Rpt. in his *Twelve* Beowulf *Papers, 1940–1960, with Additional Comments*, 135–46; new matter, 147–49.

———. *The Digressions in* Beowulf. *Medium Aevum* Monographs, 5. Oxford: Oxford Univ. Press, 1950. Rpt. Ann Arbor: Univ. Microfilms, 1982.

———. "Monsters Crouching and Critics Rampant; or, the *Beowulf* Dragon Debated." *PMLA* 68 (1953): 304–12. Rpt. in his *Twelve* Beowulf *Papers, 1940–1960, with Additional Comments*, 97–106; new matter, 107–13.

———. "On Sea Images in *Beowulf*." *Journal of English and Germanic Philology* 54 (1955): 111–15. Rpt. in his *Twelve* Beowulf *Papers, 1940–1960, with Additional Comments*, 115–19.

———. *Twelve* Beowulf *Papers, 1940–1960, with Additional Comments*. Univ. de Neuchâtel: Recueil de Travaux Publiés par la Faculté des Lettres, 30. Geneva: Droz; Neuchâtel: Faculté des Lettres, 1962.

Booth, George. Cartoon. *New Yorker*, 4 Feb. 1980, 41.

Borden, Arthur R., Jr. *A Comprehensive Old-English Dictionary*. Washington: Univ. Press of America, 1982.

Borges, Jorge Luis. "Composítión escrita en un ejemplar de la gesta de *Beowulf.*" In his *Antología personal.* Buenos Aires: Sur, 1961. 187.

Bosworth, Joseph, and T. Northcote Toller. *An Anglo-Saxon Dictionary.* Oxford: Oxford Univ. Press, 1898. *Supplement* by Toller, 1921. *Enlarged Addenda and Corrigenda to the Supplement* by Alistair Campbell, 1972.

Bowra, Cecil M. *Heroic Poetry.* London: Macmillan, 1952.

Bradley, S. A. J., trans. *Anglo-Saxon Poetry.* Everyman's Library. London: Dent, 1982.

Branston, B. *Lost Gods of England.* New York: Oxford Univ. Press, 1974.

Bright's Anglo-Saxon Reader. Rev. and enl. James R. Hulbert. New York: Holt, 1935.

British Literary Manuscripts, Series I, from 800–1800. Catalog by Verlyn Klinkenborg. Checklist by Herbert Cahoon. Introd. Charles Ryskamp. New York: Pierpont Morgan Library and Dover, 1981.

Brodeur, Arthur G. *The Art of* Beowulf. Berkeley: Univ. of California Press, 1959.

———. "*Beowulf*: One Poem or Three?" In *Medieval Literature and Folklore Studies: Essays in Honour of Francis Lee Utley.* Ed. Jerome Mandel and Bruce A. Rosenberg. 3–26.

Brooke, Christopher. *From Alfred to Henry III, 871–1272.* Edinburgh: Nelson, 1961.

Brown, Alan. "Published Works on *Beowulf*: 1971–75." New Directions in *Beowulf* Scholarship, MLA Convention, New York. Dec. 1975.

Brown, Arthur, and Peter Foote, eds. *Early English and Norse Studies Presented to Hugh Smith in Honour of His Sixtieth Birthday.* London: Methuen, 1963.

Brown, James L., trans. *Beowulf: Translated from West Saxon Verse of the Tenth Century into English Prose of the Twentieth Century Designed to Encourage Reading Based on the Text of Fr. Klaeber, with Preface, Footnotes, Illustrations, and Appendices.* Campbell, Calif.: Academy, 1973.

Bruce-Mitford, Rupert L. S. *Aspects of Anglo-Saxon Archaeology.* New York: Harper, 1974.

———. *The Sutton Hoo Ship-Burial.* Vol. 1, *Excavations, Background, the Ship, Dating and Inventory*; vol. 2, *Arms, Armour, and Regalia.* London: British Museum, 1975–78.

———. *Sutton Hoo Ship-Burial: A Handbook.* New ed. London: British Museum, 1968.

———. *The Sutton Hoo Ship-Burial: A Provisional Guide.* Rev. ed. London: British Museum, 1956.

———. *The Sutton Hoo Ship-Burial: Reflections after Thirty Years.* Univ. of York Monograph Series, 2. York: Univ. of York, 1979.

Brunner, Karl. *Altenglische Grammatik nach der angelsächsischen Grammatik von Eduard Sievers.* Rev. Karl Brunner. Tübingen: Niemeyer, 1965.

Buck, Carl D. *A Dictionary of Selected Synonyms in the Principal Indo-European Languages.* Chicago: Univ. of Chicago Press, 1949.

Burlin, Robert B., and Edward B. Irving, Jr., eds. *Old English Studies in Honour of John C. Pope*. Toronto: Univ. of Toronto Press, 1974.

Burns, Norman T., and Christopher J. Reagan, eds. *Concepts of the Hero in the Middle Ages and the Renaissance*. Albany: State Univ. of New York Press, 1975.

Burrows, Larry. "The Treasures of Sutton Hoo." *Life*, 16 July 1951, 82–85.

Bynum, David E., ed. *Bihaćka krajina: Epics from Bihać, Cazin, and Kulen Vakuf*. Collated by Milman Parry, Albert B. Lord, and David E. Bynum. Serbo-Croatian Heroic Songs, 14. Cambridge: Harvard Univ. Press, 1979.

———, ed. *Ženidba Vlahinjić Alije and Osmanbeg Delibegović i Pavičević Luka*. By Avdo Medjedovic. Collated by Milman Parry and Albert B. Lord. Serbo-Croatian Heroic Songs, 6. Cambridge: Harvard Univ. Press, 1980.

Cable, Thomas W. *The Meter and Melody of* Beowulf. Urbana: Univ. of Illinois Press, 1974.

Cameron, Angus, Roberta Frank, and John Leyerle, eds. *Computers and Old English Concordances*. Toronto: Univ. of Toronto Press, 1970.

Campbell, A. P. "The Decline and Fall of Hrothgar and His Danes." *Revue de l'Université d'Ottawa* 45 (1975): 417–29.

Campbell, Alistair. "The Old English Epic Style." In *English and Medieval Studies Presented to J.R.R. Tolkien on the Occasion of His Seventieth Birthday*. Ed. Norman Davis and C. L. Wrenn. 13–26.

———. *Old English Grammar*. Oxford: Clarendon, 1959.

Campbell, James. *The Anglo-Saxons*. Ithaca: Cornell Univ. Press, 1982.

Cannon, Charles D. "The Religion of the Anglo-Saxons." *University of Mississippi Studies in English* 5 (1964): 15–33.

Carpenter, Rhys. *Folktale, Fiction, and Saga in the Homeric Epics*. Berkeley: Univ. of California Press, 1946.

Cassidy, Frederic G. "How Free Was the Anglo-Saxon Scop?" In *Franciplegius: Medieval and Linguistic Studies in Honor of Francis Peabody Magoun, Jr.* Ed. Jess B. Bessinger, Jr., and Robert P. Creed. 75–85.

———, and Richard M. Ringler, eds. *Bright's Old English Grammar and Reader*. 3rd rev. ed. New York: Holt, 1971.

Chadwick, Hector M. *The Heroic Age*. Cambridge: Cambridge Univ. Press, 1912. Pp. 47–56 rpt. in *An Anthology of* Beowulf *Criticism*. Ed. Lewis E. Nicholson. 23–33.

Chadwick, Nora K. "The Monsters and Beowulf." In *The Anglo-Saxons: Studies in Some Aspects of Their History and Culture Presented to Bruce Dickins*. Ed. Peter Clemoes. 171–203.

Chambers, R. W. Beowulf: *An Introduction to the Study of the Poem, with a Discussion of the Stories of Offa and Finn*. Supp. by C. L. Wrenn. 3rd ed. Cambridge: Cambridge Univ. Press, 1963.

Chaney, William A. *The Cult of Kingship in Anglo-Saxon England: The Transition from Paganism to Christianity*. Berkeley: Univ. of California Press, 1970.

Chase, Colin, ed. *The Dating of* Beowulf. Toronto: Univ. of Toronto Press, 1981.

Cherniss, Michael D. "*Beowulf*: Oral Presentation and the Criterion of Immediate Rhetorical Effect." *Genre* 3 (1970): 214–28.

———. *Ingeld and Christ: Heroic Concepts and Values in Old English Christian Poetry*. The Hague: Mouton, 1972.

Chickering, Howell D., Jr., trans. *Beowulf: A Dual-Language Edition*. 2nd ed. Garden City, N.Y.: Anchor-Doubleday, 1982.

Child, Francis James, ed. *The English and Scottish Popular Ballads*. Vol. 3. New York: Dover, 1965.

Church, Samuel H. *Beowulf: A Poem*. New York: Stokes, 1901.

Clark, George. "Beowulf and Bear's Son in the *Vishnu Purana*." *Philological Quarterly* 43 (1964): 125–30.

———. "Beowulf's Armor." *Journal of English Literary History* 32 (1965): 409–41.

———. "The Hero of *Maldon*: Vir Pius et Strenuus." *Speculum* 54 (1979): 257–82.

———. "The Traveller Recognizes His Goal: A Theme in Anglo-Saxon Poetry." *Journal of English and Germanic Philology* 64 (1965): 645–59.

Clemoes, Peter. *Liturgical Influence on Punctuation in Late Old English and Early Middle English Manuscripts*. Occasional Papers, 1. Cambridge: Cambridge Univ. Dept. of Anglo-Saxon, 1952.

———, ed. *The Anglo-Saxons: Studies in Some Aspects of Their History and Culture Presented to Bruce Dickins*. London: Bowes, 1959.

———, and Kathleen Hughes, eds. *England before the Conquest: Studies in Primary Sources Presented to Dorothy Whitelock*. Cambridge: Cambridge Univ. Press, 1971.

Clover, Carol. "The Germanic Context of the Unferth Episode." *Speculum* 55 (1980): 444–68.

Collingwood, Robin G. *Archaeology of Roman Britain*. Rev. with Ian Richmond, with a chapter by B. R. Hartley. London: Methuen, 1969.

Cook, Albert S. *A Concordance to Beowulf*. Halle: Niemeyer, 1911. Rpt. Folcroft, Pa.: Folcroft, 1969.

Cox, Betty S. *Cruces of* Beowulf. The Hague: Mouton, 1971.

Cramp, Rosemary. "*Beowulf* and Archaeology." *Medieval Archaeology* 1 (1957): 57–77. Rpt. in *The* Beowulf *Poet: A Collection of Critical Essays*. Ed. Donald K. Fry. 114–40.

Creed, Robert P. "The Making of an Anglo-Saxon Poem." *ELH* 26 (1959): 445–54. Rpt. with Additional Remarks in *The* Beowulf *Poet: A Collection of Critical Essays*. Ed. Donald K. Fry. 141–53.

———. "A New Approach to the Rhythm of *Beowulf*." *PMLA* 81 (1966): 23–33.

———. " '. . . wel-hwelc gecwæþ . . .': The Singer as Architect." *Tennessee Studies in Literature* 11 (1966): 131–43.

————, ed. *Old English Poetry: Fifteen Essays.* Providence: Brown Univ. Press, 1967.

Crossley-Holland, Kevin, trans. *Beowulf.* Introd. Bruce Mitchell. London: Macmillan, 1968.

Crowne, David. "The Hero on the Beach: An Example of Composition by Theme in Anglo-Saxon Poetry." *Neuphilologische Mitteilungen* 61 (1960): 362–72.

Curschmann, Michael. "Oral Poetry in Medieval English, French, and German Literature: Some Notes on Recent Research." *Speculum* 42 (1967): 36–52.

Damico, Helen. "The Valkyrie in Old English Literature." *Allegorica* 5 (1980): 149–67.

Davidson, Hilda R. E. "Archaeology and *Beowulf.*" In Beowulf *and Its Analogues.* Trans. G. N. Garmonsway and Jacqueline Simpson. 350–60.

————. *Gods and Myths of Northern Europe.* Harmondsworth, Eng.: Penguin, 1964.

————. "The Hill of the Dragon: Anglo-Saxon Burial Mounds in Literature and Archaeology." *Folklore* 61 (1950): 169–85 and plate X.

————. *Scandinavian Mythology.* London: Hamlyn, 1969.

————. *The Sword in Anglo-Saxon England: Its Archaeology and Literature.* Oxford: Clarendon, 1962.

Davis, Norman, ed. *Sweet's Anglo-Saxon Primer.* 9th ed., rev. Oxford: Clarendon, 1957.

————, and C. L. Wrenn, eds. *English Medieval Studies Presented to J. R. R. Tolkien on the Occasion of His Seventieth Birthday.* London: Allen and Unwin, 1962.

Denholm-Young, Noël. *Handwriting in England and Wales.* 2nd ed. Cardiff: Univ. of Wales Press, 1964.

Diamond, Arlyn, and Lee R. Edwards, eds. *The Authority of Experience: Essays in Feminine Criticism.* Amherst: Univ. of Massachusetts Press, 1977.

Dietrich, Sheila C. "An Introduction to Women in Anglo-Saxon Society (ca. 600–1066)." In *The Women of England from Anglo-Saxon Times to the Present: Interpretive Bibliographic Essays.* Ed. Barbara Kanner. Hamden, Conn.: Archon, 1979, 32–56.

Dixon, P. *Barbarian Europe.* Oxford: Elsevier-Phaidon, 1976.

Dobbie, Elliott Van Kirk, ed. *The Anglo-Saxon Minor Poems.* Anglo-Saxon Poetic Records, 6. New York: Columbia Univ. Press, 1968.

————, ed. Beowulf *and* Judith. Anglo-Saxon Poetic Records, 4. New York: Columbia Univ. Press, 1953.

Dodds, E. R. *The Greeks and the Irrational.* Berkeley: Univ. of California Press, 1951.

Donahue, Charles. "*Beowulf* and Christian Tradition: A Reconsideration from a Celtic Stance." *Traditio* 21 (1965): 55–116.

————. "*Beowulf*, Ireland, and the Natural Good." *Traditio* 7 (1949–51), 263–77.

Donaldson, E. Talbot, trans. *Beowulf: A New Prose Translation.* New York: Norton,

1966. Rpt. in *The Norton Anthology of English Literature: Major Authors Edition*. M. H. Abrams, gen. ed. 3rd ed. Vol. 1. Also rpt. in *Beowulf: The Donaldson Translation, Backgrounds and Sources, Criticism*. Ed. Joseph F. Tuso.

Duggan, Joseph J., ed. *Oral Literature: Seven Essays. Forum for Modern Language Studies* 10 (1974). Rpt. Edinburgh: Scottish Academic Press, 1975.

Eliason, Norman E. "Beowulf, Wiglaf, and the Waegmundings." *Anglo-Saxon England* 7 (1978): 95–105.

———. "The þyle and Scop in *Beowulf*." *Speculum* 38 (1963): 267–84.

Engberg, Norma J. "*Beowulf* Brought Up to Date." Univ. of Nevada, Las Vegas, 1974 (unpublished paper).

Ernout, Alfred, and Antoine Meillet. *Dictionnaire etymologique de la langue latine*. 4th ed. Paris: Klincksieck, 1959–60.

Farrell, Robert T. "*Beowulf*, Swedes and Geats." *Saga-Book* 18 (1972): 225–86; London: Viking Society for Northern Research, 1972.

Feist, Sigmund. *Vergleichendes Wörterbuch der gotischen Sprache*. 3rd ed. Leiden: Brill, 1939.

Fisher, Peter F. "The Trials of the Epic Hero in *Beowulf*." *PMLA* 73 (1958): 171–83.

Florey, Kenneth. "Stability and Chaos as a Theme in Anglo-Saxon Poetry." *Connecticut Review* 9 (1976): 82–89.

Förster, Max. *Die* Beowulf-*Handschrift. Berichte über die Verhandlungen der sächsischen Akademie der Wissenschaften zu Leipzig* 61.4 (1919).

Foley, John Miles. "*Beowulf* and Traditional Narrative Song: The Potential and Limits of Comparison." In *Old English Literature in Context: Ten Essays*. Ed. John D. Niles. 117–36, 173–78.

———. "Editing Oral Texts: Theory and Practice." *Text* 1 (1981).

———. "Formula and Theme in Old English Poetry." In *Oral Literature and the Formula*. Ed. Benjamin A. Stolz and Richard S. Shannon. 207–32.

———. "Oral Literature: Premises and Problems." *Choice* 18.4 (1980): 487–96.

———. "The Oral Singer in Context: Halil Bajgorić, *Guslar*." *Canadian-American Slavic Studies* 12 (1978): 230–46.

———. "The Oral Theory in Context." In *Oral Traditional Literature: A Festschrift for Albert Bates Lord*. Ed. John Miles Foley. 27–122.

———. *The Oral-Formulaic Theory: An Annotated Bibliography*. New York: Garland, 1983.

———. "Research on Oral Traditional Expression in Šumadija and Its Relevance to the Study of Other Oral Traditions." In *Selected Papers on a Serbian Village*. Ed. Barbara Kerewsky-Halpern and Joel M. Halpern. Research Report 17. Amherst: Univ. of Massachusetts Dept. of Anthropology, 1977, 199–236.

———. "The Traditional Oral Audience." *Balkan Studies* 18 (1977): 145–54.

———. "Tradition-Dependent and -Independent Features in Oral Literature: A Comparative View of the Formula." In *Oral Traditional Literature: A Festschrift for Albert Bates Lord*. Ed. John Foley. 262–81.

————, ed. *Oral Traditional Literature: A Festschrift for Albert Bates Lord*. Columbus: Slavica, 1981.

Fontenrose, Joseph. *Python: A Study of Delphic Myth and Its Origins*. Berkeley: Univ. of California Press, 1959.

Fox, Denton, and Herman Pálsson, trans. *Grettir's Saga*. Toronto: Univ. of Toronto Press, 1974.

Frisk, Hjalmar. *Griechisches etymologisches Wörterbuch*. Heidelberg: Winter, 1960–70.

Fry, Donald K. Beowulf *and the Fight at Finnsburh: A Bibliography*. Charlottesville: Bibliographical Society of the Univ. of Virginia, 1969.

————. "Caedmon as a Formulaic Poet." In *Oral Literature: Seven Essays*. Ed. Joseph J. Duggan. 41–61.

————. *Finnsburh Fragment and Episode*. London: Methuen, 1974.

————. "The Memory of Caedmon." In *Oral Traditional Literature: A Festschrift for Albert Bates Lord*. Ed. John M. Foley. 282–93.

————. *Norse Sagas Translated into English: A Bibliography*. New York: AMS, 1980.

————. "Old English Formulas and Systems." *English Studies* 48 (1967): 193–204.

————. "Variation and Economy in *Beowulf*." *Modern Philology* 65 (1967–68): 353–56.

————, ed. *The* Beowulf *Poet: A Collection of Critical Essays*. Englewood Cliffs: Prentice-Hall, 1968.

Gallant, Roy. *National Geographic Picture Atlas of Our Universe*. Washington, D.C.: National Geographic Soc., 1980.

Gardner, John C. "*Beowulf*." In his *The Construction of Christian Poetry in Old English*. Carbondale: Southern Illinois Univ. Press, 1975. 54–84.

————. *Grendel*. Illus. Emil Antonucci. New York: Knopf, 1971.

Garmonsway, G. N. "Anglo-Saxon Heroic Attitudes." In *Franciplegius: Medieval and Linguistic Studies in Honor of Francis Peabody Magoun, Jr.* Ed. Jess B. Bessinger, Jr., and Robert P. Creed. 139–46.

————, and Jacqueline Simpson, trans. Beowulf *and Its Analogues, including "Archaeology and* Beowulf" by Hilda R. E. Davidson. London: Dent, 1968.

Gatch, Milton McC. *Loyalties and Traditions: Man and His World in Old English Literature*. New York: Pegasus, 1971.

Gibbs-Smith, C. H. *The Bayeux Tapestry*. London: Phaidon, 1973.

Girvan, Richie. Beowulf *and the Seventh Century* (1935). Rpt. with a new chapter by Rupert L. S. Bruce-Mitford. London: Methuen, 1971.

Goldsmith, Margaret E. "The Christian Perspective in *Beowulf*." *Comparative Literature* 14 (1962): 71–80. Rpt. in *An Anthology of* Beowulf *Criticism*. Ed. Lewis E. Nicholson. 373–86.

————. *The Mode and Meaning of* Beowulf. London: Athlone, 1970.

Gordon, Robert K., trans. *Anglo-Saxon Poetry*. Rev. ed. London: Dent, 1970.

Gradon, Pamela. *Form and Style in Early English Literature*. London: Methuen, 1971.

Graham-Campbell, J. *The Viking World*. New York: Ticknor, 1980.

———, and Dafydd Kidd. *The Vikings*. New York: Morrow, 1980.

Green, Charles. *Sutton Hoo: The Excavation of a Royal Ship-Burial*. London: Merlin, 1963.

Greenfield, Stanley B. "*Beowulf* and Epic Tragedy." *Comparative Literature* 14 (1962): 91–105. Rpt. in *Studies in Old English Literature in Honor of Arthur G. Brodeur*. Ed. Stanley B. Greenfield. 91–105.

———. *A Critical History of Old English Literature*. New York: New York Univ. Press, 1965.

———. "The Formulaic Expression of the Theme of 'Exile' in Anglo-Saxon Poetry." *Speculum* 30 (1955): 200–06.

———. *The Interpretation of Old English Poems*. London: Routledge, 1972.

———, ed. *Studies in Old English Literature in Honor of Arthur G. Brodeur*. Eugene: Univ. of Oregon Press, 1963.

———, trans. *A Readable* Beowulf: *The Old English Epic Newly Translated*. Introd. Alain Renoir. Carbondale: Southern Illinois Univ. Press, 1982.

———, and Fred C. Robinson. *A Bibliography of Publications on Old English Literature to the End of 1972*. Toronto: Univ. of Toronto Press, 1980.

Grein, C. W. M. *Sprachschatz der angelsächsischen Dichter*. Heidelberg: Winter, 1912.

Grohskopf, Bernice. *The Treasure of Sutton Hoo: Ship-Burial for an Anglo-Saxon King*. New York: Atheneum, 1970.

Grose, M. W., and Dierdre McKenna. *Old English Literature*. London: Evans, 1973.

Gruber, Loren C. "*Beowulf* at Simpson College." *Old English Newsletter* 11.2 (1978): 17–18.

Gummere, Francis B. *The Oldest English Epic*. New York: Macmillan, 1909.

Haarder, Andreas. Beowulf: *The Appeal of a Poem*. Copenhagen: Akademisk Forlag, 1975.

Haber, Thomas Burns. *A Comparative Study of* Beowulf *and* The Aeneid. Princeton: Princeton Univ. Press, 1931.

Haley, Albert W., Jr., trans. *Beowulf*. Boston: Branden, 1978.

Hall, J. R. Clark. *A Concise Anglo-Saxon Dictionary for the Use of Students*. Supp. by Herbert D. Meritt. 4th ed. Cambridge: Cambridge Univ. Press, 1961.

———, trans. Beowulf *and the Finnsburg Fragment*. Rev. ed. C. L. Wrenn. Pref. J. R. R. Tolkien. London: Allen and Unwin, 1950.

Halverson, John. "*Beowulf* and the Pitfalls of Piety." *University of Toronto Quarterly* 35 (1966): 260–78.

———. "The World of *Beowulf*." *ELH* 36 (1969): 593–608.

Hanning, Robert W. "*Beowulf* as Heroic History." *Mediaevalia et Humanistica* 5 (1974): 77–102.

Hansen, Elaine Tuttle. "From *freolicu folccwen* to *geomuru ides*: Women in Old English Poetry Reconsidered." *Michigan Academician* 9 (1976): 109–17.

Hart, Thomas E. "Tectonic Design, Formulaic Craft, and Literary Execution: The Episodes of Finn and Ingeld in *Beowulf*." *Amsterdamer Beiträge zur alteren Germanistik* 2 (1972): 1–61.

Hatto, Arthur T. "Snake-Swords and Boar-Helms in *Beowulf*." *English Studies* 38 (1957): 145–60, 257–59.

Havelock, Eric A. *A Preface to Plato*. Cambridge: Harvard Univ. Press, 1982.

Hernández, Ann. "*Beowulf* Lives." *Old English Newsletter* 13.2 (1980): 24–25.

Heusler, Andreas. *Deutsche Versgeschichte mit Einschluss des altenglischen und altnordischen Stabreimverses*. Paul's *Grundriss der germanischen Philologie*, 8.1. Berlin: de Gruyter, 1925.

Hieatt, Constance B. "Envelope Patterns and the Structure of *Beowulf*." *English Studies in Canada* 1 (1975): 249–65.

———. "A New Theory of Triple Rhythm in the Hypermetric Lines of Old English Verse." *Modern Philology* 66 (1969): 1–8.

———. "On Teaching *Beowulf*." *Old English Newsletter* 11.2 (1978): 18–19.

———, trans. Beowulf *and Other Old English Poems*. Introd. A. Kent Hieatt. New York: Bantam, 1982.

Hill, David. *An Atlas of Anglo-Saxon England*. Toronto: Univ. of Toronto Press, 1981.

Hill, Geoffrey. *Mercian Hymns*. London: Deutsch, 1971.

Hill, Thomas D. "The Fall of Angels and Man in the Old English *Genesis B*." In *Anglo Saxon Poetry: Essays in Appreciation for John C. McGalliard*. Ed. Lewis E. Nicholson and Dolores Frese. 279–90.

Hodgkin, R. H. *A History of the Anglo-Saxons*. 3rd ed. Oxford: Clarendon, 1952.

Hofmann, Johann Baptist. *Etymologisches Wörterbuch des Griechischen*. 1950; rpt. Darmstadt: Wissenschaftliche Buchgesellschaft, 1966.

Holthausen, Ferdinand. *Altenglisches etymologisches Wörterbuch*. Heidelberg: Winter, 1934.

———. *Gotisches etymologisches Wörterbuch*. Heidelberg: Winter, 1934.

Homans, G. C. "The Frisians in East Anglia." *Economic History Review* NS 10 (1957–58): 189–206.

Hoops, Johannes. "Die Foliierung der *Beowulf*-Handschrift. Fr. Klaeber zum 65. Geburtstag." *Englische Studien* 63 (1928–29): 1–11.

Hughes, Geoffrey. "Beowulf, Unferth, and Hrunting: An Interpretation." *English Studies* 58 (1977): 385–95.

Hulbert, James R. "The Accuracy of the B-Scribe of *Beowulf*." *PMLA* 43 (1928): 1196–99.

Hume, Kathryn. "The Concept of the Hall in Old English Poetry." *Anglo-Saxon England* 3 (1974): 63–74.

———. "The Theme and Structure of *Beowulf*." *Studies in Philology* 72 (1975): 1–27.

Huppé, Bernard. "The Concept of the Hero in the Early Middle Ages." In *Concepts of the Hero in the Middle Ages and the Renaissance*. Ed. Norman T. Burns and Christopher J. Reagan. 1–26.

Hutman, Norma L. "Even Monsters Have Mothers: A Study of *Beowulf* and John Gardner's *Grendel*." *Mosaic* 9.1 (1975): 19–32.

Irving, Edward B., Jr. *Introduction to* Beowulf. Englewood Cliffs: Prentice-Hall, 1969.

———. *A Reading of* Beowulf. New Haven: Yale Univ. Press, 1968.

Jabbour, Alan. "Memorial Transmission in Old English Poetry." *Chaucer Review* 3 (1969): 174–90.

Jessupp, R. *Age by Age*. London: Joseph, 1967.

John, Eric. "*Beowulf* and the Margins of Literacy." *Bulletin of the John Rylands Library* 56 (1974): 388–422.

Johnson, Samuel. *The History of Rasselas, Prince of Abyssinia*. Ed. Warren Fleischauer. Woodbury, N.Y.: Barron's, 1962.

Joliffe, J. E. A. *Pre-Feudal England: The Jutes*. London: Oxford Univ. Press, 1933.

Jones, Gwyn. *History of the Vikings*. New York: Oxford Univ. Press, 1968.

———. *Kings, Beasts, and Heroes*. London: Oxford Univ. Press, 1972.

———, trans. *Egil's Saga*. New York: Twayne, 1960.

———, trans. "King Hrolf and His Champions." In *Erik the Red and Other Icelandic Sagas*. London: Oxford Univ. Press, 1961.

Jordan, Richard. *Handbuch der mittelenglischen Grammatik*. 3rd ed. Heidelberg: Winter, 1968. Trans. and rev. Eugene J. Crook as *Handbook of Middle English Grammar*. The Hague: Mouton, 1974.

Judd, Elizabeth. "Women before the Conquest: A Study of Women in Anglo-Saxon England." *Papers in Women's Studies* 1 (1974): 127–49.

Kahrl, Stanley J. "Feuds in *Beowulf*: A Tragic Necessity?" *Modern Philology* 69 (1973): 189–98.

Kail, Johannes. "Über die Parallelstellen in der angelsächsischen Poesie." *Anglia* 12 (1889): 21–40.

Kaluza, Max. *A Short History of English Versification from the Earliest Times to the Present Day: A Handbook for Teachers and Students*. Trans. A. C. Dunstan. London: Allen; New York: Macmillan, 1911.

Kanner, Barbara, ed. *The Women in England from Anglo-Saxon Times to the Present: Interpretive Bibliographical Essays*. Hamden, Conn.: Archon, 1979.

Kaske, Robert E. "*Beowulf*." In *Critical Approaches to Six Major English Works: Beowulf through Paradise Lost*. Ed. Robert M. Lumiansky and Herschel Baker. Philadelphia: Univ. of Pennsylvania Press, 1968. 3–40.

———. "Hrothgar's Sermon." *Old English Newsletter* 10.1 (1976): 6–7.

————. " 'Hygelac and Hygd.' " In *Studies in Old English Literature in Honour of Arthur G. Brodeur.* Ed. Stanley B. Greenfield. 200–06.

————. "*Sapientia et Fortitudo* as the Controlling Theme of *Beowulf.*" *Studies in Philology* 55 (1958): 423–57. Rpt. in *An Anthology of* Beowulf *Criticism.* Ed. Lewis E. Nicholson. 269–310.

Kennedy, Charles W. *The Earliest English Poetry: A Critical Survey of the Poetry Written before the Norman Conquest, with Illustrative Translations.* London: Oxford Univ. Press, 1943.

————, trans. *Beowulf: The Oldest English Epic.* 1940. Rpt. in *The Oxford Anthology of English Literature.* Gen. eds. Frank Kermode and John Hollander. 2 vols. New York: Oxford Univ. Press, 1973.

Ker, N. R. *A Catalogue of Manuscripts containing Anglo-Saxon.* Oxford: Clarendon, 1957.

Kidson, P. *The Medieval World.* New York: McGraw-Hill, 1967.

Kiernan, Kevin S. Beowulf *and the* Beowulf *Manuscript.* New Brunswick: Rutgers Univ. Press, 1981.

Kirkby, M. H. *The Vikings.* New York: Dutton, 1977.

Kirschner, Ann G. "The Ph.D. Job Market: 1978–79." *ADE Bulletin* 64 (1980): 25–27.

Klaeber, Frederick, ed. Beowulf *and the Fight at Finnsburg.* 3rd ed., with supps. Lexington, Mass.: Heath, 1950.

Klein, Ernest. *A Comprehensive Etymological Dictionary of the English Language.* Amsterdam: Elsevier, 1966–67.

Kliman, Bernice. "Women in Early English Literature, *Beowulf* to the *Ancrene Wisse.*" *Nottingham Medieval Studies* 21 (1977): 32–49.

Kluge, Friedrich. *Etymologisches Wörterbuch der deutschen Sprache.* 19th ed. Berlin: de Gruyter, 1963.

Kotker, N. *The Horizon Book of the Middle Ages.* New York: American Heritage, 1968.

Krapp, George P., and Elliott Van Kirk Dobbie, eds. The Anglo-Saxon Poetic Records. 6 vols. New York: Columbia Univ. Press, 1931–54.

Lawrence, William W. Beowulf *and Epic Tradition.* Cambridge: Harvard Univ. Press, 1928.

————. "*Beowulf* and the Tragedy of Finnsburg." *PMLA* 30 (1915): 372–431.

Leake, Jane A. *The Geats of* Beowulf: *A Study in the Geographical Mythology of the Middle Ages.* Madison: Univ. of Wisconsin Press, 1967.

Lee, Alvin A. *The Guest-Hall of Eden: Four Essays on the Design of Old English Poetry.* New Haven: Yale Univ. Press, 1972.

Lester, G. A. *The Anglo-Saxons: How They Lived and Worked.* London: David and Charles, 1976.

Lewis, C[harles]. S. *The Allegory of Love.* London: Oxford Univ. Press, 1936.

Leyerle, John. "Beowulf the Hero and King." *Medium Aevum* 34 (1965): 89–102.

————. "The Dictionary of Old English: A Report to Group 1, Old English, of the

Modern Language Association, Made on December 29, 1970." *Old English Newsletter* 4.2 (1971): 3–9.

———. "The Interlace Structure of *Beowulf.*" *University of Toronto Quarterly* 37 (1967) 1–17, with 9 plates.

Lipp, Frances Randall. "The Teaching of Introductory Old English in the U.S. and Canada." *Old English Newsletter* 6.2 (1973): 7–26.

Loganbill, Dean. "Problems and Processes: Teaching *Beowulf* in Translation." *Old English Newsletter* 11.2 (1978): 26.

Lord, Albert B. "Beowulf and Odysseus." *Franciplegius: Medieval and Linguistic Studies in Honor of Francis Peabody Magoun, Jr.* Ed. Jess B. Bessinger, Jr., and Robert P. Creed. 86–91.

———. "Composition by Theme in Homer and Southslavic Epos." *Transactions of the American Philological Association* 82 (1951): 71–80.

———. "Interlocking Mythic Patterns in *Beowulf.*" In *Old English Literature in Context: Ten Essays.* Ed. John D. Niles. 137–42.

———. "Perspectives on Recent Work in Oral Literature." In *Oral Literature: Seven Essays.* Ed. Joseph J. Duggan. 1–24.

———. *The Singer of Tales.* Cambridge: Harvard Univ. Press, 1960.

———, ed. *Novi Pazar: Serbo-Croatian Texts.* Collated by Milman Parry and Albert B. Lord. Serbo-Croatian Heroic Songs, 2. Cambridge: Harvard Univ. Press; Belgrade: Serbian Academy of Sciences, 1954.

———, ed. and trans. *Novi Pazar: English Translations.* Collated by Milman Parry and Albert B. Lord. Serbo-Croatian Heroic Songs, 1. Cambridge: Harvard Univ. Press; Belgrade: Serbian Academy of Sciences, 1953.

———, ed., and David E. Bynum, trans. *The Wedding of Smailagić Meho (Ženidba Smailagina Sina),* by Avdo Medjedović. Collated by Milman Parry and Albert B. Lord. Serbo-Croatian Heroic Songs, 3-4. Cambridge: Harvard Univ. Press, 1974.

Luecke, Jane-Marie. *Measuring Old English Rhythm: An Application of the Principles of Gregorian Chant Rhythm to the Meter of* Beowulf. Literary Monographs, 9. Madison: Univ. of Wisconsin Press, 1978.

Luick, Karl. *Historische Grammatik der englischen Sprache* (1921). Rev. ed. with new chapters by Friedrich Wild and Herbert Koziol. 2 vols. Stuttgart: Tauchnitz; Cambridge: Harvard Univ. Press, 1964.

Lumiansky, Robert M. "The Dramatic Audience in *Beowulf.*" *Journal of English and Germanic Philology* 51 (1952): 545–50.

Mackaye, Percy. *Beowulf: An Epical Drama of Anglo-Saxon Times.* Leipzig, 1899.

Macrae-Gibson, O. D. *Learning Old English: A Progressive Course with Text, Tape, and Exercises.* Aberdeen: O. D. Macrae-Gibson, 1970.

Macrorie, Ken. *Telling Writing.* 3rd ed. Rochelle Park, N.J.: Hayden, 1980.

Madden, John F., and Francis P. Magoun, Jr. *A Grouped Frequency Word-List of Anglo-Saxon Poetry.* Harvard Old English Series, 2. Cambridge: Harvard Univ. Press, 1954.

Magnusson, Magnus. *Viking Expansion Westwards*. New York: Walck, 1973.

———. *Vikings!* New York: Dutton, 1980.

———, and Hermann Pálsson, trans. *Laxdaela Saga*. Harmondsworth, Eng.: Penguin, 1969.

———, and ———, trans. *Njals Saga*. Harmondsworth, Eng.: Penguin, 1960.

Magoun, Francis P., Jr. "Bede's Story of Caedman: The Case History of an Anglo-Saxon Oral Singer." *Speculum* 30 (1955): 49–63.

———. "*Béowulf* A': A Folk-Variant." *ARV: Journal of Scandinavian Folklore* 14 (1958): 95–101.

———. "*Béowulf* B: A Folk-Poem on Beowulf's Death." In *Early English and Norse Studies Presented to Hugh Smith in Honour of His Sixtieth Birthday*. Ed. Arthur Brown and Peter Foote. 127–40.

———. "Oral-Formulaic Character of Anglo-Saxon Narrative Poetry." *Speculum* 28 (1953): 446–67. Rpt. in *Essential Articles for the Study of Old English Poetry*. Ed. Jess B. Bessinger, Jr., and Stanley J. Kahrl. 319–51. Also rpt. in *The Beowulf Poet: A Collection of Critical Essays*. Ed. Donald K. Fry. 83–113.

———. "The Theme of Beasts of Battle in Anglo-Saxon Poetry." *Neuphilologische Mitteilungen* 56 (1955): 81–90.

———, ed. *The Poems of British Museum Ms. Cotton Vitellius A. XV: Beowulf (Fol. 132a–201b)* (1955). Rev. as Beowulf *and* Judith *Done in Normalized Orthography and Edited* (1959). New rev. ed., ed. Jess B. Bessinger, Jr. Harvard Old English Series, 1. Cambridge: Harvard Univ. Press, 1966.

———, and H. M. Smyser, trans. *Walter of Aquitaine: Materials for the Study of His Legend*. New London: Connecticut Coll. Press, 1950.

Malone, Kemp. "The Finn Episode in *Beowulf*." *Journal of English and Germanic Philology* 25 (1926): 157–72.

———. "Readings from the Thorkelin Transcripts of *Beowulf*." *PMLA* 64 (1949): 1190–218.

———. "The Text of *Beowulf*." *Proceedings of the American Philosophical Society* 93 (1949): 239–43.

———. "Thorkelin's Transcripts of *Beowulf*." *Studia Neophilologica* 14 (1941–42): 25–30.

———, ed. *The Nowell Codex*. Early English Manuscripts in Facsimile, 12. Copenhagen: Rosenkilde and Bagger; London: Allen and Unwin; Baltimore: Johns Hopkins Univ. Press, 1963.

———, ed. *The Thorkelin Transcripts of* Beowulf. Early English Manuscripts in Facsimile, 1. Copenhagen: Rosenkilde and Bagger; London: Allen and Unwin; Baltimore: Johns Hopkins Univ. Press, 1951.

———, and Martin B. Ruud, eds. *Studies in English Philology: A Miscellany in Honor of Frederick Klaeber*. Minneapolis: Univ. of Minnesota Press, 1929.

Mandel, Jerome. "New Directions in *Beowulf* Scholarship." MLA Convention, New York. Dec. 1975.

————, and Bruce A. Rosenberg, eds. *Medieval Literature and Folklore Studies: Essays in Honor of Francis Lee Utley.* New Brunswick, N.J.: Rutgers Univ. Press, 1970.

Marckwardt, Albert H., and James L. Rosier. *Old English: Language and Literature.* New York: Norton, 1972.

Matthews, William. *Old and Middle English Literature.* Goldentree Bibliographies in Language and Literature. New York: Appleton, 1968.

McEvedy, Colin, and John Woodcock. *The Penguin Atlas of Medieval History.* Harmondsworth, Eng.: Penguin, 1961.

McGalliard, John C. "The Complex Art of *Beowulf.*" *Modern Philology* 59 (1962): 276–82.

————. "The Poet's Comment in *Beowulf.*" *Studies in Philology* 75 (1978): 243–70.

McNamee, Maurice B. "Beowulf, a Christian Hero." In his *Honor and the Epic Hero: A Study of the Shifting Concept of Magnanimity in Philosophy and Epic Poetry.* New York: Holt, 1960. 86–117.

Mitchell, Bruce. *A Guide to Old English.* Rev. with Texts and Glossary by Fred C. Robinson. Oxford: Blackwell, 1982.

————. " 'Until the Dragon Comes . . . ': Some Thoughts on *Beowulf.*" *Neophilologus* 47 (1963): 126–38.

Mitchell, S. *Medieval Manuscript Painting.* New York: Viking, 1965.

Moore, Bruce. "The Relevance of the Finnsburh Episode." *Journal of English and Germanic Philology* 75 (1976): 317–29.

Moore, Samuel. *Historical Outlines of English Sounds and Inflections.* Rev. Albert H. Marckwardt. Ann Arbor, Mich.: Wahr, 1963.

————, and Thomas Knott. *The Elements of Old English: Elementary Grammar, Reference Grammar, and Reading Selections.* Rev. James R. Hulbert. 10th ed. Ann Arbor, Mich.: Wahr, 1965.

Moorman, Charles. "The Essential Paganism of *Beowulf.*" *Modern Language Quarterly* 28 (1967): 3–18.

Morgan, Edwin, trans. *Beowulf: A Verse Translation into Modern English.* Berkeley: Univ. of California Press, 1962.

Morris, William, and Alfred J. Wyatt, trans. *The Tale of Beowulf, Sometime King of the Folk of the Weder Geats.* (Kelmscott ed. untitled; Longman ed. titled as above.) Hammersmith: Kelmscott, 1895; London: Longman, 1898.

Moulton, William G. *A Linguistic Guide to Language Learning.* 2nd ed. New York: Modern Language Assn., 1970.

Nagler, Michael N. "*Beowulf* in the Context of Myth." In *Old English Literature in Context: Ten Essays.* Ed. John D. Niles. 143–56.

Nicholson, Lewis E., ed. *An Anthology of* Beowulf *Criticism.* Notre Dame, Ind.: Univ. of Notre Dame Press, 1963.

————, and Dolores Warwick Frese, eds. *Anglo-Saxon Poetry: Essays in Appreciation for John C. McGalliard.* Notre Dame, Ind.: Univ. of Notre Dame Press, 1975.

Niles, John D. "Compound Diction and the Style of *Beowulf*." *English Studies* 62 (1981): 489–503.

———. "Formula and Formulaic System in *Beowulf*." In *Oral Traditional Literature: A Festschrift for Albert Bates Lord*. Ed. John M. Foley. 394–415.

———, ed. *Old English Literature in Context: Ten Essays*. Cambridge: Brewer, 1980.

Nitzsche, Jane Chance. "The Structural Unity of *Beowulf*: The Problem of Grendel's Mother." *Texas Studies in Literature and Language* 22 (1980): 287–303.

Nye, Robert, trans. *Beowulf: A New Telling*. New York: Hill and Wang, 1968.

Ogilvy, J. D. A. *Books Known to Anglo-Latin Writers from Aldhelm to Alcuin (670–804)*. Cambridge: Medieval Academy of America, 1936.

Onions, Charles T. *Oxford Dictionary of English Etymology*. London: Oxford Univ. Press, 1966.

Opland, Jeff. *Anglo-Saxon Oral Poetry: A Study of the Traditions*. New Haven: Yale Univ. Press, 1980.

———. "*Beowulf* on the Poet." *Medieval Studies* 38 (1976): 442–67.

Orrick, Allan H., ed. *Nordica et Anglica: Studies in Honor of Stefán Einarsson*. The Hague: Mouton, 1968.

Owen, Gale R. *Rites and Religions of the Anglo-Saxons*. Newton-Abbot, Devon: David and Charles; Totowa, N.J.: Barnes and Noble, 1981.

Oxenstierna, E. *The Norsemen*. Greenwich, Conn.: New York Graphic Society, 1965.

———. *The World of the Norsemen*. Cleveland: World, 1967.

Page, Raymond I. *Life in Anglo-Saxon England*. London: Batsford; New York: Putnam, 1970.

Pálsson, Hermann, and Paul Edwards, trans. *Egil's Saga*. Harmondsworth, Eng.: Penguin, 1976.

Panzer, Friedrich. *Studien zur germanischen Sagengeschichte. I*. Beowulf. Munich: Beck, 1910.

Parry, Milman. *L'Epithète traditionnelle dans Homère: Essai sur un problème de style homérique*. Paris: Societé d'Editions "Les Belles Lettres," 1928. Rpt. as "The Traditional Epithet in Homer" in his *The Making of Homeric Verse*. 1–190.

———. *Les Formules et la metrique d'Homère*. Paris: Societé d'Editions "Les Belles Lettres," 1928. Rpt. as "Homeric Formulae and Homeric Metre" in his *The Making of Homeric Verse*. 191–239.

———. *The Making of Homeric Verse: The Collected Papers of Milman Parry*. Ed. Adam Parry. Oxford: Clarendon, 1971.

———. "Studies in the Epic Technique of Oral Verse-Making. I. Homer and Homeric Style." *Harvard Studies in Classical Philology* 41 (1930): 73–147. Rpt. in his *The Making of Homeric Verse*. 266–324.

———. "Studies in the Epic Technique of Oral Verse-Making. II. The Homeric Language as the Language of an Oral Poetry." *Harvard Studies in Classical*

Philology 43 (1932): 1–50. Rpt. in his *The Making of Homeric Verse*. 325–62.

Partridge, Eric. *Origins: A Short Etymological Dictionary of Modern English*. 2nd ed. New York: Macmillan, 1959.

Payne, Anne F. "Three Aspects of Wyrd in *Beowulf*." In *Old English Studies in Honour of John C. Pope*. Ed. Robert B. Burlin and Edward B. Irving, Jr. 15–35.

Pearsall, Derek. "*Beowulf* and the Anglo-Saxon Poetic Tradition." In his *Old English and Middle English Poetry*. London: Routledge, 1977. 1–24.

Pearson, Lucien D., trans. *Beowulf*. Introd. Rowland L. Collins. Bloomington: Indiana Univ. Press, 1965.

Peter, I. S. "*Beowulf* and the *Ramayana*: A Study in Epic Poetry." Diss. London 1934.

Pokorny, Julius. *Indogermanisches etymologisches Wörterbuch*. Bern: Francke, 1959–69.

Pollock, John J. "Beowulf in Jungian Perspective." *Old English Newsletter* 13.2 (1980): 25–26.

Pope, John C. "Beowulf's Old Age." In *Philological Essays: Studies in Old and Middle English Language and Literature in Honour of Herbert Dean Meritt*. Ed. James L. Rosier. 55–64.

———. *The Rhythm of* Beowulf: *An Interpretation of the Normal and Hypermetric Verse-Forms in Old English Poetry*. Rev. ed. New Haven: Yale Univ. Press, 1966.

———, ed. *Seven Old English Poems*. 2nd ed. New York: Norton, 1981.

Porter, John, trans. *Beowulf: Anglo-Saxon Text with Modern English Parallel*. London: Pirate, 1975.

Powell, Frederick Y. "Beowulf and Watanabe-no-Tsuna." In *An English Miscellany Presented to Dr. Furnivall in Honour of His Seventy-Fifth Birthday*. Oxford: Clarendon, 1901, 395–96.

Power, Eileen. *Medieval People*. 1924; rpt. New York: Barnes and Noble, 1963.

Price, Reynolds. "The Heroes of Our Times." *Saturday Review*, 12 Dec. 1978, 16–17.

Prokosch, Eduard. "Two Types of Scribal Errors in the *Beowulf* MS." In *Studies in English Philology: A Miscellany in Honor of Frederick Klaeber*. Ed. Kemp Malone and Martin B. Ruud. 196–207.

Puhvel, Martin. Beowulf *and Celtic Tradition*. Waterloo, Ont.: Wilfred Laurier Univ. Press, 1979.

Quennell, Marjorie. *Everyday Life in Roman and Anglo-Saxon Times, including Viking and Norman Times*. Rev. ed. London: Batsford, 1959.

Quirk, Randolph, and C. L. Wrenn. *An Old English Grammar*. London: Methuen, 1955.

Raffel, Burton. "On Translating *Beowulf*." *Yale Review* 54 (1965): 532–46. Rpt. in *Old English Poetry: Fifteen Essays*. Ed. Robert P. Creed. 311–25.

————, trans. *Beowulf: A New Translation*. Afterword by Robert P. Creed. 1963; rpt. Amherst: Univ. of Massachusetts Press, 1971.

————, trans. *Poems from the Old English*. Lincoln: Univ. of Nebraska Press, 1964.

Ramsey, Lee C. "The Sea-Voyages in *Beowulf*." *Neuphilologische Mitteilungen* 72 (1971): 51–59.

Rebsamen, Frederick, trans. *Beowulf Is My Name, and Selected Translations of Other Old English Poems*. San Francisco: Rinehart, 1971.

Renoir, Alain. "*Beowulf*: A Contextual Introduction to Its Contents and Techniques." In *Heroic Epic and Saga: An Introduction to the World's Great Folk Epics*. Ed. Felix J. Oinas. Bloomington: Indiana Univ. Press, 1978. 99–119.

————. "Eve's IQ Rating: Two Sexist Views of *Genesis B*." Division of Old English Language and Literature, MLA Convention, Houston. 1980.

————. "Oral-Formulaic Context: Implications for the Comparative Criticism of Medieval Texts." In *Oral Traditional Literature: A Festschrift for Albert Bates Lord*. Ed. John M. Foley. 416–39.

————. "Oral-Formulaic Theme Survival: A Possible Instance in the *Nibelungenlied*." *Neuphilologische Mitteilungen* 65 (1964): 70–74.

————. "Point of View and Design for Terror in *Beowulf*." *Neuphilologische Mitteilungen* 63 (1962): 154–67. Rpt. in *The Beowulf Poet: A Collection of Critical Essays*. Ed. Donald K. Fry. 154–69.

————. "The Ugly and the Unfaithful: *Beowulf* through the Translator's Eye." *Allegorica* 3 (1978): 161–71.

————. "*Vox Clamantis*: Human Survival and the Tradition of Letters." *Pacific Coast Philology* 16 (1981): 1–17.

————, discussant. "New Directions in *Beowulf* Scholarship." MLA Convention, New York. Dec. 1975.

Reynolds, William. "Heroism in *Beowulf*: A Christian Perspective." *Christianity and Literature* 27 (1978): 27–42.

Rice, D. T. *The Dawn of the European Civilization*. New York: McGraw-Hill, 1965.

Riché, Pierre. *Daily Life in the World of Charlemagne*. Trans. Jo Ann McNamara. Philadelphia: Univ. of Pennsylvania Press, 1978.

Riley, Samuel M. "Germanic Ethic and Poetic Craft in *Beowulf*." *Old English Newsletter* 14.2 (1981): 17–18.

Roach, Bruce V. "One Flew over the Mere." *Old English Newsletter* 14.2 (1981): 18–19.

Robertson, D. W., Jr. "The Doctrine of Charity in Medieval Literary Gardens: A Topical Approach through Symbolism and Allegory." *Speculum* 26 (1951): 24–49. Rpt. in *An Anthology of Beowulf Criticism*. Ed. Lewis E. Nicholson. 165–88.

Robinson, Fred C. "Elements of the Marvellous in the Characterization of Beowulf: A Reconsideration of the Textual Evidence." In *Old English Studies in Honour of John C. Pope*. Ed. Robert B. Burlin and Edward B. Irving, Jr. 119–37.

————. "Is Wealhtheow a Prince's Daughter?" *English Studies* 45 (1964): 36–39.

————. "Old English Literature in Its Most Immediate Context." In *Old English Literature in Context: Ten Essays.* Ed. John D. Niles. 11–29.

————. *Old English Literature: A Select Bibliography.* Toronto Medieval Bibliographies, 2. Toronto: Univ. of Toronto Press, 1970.

————, and Stanley B. Greenfield. *A Bibliography of Publications on Old English Literature to the End of 1972.* See Greenfield.

Rogers, H. L. "Beowulf's Three Great Fights." *Review of English Studies* 6 (1955): 339–55. Rpt. in *An Anthology of* Beowulf *Criticism.* Ed. Lewis E. Nicholson. 233–56.

————. "The Crypto-Psychological Character of the Oral Formula." *English Studies* 47 (1966): 89–102.

Rosier, James L. "Design for Treachery: The Unferth Intrigue." *PMLA* 77 (1962): 1–7.

————, ed. *Philological Essays: Studies in Old and Middle English Language and Literature in Honour of Herbert Dean Meritt.* The Hague: Mouton, 1970.

Rowland, Beryl. *Medieval Woman's Guide to Health: The First English Gynecological Handbook.* Kent: Kent State Univ. Press, 1981.

Russell, Josiah Cox. *British Medieval Population.* Albuquerque: Univ. of New Mexico Press, 1948.

Russom, Geoffrey. "Artful Avoidance of the Useful Phrase in *Beowulf, The Battle of Maldon,* and *Fates of the Apostles.*" *Studies in Philology* 75 (1978): 371–90.

Ruud, Jay. "Gardner's *Grendel* and *Beowulf*: Humanizing the Monsters." *Thoth* 14 (1974): 3–17.

Rypins, Stanley I. "The *Beowulf* Codex." *Modern Philology* 17 (1920): 541–47. Rpt. in his *Three Old English Prose Texts in Ms. Cotton Vitellius A. XV.* Rev. version in *Colophon* 10 (1932): 9–12.

————. "A Contribution to the Study of the *Beowulf* Codex." *PMLA* 36 (1921): 167–85.

————. *Three Old English Prose Texts in MS. Cotton Vitellius A. XV.* London: Early English Text Society, 1924.

Salu, Mary, and Robert T. Farrell, eds. *J. R. R. Tolkien, Scholar and Storyteller: Essays in Memoriam.* Ithaca: Cornell Univ. Press, 1979.

Schaar, Claes. "On a New Theory of Old English Poetic Diction." *Neophilologus* 40 (1956): 301–05.

Schibanoff, Susan. "The Crooked Rib: Women in Medieval Literature." In *Approaches to Teaching Chaucer's* Canterbury Tales. Ed. Joseph Gibaldi. New York: Modern Language Assn., 1980. 121–28.

Schmeck, Harold M., Jr. "Norsemen Did Know a Thing or Two about Monsters." *New York Times,* 10 Feb. 1981, C2.

Scowcroft, R. Mark. "The Hand and the Child: Studies of Celtic Tradition in European Literature." Diss. Cornell 1982.

Serrailier, Ian, trans. *Beowulf the Warrior*. London: Oxford Univ. Press, 1954.

Shaw, Brian A. "The Speeches in *Beowulf*: A Structural Study." *Chaucer Review* 13 (1978): 86–92.

Shippey, Thomas A. *Beowulf*. London: Arnold, 1978.

Short, Douglas D. Beowulf *Scholarship: An Annotated Bibliography*. New York: Garland, 1980.

Sievers, Eduard. *Altgermanische Metrik*. Halle: Niemeyer, 1893.

———. *Angelsächsische Grammatik*. Halle: Niemeyer, 1886.

———. "Formelzeichnis." In *Heliand*. Ed. Eduard Sievers. Halle: Buchhandlung des Waisenhauses, 1878. App. 1.

———. "Old Germanic Metrics and Old English Metrics." Trans. Gawaina D. Luster. In *Essential Articles for the Study of Old English Poetry*. Ed. Jess B. Bessinger, Jr., and Stanley J. Kahrl. 267–88.

———. "Zur Rhythmik des germanischen Alliterationsverses I." *Beiträge sur Geschichte der deutschen Sprache und Literatur* 10 (1885): 209–314.

Silver-Beck, Barbara L. "The Case against *The Rhythm of* Beowulf." *Neuphilologische Mitteilungen* 77 (1976): 510–25.

Simpson, Jacqueline. *The Viking World*. 2nd ed. New York: St. Martin's, 1980.

———, trans. *The Northmen Talk*. Madison: Univ. of Wisconsin Press, 1965.

Sisam, Kenneth. "Anglo-Saxon Royal Genealogies." *Proceedings of the British Academy* 39 (1953): 288–348.

———. "The *Beowulf* Manuscript." *Modern Language Review* 11 (1916): 335–37. Rpt. in his *Studies in the History of Old English Literature*. 61–64.

———. "Beowulf's Fight with the Dragon." *Review of English Studies* NS 9 (1958): 129–40.

———. "The Compilation of the *Beowulf* Manuscript." In his *Studies in the History of Old English Literature*. 65–96.

———. "Notes on Old English Poetry: The Authority of Old English Poetical Manuscripts." *Review of English Studies* 22 (1946): 257–68. Rpt. as "The Authority of Old English Poetical Manuscripts" in his *Studies in the History of Old English Literature*. 29–44. Also rpt. in *Old English Literature: Twenty-Two Analytical Essays*. Ed. Martin Stevens and Jerome Mandel. 36–51.

———. *The Structure of* Beowulf. Oxford: Clarendon, 1965.

———. *Studies in the History of Old English Literature*. Oxford: Clarendon, 1953. Rpt. with corrections, 1962.

Skeat, Walter W. *An Etymological Dictionary of the English Language*. Oxford, 1882.

Sklute, Larry M. "*Freoðuwebbe* in Old English Poetry." *Neuphilologische Mitteilungen* 71 (1970): 534–41.

Smith, A. H. "The Photography of Manuscripts." *London Medieval Studies* 1 (1937–39): 179–207.

Smithers, George V. "Destiny and the Heroic Warrior in *Beowulf*." In *Philological*

    Essays: Studies in Old and Middle English in Honour of Herbert Dean Meritt. Ed. James L. Rosier. 65–81.

—————. "The Geats in *Beowulf.*" *Durham University Journal* 63 (1971): 87–103.

Spencer, Hazelton, Beverly J. Layman, and David Ferry, eds. *British Literature.* Vol. 1: *Old English to 1800.* Lexington, Mass.: Heath, 1974.

Stanley, Eric G. "*Beowulf.*" In his *Continuations and Beginnings: Studies in Old English Literature.* 104–41.

—————. *Continuations and Beginnings: Studies in Old English Literature.* London: Nelson, 1966.

—————. *The Search for Anglo-Saxon Paganism.* Cambridge: Brewer, 1975.

Stenton, Frank M. *Anglo-Saxon England.* Oxford: Clarendon, 1943.

—————. *The Bayeux Tapestry.* New York: Paidon, 1957.

—————. "The Historical Bearing of Place-Name Studies: The Place of Women in Anglo-Saxon Society." *Transactions of the Royal Historical Society* 4th ser. 25 (1943): 1–13.

Stevens, Martin, and Jerome Mandel, eds. *Old English Literature: Twenty-Two Analytical Essays.* Rev. ed. Lincoln: Univ. of Nebraska Press, 1976.

Stevick, Robert D. "The Oral-Formulaic Analysis of Old English Verse." *Speculum* 37 (1962): 382–89.

—————, ed. *Beowulf: An Edition with Manuscript Spacing Notation and Graphotactic Analyses.* New York: Garland, 1975.

Stitt, Alexander, dir. *Grendel Grendel Grendel.* Victorian Film Corp., 1982.

Stolz, Benjamin, and Richard S. Shannon, eds. *Oral Literature and the Formula.* Ann Arbor: Center for the Coordination of Ancient and Modern Studies, Univ. of Michigan, 1976.

Storm, Melvin. "Genealogy in *Beowulf.*" *Old English Newsletter* 14.2 (1981): 19–20.

Storms, Godfrid. "The Author of *Beowulf.*" *Neuphilologische Mitteilungen* 75 (1974): 11–39.

Sutcliff, Rosemary, trans. *Beowulf, Dragon Slayer.* London: Bodley, 1972.

Swanton, Michael. "Heroes, Heroism, and Heroic Literature." *Essays and Studies by Members of the English Association* 30 (1977): 1–21.

—————, trans. *Beowulf: Edited with an Introduction, Notes, and a New Prose Translation.* Manchester: Manchester Univ. Press; New York: Barnes and Noble, 1978.

Sweet, Henry. *Anglo-Saxon Primer.* Rev. Norman Davis. 9th ed. Oxford: Clarendon, 1953.

—————. *An Anglo-Saxon Reader in Prose and Verse.* Rev. Dorothy Whitelock, with corrections. Oxford: Clarendon, 1970.

—————. *The Student's Dictionary of Anglo-Saxon* (1896). Oxford: Clarendon, 1976.

Tacitus, Publius Cornelius. *The Agricola and the Germania.* Trans. and introd. H. Mattingly. Harmondsworth, Eng.: Penguin, 1970.

————. *Agricola, Germania, Dialogus.* Trans. M. Hutton. Rev. E. H. Warmington. Loeb Classical Library, vol. 35. Cambridge: Harvard Univ. Press, 1970.

Taylor, Henry Osborn. *The Medieval Mind: A History of the Development of Thought and Emotion in the Middle Ages.* 4th ed. 2 vols. Cambridge: Harvard Univ. Press, 1962.

Taylor, Paul B., and Peter H. Salus, "The Compilation of Cotton Vitellius A. XV." *Neuphilologische Mitteilungen* 69 (1968): 199–204.

Terry, Patricia, trans. *Poems of the Vikings: The Elder Edda.* Indianapolis: Bobbs-Merrill, 1969.

Thornley, G. C. "The Accents and Points of MS. Junius II." *Transactions of the Philological Society* (1954): 178–205.

Thorpe, Benjamin, ed. and trans. *Beowulf, Together with* Widsith *and The Fight at Finnesburg.* Introd. Vincent Hopper. Woodbury, N.Y.: Barron's, 1962.

Tillyard, E. M. W. *The English Epic and Its Background.* London: Chatto and Windus, 1954.

Tolkien, J. R. R. "*Beowulf*: The Monsters and the Critics." *Proceedings of the British Academy* 22 (1936): 245–95. Rpt. in *An Anthology of* Beowulf *Criticism.* Ed. Lewis E. Nicholson. 51–103. Also rpt. in *The* Beowulf *Poet: A Collection of Critical Essays.* Ed. Donald K. Fry. 8–56.

————. "The Home-Coming of Beorhtnoth Beorhthelm's Son." *Essays and Studies* 69 (1953): 1–8. Rpt. in his *The Tolkien Reader.* New York: Ballantine, 1966. 3–24.

————. *The Lord of the Rings.* 2nd ed. 3 vols. Boston: Houghton, 1967.

Tonsfeldt, H. Ward. "Ring Structure in *Beowulf.*" *Neophilologus* 61 (1977): 443–52.

Trapp, J. B., et al., eds. *Oxford Anthology of English Literature: Major Authors Edition.* 2 vols. London: Oxford Univ. Press, 1975.

Treitler, Leo. " 'Centonate' Chant: *Übles Flickwerk* or *E Pluribus Unus?*" *Journal of the American Musicological Society* 28 (1975): 1–23.

————. "Homer and Gregory: The Transmission of Epic Poetry and Plainchant." *Musical Quarterly* 60 (1974): 333–72.

Tuso, Joseph F. "The Teaching of *Beowulf.*" *Old English Newsletter* 10.2 (1977): 5–6 and 11.2 (1978): 15–19.

————, ed. *Beowulf: The Donaldson Translation, Backgrounds and Sources, Criticism.* New York: Norton, 1975.

Unstead, R. J. *Invaded Island.* London: Macdonald, 1971.

Utley, Francis Lee. "Folklore, Myth and Ritual." In *Critical Approaches to Medieval Literature: Selected Papers from the English Institute, 1958–59.* New York: Columbia Univ. Press, 1960. 83–109.

Venezky, Richard L., and Sharon Butler, eds. *A Stopword Microfiche Concordance to Old English.* Toronto: Univ. of Toronto Press, 1982.

————, and Antonette di Paolo Healey, eds. *A Microfiche Concordance to Old English.* Toronto: Univ. of Toronto Press, 1981.

Vickery, John F. "The Narrative Structure of Hengest's Revenge in *Beowulf.*" *Anglo-Saxon England* 6 (1977): 91–103.

von Schaubert, Else, ed. *Beowulf.* Rev. of Heyne-Schücking ed. 18th ed. Paderborn: F. Schöningh, 1963.

Walde, Alois, and J. H. Hofmann, eds. *Lateinisches etymologisches Wörterbuch.* 4th ed. Heidelberg: Winter, 1954–65.

——, and Julius Pokorny. *Vergleichendes Wörterbuch der indogermanischen Sprachen.* Berlin: de Gruyter, 1927–32.

Walsh, Jill Paton. *Hengest's Tale.* Harmondsworth, Eng.: Penguin, 1971.

Walsh, Marie-Michelle. "Approaching *Beowulf* through the Riddle." *Old English Newsletter* 11.2 (1978): 19.

Watkins, Calvert. "Indo-European Roots." *American Heritage Dictionary.* 1969 ed.

Watson, George, ed. *The New Cambridge Bibliography of English Literature. Vol. 1 (A. D. 600–1600).* Cambridge: Cambridge Univ. Press, 1974.

Watts, Ann Chalmers. *The Lyre and the Harp: A Comparative Reconsideration of Oral Tradition in Homer and Old English Epic Poetry.* New Haven: Yale Univ. Press, 1969.

Westphalen, Tilman. Beowulf *3150–55: Textkritik und Editionsgeschichte.* 2 vols. Munich: Fink, 1967.

Whallon, William. *Formula, Character, and Context: Studies in Homeric, Old English, and Old Testament Poetry.* Washington: Center for Hellenic Studies, 1969.

——. "Formulas for Heroes in the *Iliad* and in *Beowulf.*" *Modern Philology* 63 (1965): 95–104. Rev. and rpt. in his *Formula, Character, and Context: Studies in Homeric, Old English, and Old Testament Poetry.* Ch. 3.

——, Margaret E. Goldsmith, Charles J. Donahue, et al. "Allegorical, Typological, or Neither? Three Short Papers on the Allegorical Approach to *Beowulf* and a Discussion." *Anglo-Saxon England* 2 (1973): 285–302.

Whitehead, Alfred North. *The Aims of Education.* 1929; rpt. New York: Free Press, 1967.

Whitelock, Dorothy. *The Audience of* Beowulf. Rev. ed. Oxford: Clarendon, 1958. Pp. 1–30 rpt. in *Old English Literature: Twenty-Two Analytical Essays.* Ed. Martin Stevens and Jerome Mandel. 279–300.

——. *The Beginnings of English Society.* Harmondsworth, Eng.: Penguin, 1954.

——, ed. *English Historical Documents, ca. 500–1042.* London: Oxford Univ. Press, 1968.

Whitman, F. H. "The Kingly Nature of Beowulf." *Neophilologus* 61 (1977): 277–86.

Wilbur, Richard. "Beowulf." In *The Poems of Richard Wilbur.* New York: Harvest, 1963. 148–49.

Wilson, David M., ed. *The Archaeology of Anglo-Saxon England.* London: Methuen, 1977.

——, ed. *The Northern World.* New York: Abrams, 1980.

————, and O. Klindt-Jensen. *Viking Art*. Ithaca: Cornell Univ. Press, 1966.

Wimsatt, W. K., Jr., and Monroe C. Beardsley. "The Concept of Meter: An Exercise in Abstraction." *PMLA* 74 (1959): 585–98.

Wormald, Patrick. "Bede, *Beowulf*, and the Conversion of the Anglo-Saxon Aristocracy." In *Bede and Anglo-Saxon England*. Ed. Robert T. Farrell. Oxford: British Archaeological Reports, 1978. 32–95.

Wrenn, Charles L. *A Study of Old English Literature*. New York: Norton, 1967.

————, ed. Beowulf, *with the Finnesburg Fragment*. London: Harrap, 1953; rev. and enl. 1958. 3rd ed., rev. Whitney F. Bolton. London: Harrap, 1973.

Wright, C. E. *The Cultivation of Saga in Anglo-Saxon England*. Edinburgh: Oliver and Boyd, 1939.

Wright, David, trans. *Beowulf: A Prose Translation with an Introduction.* Harmondsworth, Eng.: Penguin, 1957.

Wright, Herbert G. "Good and Evil; Light and Darkness; Joy and Sorrow in *Beowulf*." *Review of English Studies* NS 8 (1957): 1–11. Abridged version rpt. in *An Anthology of* Beowulf *Criticism*. Ed. Lewis E. Nicholson. 257–67.

Wright, Joseph, and Elizabeth Mary Wright. *Old English Grammar*. 3rd ed. London: Oxford Univ. Press, 1975.

Wyatt, Alfred, ed. Beowulf *and the Finnsburg Fragment*. 3rd ed. Rev. R. W. Chambers. Cambridge: Cambridge Univ. Press, 1952.

Yeager, Robert F. "Some Turning Points in the History of Teaching Old English in America." *Old English Newsletter* 13.2 (1980): 9–20.

Young, Art. "1979–80 Literature Electives Survey." *ADE Bulletin* 64 (1980): 28–29.

Zellefrow, W. Ken. "*Beowulf* Enhanced by Comparison with Primary Epics." *Old English Newsletter* 14.2 (1981): 20–22.

Zesmer, David M. *Guide to English Literature: From* Beowulf *through Chaucer and Medieval Drama*. College Outline Series. New York: Barnes and Noble, 1961.

Zupitza, Julius, ed. *Beowulf: Autotypes of the Unique Cotton Vitellius A. XV. in the British Museum with a Transliteration and Notes*. OS 77. London: Early English Text Society, 1882. 2nd ed., with new collotypes and introd. Norman Davis. OS 245. London: Early English Text Society, 1959.

Zweig, Paul. "The Hero in Literature." *Saturday Review*, 12 Dec. 1978: 30–35.

DISCOGRAPHY

Bessinger, Jess B., Jr. Beowulf, Cædmon's Hymn *and Other Old English Poems Read in Old English*. Caedmon, TC 1161, 1962. Reissued on cassette as Beowulf *and Other Poetry in Old English*. Caedmon, SWC 1161, 1980.

————. *A History of the English Language*. 3 records. Caedmon, TC 3008, 1973. Reissued on cassette, Caedmon, SWC 3008, 1980.

Brodeur, Arthur G. *Beowulf*. Privately recorded, 1955.

Coghill, Nevill, and Norman Davis. *Beowulf*. Spoken Arts, SA 918, n.d.

Creed, Robert P. *Lyrics from the Old English, Read in the Original, with Translations Read by Burton Raffel*. Folkways, FL 9858, 1964.

———. Untitled recording. A reading of portions of *Beowulf* with lyre accompaniment, and discussion of poem and reading by John Miles Foley, Donald K. Fry, and Bruce Rosenberg. Radio Arts of New York, n.d..

Dunn, Charles W. *Early English Poetry*. Folkways, FL 9851, n.d.

Hanson, Howard. *Lament for Beowulf* (opus 25). Victor Masterworks, VM 889, 1926. Reissued Victor, V 11–8114/6, set M889; also Mercury Records, SR 90192, n.d.

Kökeritz, Helge. *A Thousand Years of English Pronunciation*. Lexington, LE 7650, 7655, n.d.

Magoun, Francis P., Jr. *Beowulf*. Harvard Vocarium, L6000–I, 1950.

Malone, Kemp. Beowulf *(Complete), Read in Old English by Kemp Malone*. 4 records. Caedmon, TC 4001, 1965. Reissued on cassette, Caedmon, 54001, 1980.

———. *Kemp Malone on Old English Poetry: A Lecture with Readings in Old English, with the Kemp Malone Translations*. Caedmon, TC 1424, 1973.

Notopoulos, James A. *Modern Greek Heroic Oral Poetry*. Folkways, FE 4468, 1959.

Pope, John C., and Helge Kökeritz. Beowulf, *Chaucer*. Whitlock's, TV 22131, n.d. Reissued, Lexington, LE 5505 (record) and TE 9107 (cassette), n.d.

Robinson, Fred C. *Beowulf*. Lecture. Cassette Curriculum, 2302. Deland, Fla.: Everett/Edwards, 1976.

Wylie, Betty Jane, and Victor Davies. *Beowulf: A Musical Epic*. 3 records or cassettes. Toronto: Leap Frog Records, 1983.

INDEX